P9-CDA-066

A Guide to Book Publishing

A Guide to
Book Publishing

Revised Edition

by DATUS C. SMITH, JR.

UNIVERSITY OF WASHINGTON PRESS

Seattle and London

Original edition copyright © 1966 by R. R. Bowker Co.
Revised edition copyright © 1989 by the University of Washington Press
Composition by Vera-Reyes, Inc., Quezon City, Philippines
Printed by Edwards Brothers, Inc., Ann Arbor, Michigan

All rights reserved. No part of this publication may be reproduced or transmitted in any form or by any means, electronic or mechanical, including photocopy, recording, or any information storage or retrieval system, without permission in writing from the publisher.

Library of Congress Cataloging-in-Publication Data

Smith, Datus Clifford, Jr., 1907–
  A guide to book publishing / by Datus C. Smith, Jr. — Rev. ed.
    p. cm.
  Bibliography: p.
  Includes index.
  ISBN 0–295–96651–3 ISBN 0–295–96652–1 (pbk.)
  1. Publishers and publishing. 2. Book industries and trade.
3. Publishers and publishing—Developing countries. 4. Book
industries and trade—Developing countries. I. Title.
2278.S5 1988
070.5—dc19   88-5754
                                                               CIP

To IAN MONTAGNES

wise friend and generous counselor

to book people around the world

Contents

About This Book

NO ONE CAN LEARN book publishing from a book. It is learned by *doing*. There are established publishers all over the world, in both developed and developing countries, who have proved the success of that method. They have succeeded after having started with nothing except brains, energy, and a modest capital. That should give heart and encouragement to the many people just beginning careers in book publishing in the developing countries of Asia, Africa, and Latin America to whom this book is especially addressed.

This book hopes merely to explain the general principles of book publishing, to provide a kind of checklist of the things that the publisher will learn along the way. The general principles are pretty much the same everywhere, but the educational and social and economic conditions of the societies that book publishing serves are quite different in different parts of the world. The possible justification for this book is that it tries to list some of the *universals* in book publishing in broad terms applicable to any culture and—where this is possible when thinking of such varied conditions as one finds in the total of the world's developing areas—in terms especially appropriate for the intended readers in those countries.

There are some useful training courses in a number of countries, as noted in Chapter 21, and there are many books about book publishing. Although most of them focus on conditions in societies with complex publishing and printing industries, they can be of value to the readers of this book who wish to pursue their studies of particular aspects of the general problem. The chapters in this book barely scratch the surface of the subjects dealt with. Other sources, some few of which are referred to in the bibliography, will give useful detail.

But the chief message the compilers of this book would like to give to its readers is that each country must work out its book publishing in ways suitable to that country. Each of us can get ideas from observing things in other countries, and these observations are useful in themselves and as "idea starters" for our own thinking. But the final test for all of us is what we do ourselves.

This book, therefore, is humbly offered as a set of "idea starters," not as a prescription which should be or could be followed exactly in any country.

Acknowledgments

THE FIRST ACKNOWLEDGMENT must be to my former colleagues in Franklin Book Programs whose joint efforts were essential in bringing this book into being in the first place. Franklin was a nonprofit organization in international book development and felt the need for a simple handbook understandable to beginning workers in developing countries. This revised edition would not have been possible without the basic work of those pioneers. So I add at the end of these new acknowledgments the names of the friends in various countries who gave indispensable help on the first edition.

I wish to repeat, also, the acknowledgment in the first edition of the generous support of the Ford Foundation for the Franklin project, including the gathering of facts and the writing of the book.

The heroine of the present work is Naomi B. Pascal, editor-in-chief of the University of Washington Press. She has gone far beyond an editor's normal responsibilities. In addition to accepting piecemeal interpolations, catching many of the author's errors, and tolerantly accepting his second thoughts, she was the organizer of the input of a half dozen outside specialists who have generously helped in bringing this twenty-two-year-old book up to the present state of the art. She is a true professional without whom I could not have done this job.

Next mention must go to Ian Montagnes, editor-in-chief of the University of Toronto Press, for a number of years editor of *Scholarly Publishing*, and at present director of an editorial training course (with participants from Asia, Africa, and Latin America) at the International Rice Research Institute in Los Baños, Philippines. On the dedication page of this book I attempt to suggest his overwhelming international contributions. But his contributions to me and to this book have been truly remarkable. From the dozens of pages of memos and letters he has sent me I can guess the number of hours he has so generously given me. And I am sure he would say that his students at Los Baños, drawn from around the world, have taught him much that has been reflected in the continuing advice he has given me during the whole revision process.

There are many other friends, in various countries, whose suggestions and criticism I have prized. Among them are: Amadio Arboleda, United Nations University and Asian Cultural Centre for Unesco, Tokyo; Edvard Aslaksen, Universitetsforlaget and International Association of Scholarly Publishers, Oslo; S. Bodunde Bankole, University of Lagos Press, Nigeria; Julian Behrstock, Paris; Mark Carroll, George Mason University Press and editor, *Scholarly Publishing*; Elizabeth Geiser, Gale Research Co., New York; Paul Gleason, International Monetary Fund, Washington, D.C.; Chandler Grannis, *Publishers Weekly*; Czeslaw Jan Grycz, University of California Press; Sybille Jagusch, Children's Literature Division, Library of Congress; May Katzen, University of Leicester; Jerry Lamme, Atlanta; Marcia Lord, Unesco, Paris; Robert MacMakin, formerly Agency for International Development, Lesotho; Herbert Morton, American Council of Learned Societies; Sandra K. Paul, New York; Mohan Primlani, New Delhi; Louie O. Reyes, Manila; Hassan Shadily, Jakarta; Tejeshwar Singh, New Delhi.

Besides what I say about Naomi Pascal above, I want also to express deep appreciation to others at the University of Washington Press, especially to Richard P. Barden, the associate director and controller, who was so imaginative as to have suggested that his Press undertake this publication and who has carried the business responsibilities of the project. He had been an officer of Franklin Book Programs, and his understanding of the needs of international publishing and his friendship with publishers in a number of developing countries have been important assets for the project. I am grateful, likewise, to Veronica Seyd, production manager, who has given invaluable advice about modern printing technology; Pat Soden, whose wisdom about marketing has been similarly useful; Julidta Tarver, managing editor; Leila Charbonneau, who has filled the critical role of copyeditor in distinguished fashion; Dorothy Anthony, business manager and incidentally secretary of the International Association of Scholarly Publishers; and of course Donald Ellegood, the director, under whose leadership the University of Washington Press has become one of the most enlightened American publishers with an international perspective. I am honored to join the author list of that distinguished publishing house.

Chief among the people in Franklin Book Programs who helped produce the first edition of this book were: *Afghanistan*—Atiqullah Pazhwak, Robert MacMakin; *Argentina*—Roberto Couture Troismonts; *Bangladesh*—A. Mannan Chowdhury, A. T. M. Abdul Mateen; *Brazil*—Propicio Machado Alves; *Egypt*—Hassan Galal el-Aroussy, Ahmed Riad Abaza; *Indonesia*—Hassan and Julia Shadily; *Iran*—Homayoun Sanati, Dariush Hamayoun, Ali Noori, Abdol Ali Karang, Jafar Samimi; *Iraq*—Mahmud el-Amin; *Kenya*—Hilary Ng'weno; *Lebanon*—Muhammad Yusuf Najm; *Malaysia*—Ghazali Yunus; *Nigeria*—'Femi Oyewole, John Iroganachi, Mustafa Zubairu; *United States*—Alden H. Clark, Joseph Margolies, Byron Buck, Christine Jacobson, Wilbur A. Knerr, Harold N. Munger, Jr., Ruth Stein, Betsy Donley.

Among the people outside of Franklin I think especially of Peter Jennison, who formulated an original idea for a handbook of book publishing; Daniel Melcher, Horace Manges, Anne J. Richter, Elizabeth A. Geiser, William Fleming, John Kyle, Dana Pratt, Jay Daily; Lise Lebel of the Association Nationale du Livre Français à l'Etranger in Paris; Ronald E. Barker of the Publishers Association in London; Philip Harris of the British Book Development Council; Eric Taylor of Ahmadu Bello University in Zaria, Nigeria; Dina Malhotra in New Delhi; and Julian Behrstock of Unesco in Paris. And I recall with gratitude the work of Peg Cameron as copyeditor in making the book better than it would have been without her help.

DATUS C. SMITH, JR.

I

---

*Book Publishing
and National Development*

1

Grand Strategy and General Objectives

IN ANY COUNTRY, developed or developing, the book industry is a small one in monetary terms. But just as a small switch can set in motion and control an enormous machine or an electrical system carrying power to remote areas, book publishing is also a "key." Since that is not always understood and appreciated by people outside the book field, one of the important factors in the grand strategy of book development in any country is to explain to the general public, or at least to the people in charge of national planning, the way in which book publishing *is* the key to educational and social and economic development and hence to true nationhood.

At the most practical level, and in terms most easily understood by people outside of the book field, the thought is most simply stated by saying that education is the basic investment for economic development, and that books are the basic tools of education.

Furthermore, if books are to be truly useful they must respond to the actual needs and interests of the readers. Foreign books, if in the right language, can be useful in many ways for certain kinds of readers; in fact for *some* readers at the higher educational levels the world view that can be obtained through reading books from abroad is a most desirable feature. But for most of the book readers in most countries the books must grow up out of local soil.

Quite aside from questions of national pride, and the natural wish of most countries to have book industries of their own, a *local* book industry is needed, no matter how great the availability of books from abroad. This is necessary for cultural enrichment, for opportunities for self-expression by the nation's thinkers and writers and artists, and for developing a sense of national unity as well as a sense of historic tradition.

But the argument that carries weight with national leaders even if they think the points above are too "philosophical" is that young readers, or adults who are newly literate, must be *interested* if they are to enjoy the newly acquired art of reading. And they must have a feeling of enjoyment and profit if they are to keep on reading. And the reading that people do by themselves, for their own reasons, represents the cheapest kind of education and one that triumphs over all other difficulties—even a shortage of good teachers—*if good books are available that deal with understandable facts and situations in their own life experience.*

This is not to question the advantage, in somewhat more advanced reading, of having books that will reflect the culture of other countries and thus broaden the reader's horizon. But there is no point, for beginning readers in an Asian or African or Latin American village, in talking about the Métro or the Underground or the New York Subway, or in referring to geography, foods, tools, materials, articles of dress, games, toys, farm animals, trees, flowers, forms of government, or national heroes that are completely outside the readers' experience.

Once the national leaders are persuaded that a country should have a book industry of its own—or should strengthen the book industry that has started—the next thing is to persuade them of the practical steps that must be taken to achieve the objective. Among these might be such down-to-earth matters as customs duties on equipment and paper and other supplies, and foreign-exchange licenses for such purchases; postal regulations and improvement in the handling of book shipments; inclusion of graphic arts among the fields covered by vocational training schools; establishment of systems of school and village and other public libraries; permission to teachers and other civil servants to accept royalty income produced by their books; establishment of a system of small business loans for book publishers; and many other things.

The problems will differ from country to country, of course. Some countries with a large population can plunge immediately into a full-scale book publishing development; whereas some small countries that cannot expect to have, in the foreseeable future, anything like a full development can at least undertake preparation and perhaps also production of school textbooks for the lower grades.

There are possibilities of regional development among some countries using the same language; and there are possibilities of centralized production, at least in part, for neighboring countries in which the population is too small to support full production facilities in each of them. A Unesco-organized project for French-language centralized textbook production in Cameroon was designed to serve not only that country but also Gabon, Zaire, Central African Republic, and Chad. Of all the Spanish-speaking countries of Latin America, only Mexico and Argentina have developed full publishing industries with export a significant factor in the business.

Even countries of similar size may need quite different solutions. The tiny country of Lebanon, with a population of barely more than a million but a strong tradition of trading, for decades was able to maintain an active Arabic-language book industry based largely on export, until civil strife and other troubles intervened. On the other hand, Liberia, with about the same population, has a much lower literacy rate, its citizens have a variety of mother tongues, it uses a non-African language (English) as its national language, its educational system has only recently started to modernize, and it has no tradition of extensive export of consumer goods.

It would be still more unrealistic to suppose that publishing methods that have grown up slowly out of the soil of France or Great Britain through the centuries, or others that have sprung up suddenly from the special conditions in North American, can be transferred wholesale to the countries of Asia, Africa, and Latin America.

But the publisher in any country can study the experience and present techniques of book publishing in other areas and can consider which of them may, with the right adaptation, be useful at home.

The sole purpose of this book is to give the reader an idea of some of the book publishing methods that have been used in various countries, hoping that creative thinking will thus be stimulated and that the readers will develop ways of book publishing that are just right for the special situation of their own countries.

2

Partners in the World of Books

TEAMWORK IS NEEDED to produce a book and put it in the hands of readers. Each member of the team has a necessary part to play, and none of them can be eliminated. No matter what stage of development a country may have reached or how simple or complex its economy, four basic elements must exist or be created if there is to be a book industry. The first three elements are easy to understand: the *author* who writes the manuscript, the *printer* who turns the manuscript into an edition of books, and the *bookseller* who sells the books thus produced. But it is the fourth partner who is in the most central position and whose job is least understood by people outside the book field: the *publisher*, who is the grand strategist and organizer of the whole undertaking, who brings the three other partners together, and who usually serves as the basic taker of the business risk of book publishing.

Those four elements of book publishing are always needed. The fact that one individual or firm may do more than one of the jobs does not change the fact that there are four jobs to be done. To take an extreme example, for the sake of emphasis: suppose that a wealthy author who owns a printing plant writes a book, prints it, and sells all the copies. In that case, one person would perform all four functions—even that of publisher, since the same person also organized the operation, supplied the financial capital, and (in this case an easy job!) "brought the parties together." But there were still four distinct jobs to be done: those of the author, printer, bookseller, and *publisher*.

In some parts of the world, major publishers sometimes own their own printing plants and bookshops or (the other way around) printers or booksellers go into book publishing. And in areas where professional publishing has not yet developed, the authors serve as their own publisher, simply arranging with a printer to manufacture the books, which the authors then sell to bookshops or directly to individual purchasers.

But, to repeat, every book issued for sale has an author, printer, bookseller, and publisher; and it is the purpose of this chapter to look at the function of each, and especially at the relation of the first three partners to the central figure in the partnership, the publisher. Elsewhere in the book we shall examine briefly the functions of others who may or may not play a part in particular book publishing situations: literary agents, wholesalers, mass distributors, and so forth. And the work of the teacher and the librarian of course underlies everything else. But first we will discuss the four basic active partners in book publishing.

The Author

The author is the creator or formulator of the ideas to be given to the world through a book, the arranger of the words, pictures, charts, tables, and so forth, in which the ideas are to be presented. Although we usually think of the author as being an individual—such as Shakespeare, al-Ghazzali, Cervantes, or Camoëns—the "author" in a legal sense and in contract relations with a publisher may be a group or an institution or even a government.

The author is the first owner of the right to publish the work created, and will usually try to sell that right—or lease it or assign it—to a publisher to reproduce the manuscript in some way for distribution to the world under one or another of the business arrangements we shall later examine. But until permission is given to someone else, the author is the sole proprietor of the right of publication; and there is nothing to prevent the author from hiding the manuscript or burning it up rather than sharing it with the rest of the world.

But the author who *does* want to share it is entitled to some reward from society. That is recognized in a general way in the custom of most developed countries, and specifically in the laws of countries having laws on the subject. Things do not always work out just right, but it is generally recognized that there should be some relation between the number of people using the book and the size of the reward that the author gets.

Protection of the author's rights under that general principle is the purpose of copyright laws and of many book trade practices even when not required by law. The reason behind these laws and customs is not merely to ensure common justice for individuals but to encourage authorship for the general good of society.

In effect, society means to give the author a monopoly on the work produced. It is intended that only by the author's permission—and under business arrangements and other conditions agreed to—may others have the privilege of making copies of the work. Although there are differences between copyright law and patent laws relating to mechanical invention, there is a basic similarity: the author is the "inventor" of the book; and because society wants to encourage both authorship and mechanical invention, it tries to help both the writer and the mechanical inventor protect their property rights in their creations.

Of course there can be theft of literary property as well as of other kinds; and the publisher who issues a work without the author's permission, and without paying any royalty or fee, is a thief, a "pirate." (An author *may*, through generous intention or plain carelessness, give the work to the world free, by deliberately or inadvertently authorizing anyone who wishes to do so to reproduce and sell the work. Or the lack of copyright laws or poor administration of them may make it difficult for the author to protect the supposed rights. Or, through contract, an author may have assigned all rights to a publisher or someone else. But that does not change the principle that publishing rights start with the author, from whom all others get their rights.)

The main argument against piracy—frequently ignored in developing countries—is that piracy prevents the growth of the indigenous book industry. It might be noted in passing that the earliest pressure for copyright legislation in the United States was from publishers who recognized that piracy was against the interest of an American book industry that was trying to develop.

The chief international copyright agreements are the Berne Convention and the Universal Copyright Convention (UCC), each with about eighty members (not identical groups). Both Conventions were modified by the so-called Paris Revisions of 1971, providing under some circumstances for a system of "licensing" intended to make it easier for publishers in developing countries to get translation and publication rights. Changes are taking place so often that it is impossible to guess just what the situation will be even a few years ahead. For a good description of the international copyright problem and its background, see Paul Gleason's article, "Copyright, Licensing, and Piracy," in the Appendix.

Copyright was not created to restrict information. It was created nearly 400 years ago to ensure common justice for individuals and to encourage authors for the general good of society. Without authors there could be no publishing for education and social enrichment. And without the protection of copyright, it is fair to say, the world would never have had the explosion of knowledge that has come through books.

There is a great deal of not-for-profit publishing in both developed and developing countries. Some of that is by individual authors, but more is by institutions. These persons or groups may wish to copyright their works not for reasons of profit but to retain some control over the use to which they are put. Sometimes a warning against reproducing without permission is followed by wording such as, "This permission will not be unreasonably withheld if the proposed use is for noncommercial purposes."

Details about publishing rights and contracts are given in Chapter 18, but it is sufficient here to say that, according to the most normal pattern, the author makes a contract with a publisher, permitting the publisher to have copies of the book printed and to sell them, with specified payment to the author, often on the basis of the number of copies sold.

In theory, once the contract is signed, the author turns the manuscript over to the publisher, the publisher has copies printed and distributed, and the author merely sits back waiting for royalty payments while working on the next book. In actual practice, however, the situation is very different. Not only does the author have heavy responsibilities, shared with the publisher, of making the manuscript truly ready for the publisher to turn over to the printer, and of proofreading to make sure that the printer has reproduced the manuscript accurately (see Chapter 5), but the author can also be of great help to the publisher in promotion (Chapter 9). And even in the earliest stages, when the manuscript is planned and written (see Chapter 4), the wise author is not entirely alone. A creative and imaginative publisher can be of great help to an author in seeing ways in which knowledge and writing skill can be applied to a particular book project for which the world has need and—unfortunately not always exactly the same thing—for which there is a ready market.

No respectable author is willing to be ordered around about what to say or how to say it. In such fields as fiction, criticism, drama, and poetry the sensitive writer will find it difficult to accept ideas from others, even when the publisher is qualified to offer advice to established authors. But in many fields of writing, especially in those relating to presentation of facts, the author and eventually the readers can benefit greatly from the suggestions and vision of a creative publisher. There are many examples of famous writers who have publicly acknowledged the part played in their success by the inspiration and wise guidance of an imaginative publisher.

Each author has to decide how far to go in accepting the publisher as partner in the planning stage, and much will depend on the spirit of mutual confidence established. When that partnership happens to work, however, it can bring thrilling results for the author, publisher, and the public alike.

Through most of the ages of man, and in most countries, authorship has been a poorly paid profession; and very few authors out of the total number, even in prosperous countries with a high rate of literacy, are able to support themselves solely on the earnings of their writing. Even at the present time, when one reads reports of truly enormous sums paid to a few authors in some countries, the situation is not very different. The overwhelming majority of authors are people in other lines of work for whom writing is incidental.

Money is as important to authors as it is to other people, and the author properly demands that the financial relationship with a publisher be properly and honestly handled. But because the *chief* purpose in writing is a desire to communicate, the wise author gives first thought to the integrity and effectiveness with which a publisher presents the message to the world. All the other qualities that an author hopes to find in a publisher—including the ability to earn money for the author—follow from these.

Other comments on the relations between publishers and authors are found throughout this book, and specific discussion of the money side of the relationship is in Chapter 18. But the main point for the publisher, printer, and bookseller to remember is that without the author they would have nothing to do; and that unless they do an efficient job, other authors will not feel like entrusting them with books in the future. The chief thing for the author to remember is that no matter how golden the written words are, no one except family and friends will read them unless the whole machinery of the book industry helps to present them to the world.

The Printer

The printer is the manufacturer. The printer receives the manuscript from the publisher, composes and prints and binds an edition, and sends the manufactured book back to the publisher. Under all normal circumstances, the printer plays no part in deciding what to print but merely does the job requested by the publisher and gets paid for it. The printer is not a risk taker on any specific book project. The printer takes a business risk, of course, in establishing a printing plant in the first place when uncertain how much business there will be; but payment for producing any specific book is a matter of firm agreement between publisher and printer and does not depend (as does the profit of the publisher and the royalty income of the author) upon the sale of the book.

If the printer knows that the publisher is sufficiently honest and sufficiently prosperous to assure payment (the printer will probably demand payment in advance if that assurance is lacking), the printer has a certainty of profit that is denied to the author and publisher. In terms that an economist would use, the printer, although an entrepreneur in setting up and running the printing plant, is not formally a participant in the "entrepreneurial enterprise" of publishing any particular book. As we shall see below, the risks and the possible profits and losses of that enterprise are the publisher's.

But this theoretical statement of the relationship is not always true in practice. Even aside from the cases in which the publishing house and the printing plant are commonly owned, or in which the printer becomes the publisher as well as the manufacturer of a book, the printer has major contributions to make to the successful publication of particular books, as well as to the strengthening and developing of the book publishing industry generally.

The quality of the printing, the supply of appropriate paper, the conscientious following of production schedules, the care in proof-reading, and so forth, are obvious factors in the success of any given book, often affecting the sales and always having some effect on how clearly the author's message gets through to the reader. In the case of production schedules, a failure by the printer may prevent the message from getting through at all if the book (for instance, a textbook) must be available at a certain time for use by its intended customers or they will not buy it. Further comment on the normal publisher-printer-author relationship is given later, but mention should be made here of the major contributions that an intelligent printer can make to the publisher's welfare by special cooperation outside normal responsibilities.

One such contribution is in the field of book design: type arrangement, page layout, colors of ink, selection of paper, kind of binding, and so forth. In countries with developed book industries, every publisher has a designer, either on the payroll or available on a regular consulting basis, and the printer follows the designer's instructions as a builder follows an architect's. In many of the developing countries of Asia, Africa, and Latin America, however, the profession of book designer is unknown, or at least designers are not regularly available. The matter is left entirely to the printer.

The printer who recognizes a stake in the improvement of book publishing will not merely "throw the book together," but will attempt not only to design the particular book tastefully but also to elevate general standards of design and manufacture at the same time. More important than anything else, the printer can help educate the publisher in the problems and techniques of design and manufacture and lead the publisher gradually into accepting full responsibility. This cannot be done all of a sudden, and in the meantime the publisher should be duly grateful for the way in which the printer is doing part of what, in developed countries, is regarded as the publisher's job.

There is another field besides design in which the publisher's neglect of publishing responsibility imposes an extra job on the printer and—in this case—greatly increases the cost of book printing for the publisher. That is the field of copyediting and proofreading, as well as general relations with the author while the manuscript is going through the production process.

In developed book industries it is the publisher who receives the manuscript from the author and, after copyediting (see Chapter 5), turns it over to the printer; and the printer sends proof to the author *through* the publisher, and receives back the corrected proof by the same route. In many developing countries, on the other hand, the publisher has no copyeditor and often merely refers the author to the printer, leaving it to those two to work out all problems until the book is finished.

Because few authors know about the mechanical problems of printing (and most of them are not even very good proofreaders of their own works), and because printers cannot be expected to maintain an editorial staff in addition to their mechanical workers, the result of carrying on author relations without help from a publisher is usually unsatisfactory. It can be a frightful experience for the printer and the author and very costly to the publisher, who will eventually pay the bill. Here again, the printer can help educate the publisher to the economic advantages of taking back this part of the publisher's job that the printer has been performing.

The publisher, at the same time, can insist that the printer make good a major neglect in the field of proofreading. As explained more fully in Chapter 5, in developed book industries the printer is supposed to provide proofs in which the type conforms to the manuscript. The main purpose of proofreading by the author and publisher is to give the author a chance to catch the *occasional* typographical errors missed by the printer's proofreaders. But in most countries of Asia and Africa, even in several with well-developed book industries, the printer does no proofreading, or none of any professional standard. Thus a galley sheet returned to an Asian or African printer after proofreading by the author may call for a hundred or more corrections in the same space that might have needed only a half dozen in Great Britain or Germany. Further errors of course occur in correcting the first ones, and the process goes on and on.

If the printers can persuade the publishers to assume their responsibility for copyediting and author relations, the publishers would be justified in demanding, in turn, that the printers develop a professional proofreading staff able to send out proof that, insofar as it conforms to the manuscript, is nearly perfect.

Still another area in which the printer's and publisher's functions become mixed is that of finance capital. Although the publisher is supposed to supply the capital for a book project, and in fact does so eventually, many books take a long time in production, and unless there is an arrangement for the publisher to pay in installments, it may prove to have been the printer who provided much of the capital investment during the whole production period, through advancing the funds to buy paper, pay the workers, and so forth. Printers know this, of course, and, if they have a sound accounting system, they include the cost of the interest on that capital in what they charge the publisher for printing his books. But the publisher should be equally aware of the printer's contribution and must be prompt in paying the printer at agreed times. Each party can help through common analysis of the problem of short-term capital requirements and common seeking of solutions helpful to both.

A final point on publisher-printer relations is their joint interest in modernization and technical improvement in book manufacture. The printer would be foolish to undertake a large project in modernization for cheap production of large quantities of books without any idea where the business would come from. On the other hand, the publisher with a vision of mass distribution could do nothing about it if the country had nothing except antique equipment incapable of producing books in large quantities at low prices.

Joint study of such possibilities, and recognition of a common interest in solving the problems, are necessary. The book printer with a clear vision of future economic welfare, possibly increased by a sense of patriotism, will be concerned with the whole development of the book industry and with the factors influencing it, including such subjects as reading development and libraries (discussed in Chapter 16), the expansion and improvement of education, better facilities for postal shipment of books, and the economic well-being of retail booksellers. The printer alone cannot achieve the needed reforms, but should see both the commercial and patriotic incentive for joining with other branches of the book industry, perhaps in some ways along lines suggested in Chapter 17.

The Bookseller

The bookseller receives the books directly or indirectly from the publisher, buying them at a discount and selling them at a higher price to purchasers in a bookshop or in other ways. The bookseller is customarily the last person before the final purchaser in the chain that began with the author.

The problems of a normal kind of retail bookshop are dealt with in Chapter 20, but for the purposes of this chapter we mean "bookseller" to include not only the conventional bookshop but also all the other retail sellers of books who stand between the publisher and the ultimate consumer, thus including even the illiterate proprietor of a bicycle repair shop who has a wire rack of paperbound books for sale hanging on the wall or a peddler with a sack of books in a rural village.

Constant availability of books for purchase is one of the most important keys to expansion of the market for books, whether in developed or developing countries, and of equal interest to the commercially minded member of the book industry and to the educational statesman interested in the spread of knowledge among the citizens.

It is greatly in the interest of the publisher, as well as of the public generally, to have a flourishing retail book trade. Every step considered by a publisher for increasing direct sales to consumers, or for selling through new channels, should be carefully considered in terms of possible bad effects on the retail bookseller. As in Europe and America, there will undoubtedly be occasions in the developing countries when the publishers feel that a new distributing method (for instance a mass distribution plan such as described in Chapter 13) will produce so many new readers and carry sales so far into new areas that it must be attempted anyway, in spite of the opposition of booksellers. But there will be other occasions when no new readers would be added, though the publisher would gain a small additional profit, for instance by selling to a library directly instead of through a retail bookseller. In such cases the publisher should think long and hard before taking a step harmful to the bookseller, who is the publisher's strongest economic supporter and the source of so much future profit.

New methods of distribution hold great promise for Asia and Africa and Latin America. But they must be examined carefully.

Neither the publisher nor the public should lose sight of the invaluable contribution to the interest of both by the conventional bookseller with a large stock of books on many subjects and drawn from the lists of many publishers. Such a bookshop is an educational institution next in importance only to a school or library. It is a prime encourager of reading and producer of book sales. No matter how effective the development of mass-distributing methods may become or how widely book club memberships are spread, it is only a bookshop that can offer for sale a wide enough variety of books to stimulate all interests and serve all tastes.

Both the publisher and the public should appreciate the enormous cost borne by a proper bookshop in having available at all times so large a collection from which the purchaser can make a choice. Most of the books in the shop will have been bought from the publisher, and paid for, months or often years before the money comes back to the bookseller from a retail purchaser. There are various ways in which the publisher can help the bookseller carry that heavy cost. In countries that have a tradition in which most publishers serve also as booksellers there may be methods of barter among the firms to avoid use of direct cash for the booksellers' investment in inventory.

Whatever the business relations, neither the publisher's economic interest nor society's interest in reading and education can permit neglect of retail bookselling. It is the money counted up on the abacus or cash register of a nation's retail distributors that decides the ultimate fate of the book industry in any country.

II

The Book Publishing Process

3

The Economics
of Book Publishing

THE BOOK PUBLISHER is an investor in books. The publisher is the one who pays out money to the author, translator, artist, editor, printer, papermaker, and others for producing the books, and to the salespeople, advertisers, and those who help in marketing them, and takes in money from booksellers and others who buy the books or who buy the right to use the books' content in some way. The publisher hopes to take in more money than is paid out.

That is the whole story of "the economics of book publishing." Everything else here, and in the millions of words in many languages written on the subject through the years, is only a refinement of that basic theme.

As in any business, the book publisher tries to reduce costs and increase income but realizes that "you have to spend money to make money." It is the purpose of this chapter to look at some of the relationships of cost to income and final profit.

The surest way to increase income is to sell more books. More income should increase profit, if the publisher is a commercial house, or reduce the need for subsidy, if the publisher is a nonprofit organization. That is a more profound statement than appears at first glance, for it rests on a fundamental principle of book publishing: manufacturing *costs per copy* go down not just a little bit but often sensationally as the quantity increases. As we shall see in a moment, that is dramatically true for manufacturing costs, but it is also true in greater or less degree for many other of the publisher's expenses.

The successful publisher is the one who recognizes that principle, and learns how to make use of it. That is what makes the difference between a vigorous and expanding and profitable book publishing industry and one that plods along with the same old high prices, low sales, and low profits—and, incidentally, small contribution to the national welfare.

Cost

There are two ways of looking at the items of the book publisher's cost. The first way considers merely what is done in the various operations, and the costs fall into three main groups:

Editorial preparation costs. This category includes the publisher's payment to the author and salaries or fees to the illustrator, editor, translator (if the book is to be a translation rather than an original work), designer, and others.

Physical manufacturing costs. This includes payment to the printer for printing the books and (either directly or through the printer) to the manufacturers of paper, ink, cloth, thread, glue, and so forth.

Marketing and distribution costs. Included here is the work of sales representatives, order clerks, shippers, advertisers, promoters, and others.

That is a perfectly logical way of looking at costs, and for some purposes it is the best way. But there is a more useful method for analysis of how the factors can influence the cost of a book and, eventually, the size of the publisher's profit.

This second method of studying costs is the one a farseeing publisher uses when deciding how many copies of a book should be printed, what selling price to charge, how far to go in meeting an author's demand for a higher rate of royalty payment, and so forth. Under this other method of listing the kinds of expense, they are divided into groups showing how their size is influenced by the number of copies:

Automatically varying costs. These are costs that automatically increase for a given book if the number of copies is increased.

1. Royalty payments to the author, usually based on number of copies sold; sometimes a flat amount based on the size of the edition printed.

2. Payments to the printer for presswork and binding (this does

not include the cost of composition, which is an unvarying cost in the category below).

3. Payment for materials, through the printer or directly to the supplier of paper, ink, cloth, thread, staples, glue, and so forth.

4. Storage and shipping.

Unvarying costs. These are, costs that do not vary for a given book, whatever the number of copies printed.

1. Editorial preparation, including editing, illustration, cover design, and so forth.

2. Composition, that is, the typesetting, calligraphing, and plate-making—in other words the preparatory stage of bookmaking up to the point when the press starts putting ink on paper.

Promotion costs. These vary according to the publisher's policy decision, naturally influenced by the number of copies but not automatically following it.

Overhead costs. These can be controlled by the publisher to some extent in view of expectation of sales for all the books published, but in general are fixed costs: administration, accounting, taxes, rent, interest on borrowed capital, and so forth.

Each of these kinds of expense is discussed in one of the chapters of this book, but the following comments provide one example from each category to help make the distinction clear.

Automatically varying costs. Paper is a clear case of an expense that goes up or down almost directly in proportion to the number of copies. There are ten times as many kilograms of paper in an edition of 10,000 books as in one of 1,000. And although there is some variation in the price per kilogram depending on whether a little or a lot is bought at one time, one may say in general that the cost of paper is in direct proportion to the number of copies.

Unvarying costs. On the other hand, typesetting is a good example of a cost that is the same for a given book whatever the number of copies. When the compositors set the type, their job is no more difficult, and the cost no greater, whether one copy is to be printed or a million. And because the *total* typesetting cost is unchanged, the cost *per copy* of course goes down as the quantity increases. For instance, if it costs §1,000[1] to set type for a book that is to be printed in an edition of 1,000 copies, the typesetting will be §1 *per copy*; or if an edition of 10,000 copies, then the typesetting cost goes down to §0.1 *per copy*; and so on.

Promotion costs. Advertising is an item of expense for which the publisher's policy judgment will be *influenced by* the number of copies, but there is nothing automatic about it. Many publishers plan on spending a fixed percentage of the year's sales income on advertising, and they use that figure for overall estimating. But the expenditure for any particular book is decided in the light of many factors, including the kind of book as well as the quantity the publisher thinks can be sold, how the public is expected to respond to different kinds of advertising, and so forth.

Overhead costs. It is clear that most such costs are relatively fixed and, in the short term, cannot be changed very much, or at least not with respect to any one book. Although the publisher may engage or discharge administrative staff or accountants and thus make some adjustment for increases or decreases in the overall business, it is not possible to cut off and sell half the office or warehouse or delivery truck if business suddenly declines by 50 percent. It is in this sense that we call these costs fixed.

The publisher wants to include, in the price purchasers are asked to pay for the book, a sufficient allowance for overhead cost. It is never possible to calculate exactly what should be charged to each book, but the year's total overhead expense to be charged to *all* of the publisher's books can be estimated; and then it can be assigned to individual books in various ways. A common method is to assume the overhead cost in the future will be about the same percentage of net sales income as it was in the previous year. If last year's sales totaled §400,000 and overhead costs totaled §100,000, the publisher assumes that the overhead in the coming year will probably again be 25 percent of net sales income. To complete this illustration by applying it in a specific case: if the publisher guessed

---

1. Throughout this book we will use the symbol "§" for all money figures, as a generalized representation of a money unit of any country.

that there would be §10,000 sales income from a particular book it could be roughly estimated that the overhead cost of that book would be 25 percent of §10,000 or §2,500. The 25 percent figure used here is merely an example; the overhead percentage varies widely from one country to another and from one publisher to another as well.

We will come back to the question of cost when putting the expense figures and incomes figures together in a later section of this chapter. But first, let us see what determines how much sales income the publisher gets.

Income

The main influences on the amount of sales income are only vaguely imagined by most people outside the book business. The typical layman, upon hearing that a publisher has brought out an edition of 5,000 copies of a book with a selling price of §3 does some quick figuring and decides the publisher has an income of §15,000. How wrong that is! Discussed below are the four major factors a publisher has in mind in calculating possible income.

1. *Selling price*. For reasons we shall study later, the relation of the manufacturing cost of a book to the selling price is quite different in Asia and Africa from what it is in Europe and the United States. Many Asians have a general rule of multiplying the manufacturing cost by only 3 to 3.5 to determine the selling price, whereas in publishing industries in other parts of the world the factor may be 4, 4.5, 5, 6, or even more for certain kinds of books.

2. *Number of copies sold*. This is, of course, the major risk in any book publishing project. If a large part of the edition is unsold, all the calculations are thrown off. But even if the edition is sold out, that will not be the full number of copies because of the free copies given away for promotion and the damaged copies.

3. *Discount to booksellers and other purchasers*. Booksellers always receive a discount from the publisher; jobbers and wholesalers get an additional discount; and other kinds of purchasers get discounts of different kinds and sizes. Although some purchasers pay the full listed price, the average is brought down by the large purchasers

with large discounts. In the United States discounts may run as high as 55 percent or more, and the average for many general books can be about 44 percent; in Europe the discount sale tends to be lower and in Asia and Africa very much lower.

4. *Incidental cost of marketing.* These costs include commissions to certain kinds of sales representatives, uncollectable debts from purchasers, postage in those cases where the publisher pays the carrying charge, and so forth. Such costs can run from a very low figure to more than 15 percent.

For the example above of an edition of 5,000 copies of a book selling at §3, let us assume that 100 copies of the book are damaged or given away free, so there are only 4,900 to sell; that average discounts are 25 percent; and that incidental selling costs are 3 percent. We would then get this result:

Selling price of 4,900 copies @ §3	§14,700
Less average 25% discount to purchasers	3,675
Total paid by purchasers	§11,025
Less incidental selling costs, 3% of sales	§　330
Net sales income for the publisher	§10,695

That is quite different from the §15,000 predicted by the naive person outside the book industry! And this particular example is more favorable to the publisher than the average in most of the world's book industries because of the low average discount we have assumed.

Cost versus Income

Thus far we have been considering cost and income separately. The real test of publishing wisdom comes when you try to fit the two together. You would like to charge more for the book, but the higher selling price might decrease the number of sales; you would like to encourage booksellers by allowing more discount, but that would reduce the sales income per copy sold; you would like to use cheaper paper, but the less attractive book may be so much less appealing to the public that your loss of sales may be greater than your saving of expense.

There is a never-ending series of such relationships for all books, as well as surprises in the performance of particular books. The genius of book publishing lies in the vision and analytical intelligence with which the publisher sees how to increase quantities, reduce prices, and get more profit, all at the same time.

As suggested earlier, the most important key to achieving this is the principle of how per-copy costs decline as quantities increase. The saving in per-copy costs when quantities increase is not, at present, as great in Asia and Africa as it is in Europe and the United States and, to some extent, in Latin America because (1) the developing countries do not yet have enough equipment giving the full saving for long press runs compared with short ones, and (2) in view of the high cost of paper and the relatively low cost of labor in most Asian and African countries, paper cost (which we have seen does not vary much per copy) is a larger element in the cost of a book than printing cost (which *does* become less per copy with increasing quantities) in countries with more developed book industries.

Even so, in every country on earth the important fact to note at all times is: *per-copy costs go down as quantities go up.* See how the principle works out in the example in Table 1—an imaginary one based on actual figures from a combination of Asian, African, and Latin American countries. The actual figures would not be right in any one country because of differences in printing and paper costs, in publishing practices, in discount schedules, and so forth, and especially in the completeness with which the publisher does the job and bears the cost of his full publishing responsibility. But the example illustrates the basic fact.

Another way of stating the per-copy saving when producing the larger quantity is to say that although the first thousand copies cost §0.46 each, an additional 4,000 copies could be produced at the same time at a cost of only §0.17 each.

TABLE 1
Cost of Producing Books

	1,000-copy edition	5,000-copy edition	10,000-copy edition
Composition (typesetting) cost unaffected by quantity	§237.00*	§ 237.00	§ 237.00
Presswork and binding	121.00	400.00	746.00
Paper	103.00	500.00	1,000.00
	§461.00	§1,137.00	§1,983.00
Cost per copy	§ 0.46	§ 0.23	§ 0.20

*§ = a generalized representation of a money unit of any country.

The most important element in this critical fact of low *run-on costs* is the decreasing cost *per copy* of composition as the size of the edition increases. Figure 2 shows this.

Or the facts can be presented in another way, showing directly the low run-on costs of additional copies manufactured at the same time. In the next chart (Figure 3) the three bars show the per-copy cost of the book in editions of the three sizes. The costs of composition, presswork, and paper make up the total in each case. As noted above, the composition cost *per copy* goes down greatly as the edition becomes larger. Presswork and paper are the run-on costs.

Publishing Cost

The cost of production, just discussed, is only one part of the publisher's cost; and of course income has to be calculated to consider the profit or loss on a book.

Because some of the publisher's costs relate directly to the selling price (for instance, the author's royalty is usually a percentage of the selling price), the price at which the book is to be sold has to be decided before doing the rest of the figuring.

 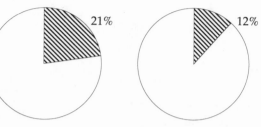

Composition cost in a
1,000-copy edition

Composition cost in a
5,000-copy edition

Composition cost in a
10,000-copy edition

Figure 2. Composition costs shown as a percentage of total book manufacturing cost. Full circles represent the cost of manufacturing one copy in editions of three different sizes. Shaded areas show the varying cost of composition (figures indicate the composition cost as a percentage of the full manufacturing cost).

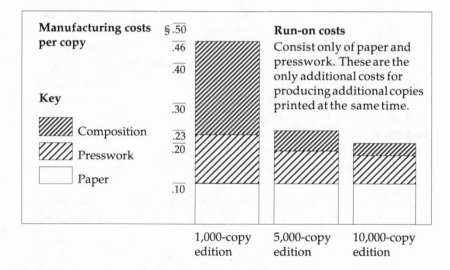

**Manufacturing costs
per copy**

Key

Composition

Presswork

Paper

Run-on costs

Consist only of paper and presswork. These are the only additional costs for producing additional copies printed at the same time.

1,000-copy
edition

5,000-copy
edition

10,000-copy
edition

Figure 3. Manufacturing cost of one copy in editions of three different sizes.

TABLE 2
Selling Price and Sales Income

	1,000-copy edition	5,000-copy edition	10,000-copy edition
Production cost per copy (see Table 1 above)	§0.46	§0.23	§0.20
Selling price	§1.50	§0.80	§0.75
Average sales income per copy (70% of selling price)	§1.05	§0.56	§0.53
Number of copies available for sale (after deducting free and damaged copies)	950	4,900	9,850
Total sales income	§998	§2,744	§5,220

In the case of this hypothetical book, we assume the publisher might apply a multiplying factor of something like 3.5 to the per-copy manufacturing cost shown in Table 1—that is, that the selling price would be fixed at three and one-half times the per-copy manufacturing cost. And we assume that in the country of publication a publisher's average income from sales (after allowing discounts to booksellers, etc.) is about 70 percent of the selling price. And, finally, we assume that the free copies given away for promotion and the damaged copies will reduce the number of copies for sale somewhat below the number printed. These hypotheses are calculated in Table 2.

The publisher's full cost can then be put together as shown in Table 3.

Finally, putting together the income from Table 2 and the publishing cost from Table 3, we see the profit situation for the editions of different size (if all copies are sold) in Table 4.

The relationship of cost to profit in editions of different size is of course a key point. Note that: for the 5,000-copy edition the *cost* is 2.5 times the cost of the 1,000-copy edition, but the *profit* would be 7.5 times as great if all copies were sold; for the 10,000-copy edition

TABLE 3
Full Publishing Cost

	1,000-copy edition	5,000-copy edition	10,000-copy edition
Selling price	§1.50	§ 0.80	§ 0.75
Number copies to sell	950	4,900	9,850
Production cost (from Table 1)	§ 461	§1,137	§1,983
Author's royalty (10% of selling price for first 5,000; 12.5% after that)*	142	392	831
Advertising, estimated	100	200	300
Overhead, estimated at 25% of the net sales income shown in Table 2†	250	686	1,305
Full publishing cost	§ 953	§2,415	§4,418

*The royalty figure here is just an example. There are many different royalty rates, and in recent years there has been a tendency to fix the royalty as a percentage of the publisher's net receipts, rather than of the list price of the book. There are also different rates for paperback editions, for export sales, and so forth.

†The overhead estimate of 25% is also just an example. In many developed book industries a 40% overhead allowance is more usual.

TABLE 4
Possible Profit

	1,000-copy edition	5,000-copy edition	10,000-copy edition
Income from Table 2	§998	§2,744	§5,220
Publishing cost from Table 3	953	§2,415	§4,418
Profit if all copies sold	§ 45	§ 329	§ 802

1,000-copy edition   5,000-copy edition   10,000-copy edition

Figure 4. Profit as percentage of production cost. Full circles represent production cost; shaded areas indicate profit.

the *cost* is about 4.5 times the cost of the 1,000-copy edition, but the *profit* would be nearly 18 times as great if all copies were sold.

If all copies are sold, in other words, the publisher's *profit in relation to the amount risked in paying for production* increases greatly as the size of the edition goes up. The charts in Figure 4 give the picture.

Calculating the Break-Even Point

A method of figuring that publishers sometimes use when deciding printing quantities and selling prices is that of calculating what is called the break-even point—that is, the number of copies that will have to be sold in order to recover manufacturing cost. The trouble with the method is that it does not necessarily include correct overhead costs for selling part of an edition; but applications of overhead to particular books are inaccurate in other ways as well, and this break-even approach has value for rough estimating.

The publisher first calculates what margin per copy, after paying other expenses, will be left over for meeting production costs. That margin figure is then divided into the total production cost, thus giving a rough idea of how many copies must be sold before breaking even. Here is an application of the method to the above book in the 5,000-copy edition:

Selling price of the book (5,000-copy edition)   §0.80
Less average discount estimated at 30%   0.24
    Net sales income per copy   §0.56

Less (per copy):
    Author's royalty (10% of selling price)   §0.08
    Overhead (25% of net sales income)   0.14
    Advertising   0.05

    0.27

Margin per copy for paying for production   §0.29
Break-even point: §1,137 ÷ §0.29 = 3,921 copies

Thus if the book is published in a 5,000-copy edition at a selling price of §0.80 and with the other conditions as given, the publisher can recover the manufacturing cost by selling 3,921 copies. The reader may enjoy making a study of the break-even point for the 10,000-copy edition.

Subsidiary Rights

The income discussed in all of the examples above has been entirely from the sale of books. But there is another kind of income to be kept in mind, though it is often of a minor sort in a book industry that is not highly developed: income from the sale or licensing of what are called subsidiary rights, including permission to other publishers to bring out reprint editions; the granting of translation rights; authorization to include excerpts in anthologies or books of readings which other publishers are issuing; and (although this particular income often goes entirely to the author and none to the publisher) authorization to present the work on the stage or on film, radio, television, tape, or videotape.

More is said about these subsidiary rights in Chapter 18, and especially about the sharing of this income between publisher and author. But it should be noted here that there has been a tendency in some developed book industries in recent years, notably that of the United States, for income from subsidiary rights to make a great difference—often the whole difference—between the publisher's profit and loss. That is, many American publishers make a profit of only 2 or 3 percent—or actually sustain a loss—on their regular operations in publishing books, but have a large profit overall because of very substantial income from subsidiary rights.

At present, there is not much income from subsidiary rights for book publishers in Asia, Africa, and Latin America. It can become increasingly important, however, especially as mass distribution schemes are carried out, with a natural increase in cheap reprintings in large quantities of books that may have been issued originally by other publishers. If book publishing in other countries follows the line of development it has taken in Europe and North America, royalty income paid to the original publisher from the mass distribution and book club reprint rights can—at least in theory—become a major source of income. It must be recognized, however, that there has been little progress along this line in the last twenty years. As the West becomes more interested in the literature of developing countries, however, there will be increasing quotation from that literature in anthologies and other possibilities of subsidiary rights, with income for Asian and African and Latin American publishers from that source.

Economies for the Publisher

There are a thousand ways for the publisher to increase profits besides the basic major way of selling more books. Merely to reduce expenses in the editorial department, in production, in the sales department, and so forth, will not necessarily increase profits, because sales income may be reduced as a result of an unwise economy. Examples of wise and unwise economies will be studied in different chapters of this book. Special mention, however, is made in the following section of the two kinds of expense that are indispensable and are related to each other—long-range development and the cost of interest on capital needed if the publisher is going to build for the future.

Capital and Interest

A constant expense in any business is the cost of the capital required—the interest that has to be paid on the money invested in a project from the time the expenses are met until the money comes back in the form of income. Interest is a cost of investment even if the publisher does not have to borrow. Even if the publisher is so lucky as to have plenty of available cash, making it unnecessary to borrow from banks or elsewhere, the capital still costs something because the money could be profitably invested somewhere else, if not in book publishing.

This is perhaps a good place to say that most of the principles in this book, and specifically in this chapter, are as applicable in a socialist as in a capitalist economy, though they are expressed here in terms of a private enterprise system of book publishing. The methods, value judgments, and objectives in the two systems differ in particular circumstances, but an able professional book publisher in either system will look at many of the factors in the same way, and especially the factors of cost.

The question of interest on capital is a case in point: even if, in a state publishing enterprise, the publisher has merely to request an appropriation from the national treasury, that is still part of the national wealth which could be put to good use in some other way if the state did not invest it in book publishing. The conscientious state publisher, as a temporary caretaker of public funds, will regard interest on capital as a true cost of the operation, especially in thinking about long-term investments, whether or not "interest" is an actual entry in the book of account.

To return to the general question of interest on capital as a cost of book publishing, the picture is clearer if we think of interest costs of three sorts: (1) interest cost of normal operations, (2) investment in inventory, and (3) long-term development.

Interest cost of normal operations. This category includes advance payments that the publisher may make to the author, and those almost surely to be made to the printer and paper merchant; and the credit to be extended, for at least some period of time, to at least some of the purchasers; and of course the normal running expenses of the publishing house.[2]

Investment in inventory. Remembering the inexpensiveness of producing additional copies of a book at the time of first printing, the publisher may think it wise to print more than just a year's supply. For some kinds of books, this can be a wonderful benefit in future years, as steady income is received without further printing cost. But it ties up capital in the meantime, and that cost must be balanced against printing economy. Storage and insurance costs are likewise incurred, as well as the risk of damage from mold and insects. And the high cost of paper in developing countries makes long-term investment less attractive in those areas.

Long-term development. This kind of investment, though perhaps bringing no return at all in the year in which the money is spent, can be more important than any other kind for the ultimate good of the individual publisher and of the national book industry of which he is a part. Included in this category are such things as (1) experiments in new distributing methods, (2) long-term projects in editorial development, such as series, new kinds of textbooks, subscription projects, and large reference works, (3) cooperative efforts, with others, in developing more readers and more book purchasers, better schools, additional libraries, and so forth, and (4) projects in industry betterment, such as publishers' associations, trade magazines, a cooperative credit bureau, and exchange of industry information.

All of those projects in the category of long-term development are discussed elsewhere in this book, but it must be emphasized here that the publisher who entirely neglects such projects not only fails in public duty but accepts a dull future, without hope of real expansion in either business or public service.

---

2. Note, by the way, that, to the extent to which the publisher extends credit to purchasers, the publisher is in effect providing them with finance capital; and to the extent to which authors or printers or paper merchants provide their service or material to a publisher without advance payments, they are helping to provide the publisher with finance capital.

The Need for Publisher's Credit

The lack of risk capital, or at least of capital that its owners are willing to invest in the future of their own countries, holds back development in many parts of Asia, Africa, and Latin America. The problem is especially acute in the book publishing industry (though less so in the printing industry, perhaps because the potential investors can see tangible machinery), and undercapitalization is perhaps the most serious single obstacle to book publishing development in the developing countries. This is not merely because the lack of capital forces the publisher to print in small quantities at high prices, but because it prevents all the other long-range efforts at building for the future—not only the future economic welfare of the publisher, but also future service to society.

Because book publishing is so small an industry—so small an economic fact in direct terms—in comparison with agriculture, armament-manufacturing plants, and port facilities, the people who draft national financial and economic plans rarely consider the publisher's need for credit. Yet if, for lack of a business loan at a sensible rate of interest, the publisher is forced to go to bazaar moneylenders and pay 25 percent or more, the result is clearly against public welfare. Not only does the publisher have to charge more for books, forcing up the price of textbooks and other basic tools of national education, but in view of that terrible cost of borrowed money, the publisher dare not print more than the minimum number of copies certain to be sold. The publisher is thus prevented from using the principle we studied earlier concerning per-copy costs when quantities are increased.

One of the special reasons for cooperation among publishers is to present facts like these to national planners and financial officials, in terms not of the publishers' desires but of national necessity. They need also to enlist the help of others, notably the ministry of education and the intellectual leaders of the country, in giving the public some understanding of how the public welfare is tied up with the economic welfare of this small but critically important industry.

Economic and Public Service

But the publisher has no right to claim public support unless truly serving the public interest, not merely from day to day but also in building for the future in the ways mentioned above. And there are some other ways as well.

A special form of long-term investment is a deliberate decision a publisher sometimes makes to pass on to the consumer through a lower selling price an economy achieved in producing a book, even though, in pure theory, the extra profit could be pocketed. Another form of long-term investment is made sometime or other by every publisher whose sense of financial interest is based on a sense of honor and a concept of public service: the cool decision to go ahead and publish a book that society needs, or that will give a start to a writer of great promise, even though the publisher is pretty sure no money will be made on that particular book.

This talk about the publisher's obligation to society might seem better suited to a philosophical discussion than to this chapter on economics, but in fact it is appropriate here. Most of the truly successful book publishers in the developed book industries of the world have won their most priceless financial asset—the respect and loyalty of authors and booksellers and readers and educators—because they have had so clear a view of the relation between the public interest and their own commercial interest. They have not been unbusinesslike, nor have they turned away from the hard facts of economics. But they know that a firm that is hoping for a long future must think of the consumer at all times and must take risks.

The book publisher, like other people in business, has a kind of license from society to make money in the publication of books. Risk-taking is the fee paid to society for that privilege.

4

Editorial Development: Ideas into Books

THE PUBLISHER WHO sits waiting for authors and translators to bring in manuscripts is going to publish an undistinguished list of books—and have small profit. On the other hand, the publisher who wants to give good service both to the public interest and to the firm's profit goes out and gets manuscripts. Such a publisher not only tries to bring in the best manuscripts that are already written but stimulates and encourages and guides the writing of new manuscripts for which there is an apparent need, and therefore a market.

This whole process is called editorial development or, more vividly, "turning ideas into books." It is when carrying out the work of editorial development that the publisher acts most clearly in the double capacity of cultural statesman and farseeing businessman. The two can never be separated. The long view is as necessary for the publisher's economic welfare as for what society expects the publisher to do for the general welfare.

The Editor's Job

The editorial department of a publishing house—whether that means a large staff of specialists of different kinds or only one corner of the mind of the publisher in a one-person firm—is the key to success or failure. The manuscript is the foundation on which everything else in book publishing is built. Unless there are ideas that will be interesting or useful to the public, and presented in ways that the public will accept, there is no point in book publishing at all.

This chapter deals only with the strategic role of the editor. The next chapter describes another editorial function, copyediting, or preparing the manuscript for the printer; but that important work comes after the editorial strategist has decided what books will be published.

In making those decisions the wise editor does not work alone. There are many other talents to be called on, even if the firm is a small one. If a firm is large enough to have separate departments for production and sales, the editor calls them in, but in any case tries to get the kind of information that such departments would have supplied.

The main point is that in the work of editorial development the points of view of *all* branches of book publishing must be represented; the decision cannot rest solely on the editor's own intellectual judgments about the literary quality of a manuscript.

To illustrate that point: if the production department estimates the cost of printing a manuscript, and the sales department then says that the selling price necessary in view of that cost would be too high for the public, the editor may be less certain that the manuscript is publishable than before getting those economic judgments. Or—the other way around—the editor may fear that an exciting manuscript is hopeless in practical terms until the production department thinks up some practical way of giving it physical form at an unexpectedly low price; or until the sales department invents a new method of selling to reach a large market.

Although the basic editorial requirement is to have good manuscripts coming into the publishing house, it will aid our study of the editor's function if we look first at what happens when the manuscripts arrive. We shall then return to the steps the editor can take to make sure that more and better manuscripts are in that incoming stream.

The Handling of Incoming Manuscripts

The purely housekeeping side of handling incoming manuscripts is worth careful attention. One reason is to avoid the unhappiness and public ill will that can result from lost manuscripts, delay in reporting back to authors about acceptance or rejection, and other problems. But the second reason is even more important. That is to ensure orderliness and intelligence in moving toward the single most important act in book publishing: the decision whether to publish the book. Careful manuscript handling, though "only house-keeping," can be the basis of a good editorial development.

Simple record keeping can show the editor when a manuscript was received, when sent to an outside reader, when returned to the author, and so forth. This can be done in a number of different ways—on cards, in a ledger book, and so on. A card catalogue system has some advantages because then you can keep in alphabetical order the dozens or hundreds or thousands of cards for manuscripts considered previously. If that plan is used, the cards for manuscripts still under consideration are not usually put in the main alphabet, where they might be lost in view unless specially flagged. Instead, they can be kept in a small separate section, often filed according to date of receipt, until the decision is made. Incidentally, the main listing of a manuscript should be under the author's name (indexed under first or last name according to the custom of the country); that is because the author's name does not change, but the title may change or be forgotten, or you may not recall whether a manuscript was call "General Sociology," indexed under G, or "*Introduction to* General Sociology," indexed under I.

A new publishing firm naturally has few incoming manuscripts at the beginning, but the number grows hugely as time goes on and as the firm becomes well known. In the United States a publishing house of modest size that issues only 50 new books a year may receive as many as 1,500 manuscripts a year. Young publishing firms are less likely than the older ones to be staffed with people competent to dispose quickly of the vast majority of the incoming manuscripts that have no chance of publication at all.

That leads to the next subject for our attention, the way in which an editor considers a manuscript for publication, and how other people can help him in making the tremendous decision of Yes or No.

Considering Manuscripts for Publication

Consideration of manuscripts you are *not* going to publish can be a very costly business. You have to accept some of that cost in order to find the manuscripts you *will* publish. But the heart of efficiency in an editorial department is to find ways of holding down the waste of time and money in editorial consideration of manuscripts on which you will finally say No. The objective is to confine your use of time and money as much as possible to a small fraction of the total incoming flood—that is, to those manuscripts on which you will eventually say Yes, or at least Maybe. Of course it is never possible actually to do that, as no one can be certain ahead of time which manuscripts are in the Yes or Maybe groups. But a lot can be done in reducing the waste in considering the manuscripts that are certain to end up in the No group.

Many manuscripts can be rejected immediately, without worrying about their quality, if they are the wrong kind for your particular firm—for instance, a manuscript on a religious subject offered to a medical publisher. Or they can be turned down without further thought if they are not in physical condition for easy reading, or if they are impossibly long or impossibly short for the particular kind of book (with a possible slight hesitation here, however, because of the possibilities in adaptation as a form of editorial development, as will be discussed later). Perhaps one-half to two-thirds of the incoming manuscripts can be eliminated simply on grounds of unsuitability.

First reading. In many publishing houses, after the "impossibles" have been set aside, the other manuscripts have a first reading by someone on the editorial staff. That first reading may be just a sampling and overview, and is for the purpose of deciding whether the firm is willing to accept the cost of real consideration through readings by other staff members and by outside readers. If it is a one-person editorial department with limited funds, the editor may drop everything else and reread the manuscript—this time the whole thing and with great care. With further encouragement from the additional staff readings, the editor may then decide it it time to engage an outside reader.

Outside readers. The outside reader will usually be a specialist in the subject matter of the particular book or an authority on literary style or having some other special qualification.

Especially if a publisher is hard pressed for cash, it sometimes seems extravagant to pay an outside reader when the firm has its own editorial staff. But the small amount of a reading fee is nothing compared with loss that will come from a wrong editorial decision in accepting a book that should have been rejected. Common sense must of course prevail, for a publisher who is not careful could waste resources on readings of manuscripts that will never be published. On the other hand, the outside reader's different point of view can make the final difference not only in deciding for or against publication but also in suggesting revisions that may turn a merely good book into one of outstanding quality.

Other considerations. Even after all the readings by staff members and outsiders, and even if all of them agree about the quality of the manuscript, the editor may still be a long distance from a final decision. For one thing, it is not often that a publisher can consider a particular book all by itself. Usually one has to compare the merits of several manuscripts because of a feeling that, without increasing staff or office space, only a certain number of new books can be published in the coming year. Or very often in developing countries where bank loans to publishers are rare and other kinds of borrowing incredibly costly, working capital may prevent as much new-book production as would be desired. Or—and this is a cruel frustration when the publisher's staff and capital are large enough for increasing production—there may be a shortage of available book paper or of printing facilities.

For all these reasons, frequently encountered anywhere but especially in developing countries, there is a need for real genius on the part of the editor in balancing all the different factors. First the merit of the book itself must be considered and then—second but equally important in practical terms—how the book fits into the general picture of the publisher's whole business, not only in the light of hopes and plans but also of the general economic situation. To summarize, these are the resources upon which the editor may call in making the No or Yes decision:

1. Personal knowledge of books and education and culture; knowledge of what is going on in the world; and an experienced "feel" for public reactions.

2. Specialized editors within the firm, if there are any. A large firm

may have people with special talent in fiction, in children's books, in science, or in other fields.

3. Outside readers, that is, people who, for a fee, read manuscripts and advise the editor confidentially about them. Careful selection of the outside readers is one of the editor's most important jobs. They are useful in two ways: in providing special talents the editor does not happen to have on the regular staff, and in giving other points of view to correct or confirm opinions of the staff within the house.

4. Production and sales departments, to advise in practical terms in the ways suggested above.

5. The financial department (which in a small firm may mean no more than the publisher thinking about the firm's bank account, commitments, and hopes for income). This step is of great importance, whether or not the firm actually has a separate "financial department." This would be obvious in general, but we shall see later in this chapter that there is special relation between "tying up capital" and the cost of editorial development.

6. In some cases the editor and the sales department may want to test their own guesses about the market by some kind of market research. For a small project, that may mean no more than asking questions of some booksellers, school principals, and others. But for a proposed series of books or for projects needing large financial investment it may seem worthwhile to have more elaborate surveys or studies or actual testing in pilot projects.

When all the judgments have been received from sources such as these, the critical fact is the way in which an editor puts the elements together and makes the final decision. And the total of all those decisions over the years is an expression of the publisher's personality.

Publishers do not all have to publish the same kind of books. One firm may decide to give special attention to textbooks, another to literature, and another to popular science, while having a general list at the same time; or a firm may limit itself to one or a few of the specialities; or a very large firm may be divided into departments, each with its own editor who follows particular lines.

The important thing is for the publishing firm, or its departments, to have *personality and editorial integrity*. Creative book publishers, such as Dina Malhotra in India, Alfred Knopf in the United States, Sir Allen Lane in the United Kingdom, Santiago Salvat in Spain, Sobhy Griess in Egypt, Gonzalo Losada in Argentina, José Olympio in Brazil, acquired their reputations not just as good businessmen but because the names of their firms on a title page meant something to the reader.

The strongest argument in favor of accepting a manuscript in an editorial conference in any country should be "It's *our* kind of book."

How Manuscripts Come to a Publisher

Not many manuscripts come in all by themselves. Even when it seems that the publisher had no part in persuading the author to send in the manuscript, careful investigation would probably show that the author sent the manuscript to that particular publisher on the suggestion of someone else. It might be a bookseller or librarian or teacher or another author or some other person who knew the publisher's competence, special interest in that kind of book, or previous record for good handling of books on that subject.

This emphasizes that, in editorial matters as well as in everything else, the publisher's reputation is the most valuable asset. A new publisher lacks that advantage, of course, but sincerity of intentions and intelligence of planning can to some extent be judged by authors; and good performance with the first few books can quickly build up a chain reaction of good opinion among the country's writers.

But the publisher who counts only on the manuscripts that come in because of the firm's general reputation will not get a publishing list of much distinction. The publisher must take vigorous initiative, especially if the firm is a new one not yet well known to authors or to the people who influence authors, whether the purpose is to make a profit or to serve society through the spread of knowledge.

The staff. The editorial department—one individual or a whole group of people, depending on the size of the house—has the main responsibility for bringing in manuscripts. But in a lively organization *everyone* in the house knows that the editors will give sympathetic consideration to manuscript suggestions they bring in. The members of the sales department, especially those who are in frequent contact with booksellers, librarians, and educators, are often a source of good editorial suggestions. And, as explained more fully in Chapter 11, the sales staff and the editors of textbooks have an especially close and useful relationship.

Literary scouts. Besides the publisher's own staff and the volunteer advisers, however, there may be a formal professional relationship with scouts who act on the publisher's behalf in finding manuscripts and directing them to the publisher's editor. Or the publisher may appoint an outside *subject editor* (often a university scholar who does the work on a part-time basis) to keep in touch with books being written, or needing to be written, within a subject field, whether it be fiction, economics, psychology, or something else. Another arrangement of the same general sort is appointment of an outside *general editor* for a series, with that outside editor doing much of the work, with respect to the books in that series, that the publisher's own editor would have done otherwise.

The publisher's payment to the different kinds of scouts is usually a small royalty which, like the regular royalty paid to the author, is based on the number of copies that the book sells.

Prizes. Most of the literary prizes in the world give general encouragement to authorship by awards *after* books have been published. That is the case with the famous national and international awards. These are of high usefulness to society through calling attention to deserving books and through public emphasis on the importance of books in general. Publishers interested in the long-term welfare of their national book industries recognize the usefulness of encouraging and supporting such prizes, as we shall mention in Chapter 17.

But there is another kind of literary prize, offered by individual publishers for the best manuscripts of specified sorts that are *submitted to them* before publication. Such prizes are especially frequent in the field of fiction, and they are regarded by their sponsors as useful not only in attracting the manuscript that will eventually win the prize but in bringing in many others. And the fact that a publishing house offers a fiction prize, for example, is an effective way of saying to the public, "This house is interested in publishing the best novels this country can produce." These publishers' prizes for unpublished manuscripts are often in two parts—an outright sum, plus an additional amount that is an advance against the royalty that the publisher believes will eventually be due the author based on the sale of the book.

Literary agents. To complete the account of different ways in which manuscripts come to publishers, we must mention the literary agent, even though that is not now an important factor in Asia, Africa, and Latin America. Opinions on the value of the agency system differ, even in the United States where the great majority of manuscripts by established professional writers go to the publishers through agents. The agents cannot, in any event, afford to spend time on authors who do not promise to become good income producers.

The literary agent works for the author rather than the publisher, receiving the manuscript from the author, showing it to various publishers, and, if successful, eventually negotiating contract terms with one of the publishers on behalf of the client, the author. The agent's job, in other words, is the opposite side of the coin from the job of the publisher's scout. Because the agent serves the author, it is the author who pays for the agent's work, usually by giving the agent some fraction of the royalty the author receives from the publisher when the book is finally issued.

Developing Individual Manuscripts

All of the people interested in encouraging the writing of good books—the publishers' editors, the scouts, the literary agents— think constantly not only about manuscripts on which writers are already at work, but about books which authors' interests and talents and experience equip them to write. If these ideas still seem good after study, the editor may discuss them with the possible authors, and together the author and editor can work out the basic plan. As an encouragement to the author, and as proof of good intentions, the publisher may at that point offer a contract and make an advance payment of royalty that—they both hope—the book will eventually earn.

Publishers will of course have widely different ideas about what fields are best for them, but it is important to focus on a relatively small number of subjects, rather than a broad list with only a few books in each area.

Ideas for an author to convert into books can be of the widest variety, and may occur to the editor in many different ways. Some examples:

1. A respected public figure, long his country's delegate to the United Nations where he played a leading part in world events, is about to retire and may be persuaded to write his memoirs.

2. A writer of short stories who has been coming more and more into public notice as each story appears may be nearing the time when a volume of collected stories could be published.

3. A leading scientist has gained a reputation as a public speaker and radio broadcaster with a special talent for giving laymen a clear explanation of modern science; so the publisher persuades the scientist to convert some of the best speeches into chapters for a book, and to write new ones to fill in gaps in the subject; and in discussing the idea with the author it comes out that the author had admiration for a certain artist skilled in making simple drawings on scientific subjects, so the artist is commissioned to work with the author in making the illustrations for the book.

4. The country's most distinguished sociologist had publicly criticized the sociology textbooks use in the local university because all of the examples and case studies in the books are from a foreign culture; the editor may encourage the writing of a new sociology text in which the examples are based on social conditions in the local culture.

5. A talented painter, never before a book illustrator, has made drawings illustrating the works of the most popular national poet; the editor may work out an arrangement with the illustrator and the poet to do an illustrated edition of a selection of the poet's verse.

6. One of the country's greatest writers, known to have been working for years on a new novel, is reported to be "bogged down" in a state of psychological frustration; a gifted, sympathetic, and

imaginative editor *may* be able to help the author find a way out of the dead end.

7. A popular teller of folk stories for children on the radio might be persuaded to write them down, with suitable illustrations, for publication as a supplementary reader for school libraries.

8. A brilliant photographer has been making pictures of national shrines and monuments for many years and may be prompted to turn them into a picture book for supplementary use in schools.

9. A scientist who has studied for years the best methods of growing rice (or who has worked for years to develop economical use of a gas produced from waste for family cooking and heating) might be persuaded to set down his findings in a simple, clear way that can be use by extension workers and farmers.

It is clear from those examples, and from the many others that will occur to the reader, that the former concept of an editor as an unworldly hermit working in remote seclusion from the world is far out of date. A truly creative editor must be alert not only to cultural and intellectual trends but to the whole movement of events in the modern world.

Vision is needed in everything relating to editorial development, but in no phase is it more important than in the major development projects such as we will now discuss.

Major Development Projects

We deal in this section with the development projects which are such major undertakings that they may stretch over a long period of years and may involve many authors, the talents of every department of the publishing house, and (usually) a large investment of capital that may be a long time in coming back. The question of the financing of the development projects is discussed in a special section below, and it will be seen that there are ways of reducing the seriousness of the problem, even for very large projects.

Series. The most obvious kind of major development project is a series of books on a general subject or of a general sort, such as biographies of world figures, treatments of historical events, children's stories with the same main characters or related themes, and introductions to the major sciences for supplementary reading. Some series may have clear limits—such as a series on the nations' presidents—but some are open-ended, and can go on and on as long as they are successful. Similarly, some series need specific planning and public announcement from the beginning, while others can grow naturally, perhaps without even referring to a "series" until two or three successful books have been published. A series of the latter kind is obviously easier for a publisher to launch, both editorially and economically, but it also lacks the great public impact of bold announcement of a new series.

Referring back to our earlier comment on subject editors and general editors who aid the publisher's editor in editorial planning, it is clear that the service of those outside specialists is of special value in the planning of series.

In any event, a series not only has the sales advantage we shall examine in Chapters 8 and 9 but also a clear editorial advantage in tending to attract to the publisher the best manuscripts on the subject dealt with in the series.

Textbooks and school readers. The special problems and special opportunities presented by series of textbooks and supplementary readers for school use are discussed in Chapters 11 and 12. But we should note here that these give the clearest example of major development projects, often in series form, that involve great effort over a long period.

Reference works. Projects such as dictionaries, encyclopedias, and atlases, even if only single volumes instead of series, can be major undertakings with years required for their preparation and enormous investments before the money finally starts coming back in the form of sales income.

The editorial problems of such projects are so different from those met in preparing other kinds of books that publishers often set up a special department for the purpose. And, unlike the usual situation, much of the work may be done in the publishing house by the publisher's own employees.

The Financing of Editorial Development

Editorial development costs money in advance of income in any event, if only because of the expense for the publisher in maintaining a staff qualified to plan and carry out the development projects. But there can also be great out-of-pocket costs through advance payment to authors, artists, mapmakers, and others; market research in the detailed planning; advance promotion by the sales department; the possible large cost (especially in the case of series) of advance bulk purchase of paper and of paying the printer for typesetting and platemaking even before a single copy has been printed; and (in the case of a series in which all the volumes are to be published at the same time) a huge investment in complete manufacture of the entire series before even one rupee or piaster or peso is received as sales income.

Schedule of needs. Faced with the large problem of financing a major project, the publisher tries to work out not only an estimate of overall cost and overall income but also a time schedule of *when* payments have to be made and *when* income can be expected to come in. In the case of many series of semi-independent books, the need may be only to finance the first few volumes in the series, as the publisher may see that—once the process is properly started—income from earlier volumes will finance the succeeding ones. But there are projects, especially textbooks and reference books, that cannot be broken into parts that way. The publisher has to make the whole commitment at the outset, tying up portions of working capital and often having to go out and borrow money from investors who have faith in the firm and its project.

Loan capital. We spoke in Chapter 3 of the need for a system of business loans for book publishers if they are to build for the future. That need is obvious in general, but the need is absolutely critical in connection with major projects of editorial development because of the length of time over which the investment must be made. It is unthinkable for a publisher to pay the rates of interest charged in the bazaar on capital invested in a project stretching over a period of years.

Relation between Editorial Development and Plans for Marketing

For any book project the editor will always think, "Who will buy it?" in addition to considering literary quality, tastes and interests, and other factors. For all books—and especially for major development projects such as we have been discussing—it can be absolutely fatal for the editor to undertake planning without the fullest participation by colleagues in the sales department.

Teamwork with the sales staff. The editor may have a brilliant idea for a series of books intended to appeal to a wide general audience, but it would be senseless to start commissioning authors to write the books until the sales department had worked out a plan of mass distribution at low prices, perhaps along one of the lines suggested in Chapter 13.

Or the editor may have a wonderful plan for a group of supplementary reading books for use in school, but unless the sales department can see how the books can actually be sold to the schools, or to individual students on the schools' recommendation, there would be no point in starting the development project. As a matter of fact, everything relating to development of books for specific educational use demands closest cooperation between the editors and the sales staff, and between the publishing house in general and the educational authorities of the country.

Subscription books. A method of marketing that has not been used extensively in most developing countries but through the years has been important in the United States and Europe and Latin America is called "subscription selling." This method, which is used most frequently for multivolume series such as encyclopedias, is described in Chapter 14, but it should be stated for our purposes here that editorial planning and market planning have to go hand in hand.

Current Books versus Backlist

Other examples of teamwork between editors and sales staff will be encountered as we go through this book, and we shall see constantly that the teamwork operates in both directions. The sales staff, perhaps especially in connection with educational books, can be one of the most important sources of ideas for the editor. Both members of the team will think always of the sale not only in the year of publication but also through succeeding years, whether from the original edition or reprintings.

The "strength of the backlist"—that is, the salability of books first published in previous years—is one of the critical factors affecting the continuing profit of the publisher and continuing service to the public interest. In some kinds of publishing, for instance books of scholarship, "publishing for the backlist" is almost the whole responsibility. (Oxford University Press proudly boasts that its edition of the Coptic Bible finally sold out of print, after 150 years.) For any publisher the backlist is a key to success through the years, a badge of pride and a source of continuing income.

5

Editing the Manuscript

THE EDITOR HAS two jobs. The first, just described in the previous chapter on editorial development, is to find manuscripts to publish, or to get authors to write them. The second job, the subject of this chapter, begins only after it has been decided to publish a manuscript. That task is to edit the manuscript and prepare it for the printer.

The work of preparing the manuscript for the printer is called *copyediting*. The copyeditor's purpose is to help the author put ideas into print in the clearest, most orderly, and most effective way; and to have the manuscript so neatly and accurately prepared and so clearly marked with instructions for the printer that the cost of corrections will be as low as possible. This is of course an advantage for the publisher who pays the bill and, in the long run, for the public.

As with everything else in this book, the general principles apply to a publishing firm of any size. A very large firm may have not only a full "editorial department" but divisions within it specializing in books in particular fields such as science, economics, and children's books. However, what we say here is just as true for a solitary editor in a small firm, or even for a one-person firm in which a single individual does all the jobs.

Some people think it is best, even in a large firm, if the editor who carried on the prepublication negotiations with the author is also the copyeditor who deals with the manuscript right up to the moment of publication. That is one of the arguments for a small publishing firm, so that direct personal relations can be maintained from beginning to end, rather than giving a manuscript assembly-line treatment in a large impersonal department. The personal relationship is

56

so valuable that the editor-in-chief or the president of the company, even in some large firms, sometimes serves as copyeditor for important authors.

In some large firms the copyeditor marks the manuscript but then another person, called the *production editor*, serves as the coordinator with artists and the printer, and oversees the actual production, including the handling of proofs. For our purposes here, however, it is simplest to assume that the copyeditor is responsible for everything of an editorial sort from the moment the firm has decided to publish a manuscript until the printer has delivered the finished book. The copyeditor is the one member of the publisher's staff who knows everything about a book while it is in production. During that period the copyeditor handles all relations with the author or translator, illustrator, designer, and printer.

The author or translator is supposed to turn in the manuscript in a form ready for the printer. But no author, in the history of printing, has been able to do that; and the publisher who fails to do a thorough job of copyediting incurs needless extra expense, besides lowering the quality of the book and serving the public badly.

Because the readers of this book are concerned with publishing in so many different languages, written in different scripts and even reading in different directions, there would be no point in saying much about the specific details of the copyeditor's job. Whatever the language, the copyeditor tries to prepare the manuscript so that, if the printer copies it exactly, that will be the message the author wants the book to convey in print. That process may sound easy, but in fact is one of the most difficult jobs of publishing because it involves so many thousands of details which even the author cannot think of ahead of time.

We say "even the author" may overlook editorial details; but maybe it would be better to say "especially the author," because few authors are good copyeditors of their own books. They are so intent on what they *meant* to say that they may be unable to see the mistakes and inconsistencies in what they actually wrote.

The publisher's copyeditor, aside from learning to be a professional in watching out for these things, has an advantage over the author in bringing a new eye to the work. The wise author will be grateful for this if convinced that the copyeditor's aim is to give clearer and more accurate presentation of the author's own ideas.

The things a copyeditor has to do can be summed up under these seven headings, which will be discussed in order in this chapter: (1) legibility, (2) consistency, (3) grammar, (4) clarity and style, (5) factual accuracy, (6) legality and propriety, and (7) production details.

Legibility

Every letter of every word of the manuscript must be not only readable but so quickly and easily read that the printer can concentrate entirely on the difficult technical job of setting type without worrying about what the author *meant* to write. There are many developing countries in which typesetters, though quick at distinguishing individual letters, are almost illiterate, so it is of special importance that the manuscript be clear.

If too many corrections and insertions have to be made in the manuscript, the copyeditor should have the messy parts retyped or, if the manuscript is in a script for which typewriting is not normally used, rewritten in a clean copy.

If the manuscript is in hopeless condition when first received from the author, the copyeditor will ask the author to take it back and resubmit in better form. This is in the author's own interest (besides being required by the contract), because of the number of errors that will result if the printer has to work from a mixed-up manuscript that is hard to read.

In scripts using roman letters (the Western European languages, Turkish, Indonesian, Malay, Swahili, Yoruba, Igbo, Hausa, and most other sub-Sahara African languages) manuscripts should always be required in typewritten form. In the scripts such as Arabic and Persian in which typewriting is often but not automatically used, two special arguments for typewriting can be given to the author: (1) although *good* Arabic handwriting is more attractive and may be easier to read than typewriting, handwriting varies widely, and the *uniformity* of typewriting helps the printer to work more quickly and more easily; and (2) with a typewriter and carbon paper or a photocopier it is cheap and easy to have a duplicate manuscript made at the same time; and that duplicate can be invaluable, not only as insurance against loss of the other copy but also for the author's convenience in reference while the master copy is in the hands of the printer.

The requirement of legibility applies, of course, to the copyeditor's own notes of instruction to the printer (see the section on Production Details later in this chapter) quite as much as to words in the author's original manuscript. It is, moreover, essential for the copyeditor to know and to follow whatever system of marking for the printer is customary in that country.

The copyeditor's overall responsibility is to prepare the manuscript so clearly that *without having to stop to think* the printer can see what is to be set in type.

Consistency

Some people talk about a copyeditor "correcting" a manuscript, and some actual corrections are made as we shall note below. But a much bigger job is the effort to give the manuscript some sort of consistency in the choice between alternate forms of spelling, punctuation, and so forth. Even if both of two alternate spellings, for instance, are "correct," that does not justify the author in varying back and forth between them in the course of one book. Such inconsistency can be very disturbing to the reader, and its upsetting effect on the typesetter is almost sure to increase the cost of printing.

In languages for which there are well-established and generally accepted dictionaries, such as Oxford, Larousse, or Merriam-Webster, for instance, the copyeditor's job is much easier than in languages for which there are no dictionaries with such wide coverage and general acceptability. Even in European languages, however, dictionaries in the same language may differ from one to another. Publishers in those languages often announce that their *house style* is based on such-and-such a dictionary, or on one of the well-known publisher's *style books* issued for public sale, such as *Rules for Compositors and Readers at the Oxford University Press, The*

Chicago Manual of Style, and *U.S. Government Printing Office Style Manual*. And there are, of course, specialized style books for particular fields, especially in the sciences.

As suggested in the chapter on translation, it is often useful, especially in the case of scientific books, to translate the index first, so the terms will be fixed from the start.

The copyeditor—whether accepting some reference work as a guide or making up rules along the way—is responsible for seeing that the manuscript has consistency from beginning to end. We shall try to suggest in the paragraphs below some of the ways in which the problems of consistency arise. Because there are such wide differences among the traditions and customs of various languages, it would be impossible to give examples from all of them, but the general nature of the problems can be suggested by illustrations from English in those cases in which examples are presented.

Spelling. This is not merely a question of systematic differences within a language, such as the British "labour" versus the American "labor," but especially problems of plurals ("buses" versus "busses") or of forms with suffixes ("travelling" versus "traveling"). And of course in addition to choosing between alternate correct forms, the copyeditor must correct the many wrong spellings of which most authors are guilty.

Transliteration. Especially in the modern world, with so much exchange of ideas and cultural information between areas using different languages, a special aspect of spelling—and one of the most difficult—relates to transliteration from one script to another. The problem is even more difficult when the transliteration into another language is from English, which uses a largely irrational method of spelling, frequently with big differences between the spoken and written forms. Asian editors differ among themselves as to whether the transliteration into their language should try to copy the sound or the spelling of the English original; and the lack of good bilingual dictionaries makes the problem even more difficult. All we can do here is point to the transliteration problem as a major one in intercultural relations, and warn copyeditors in both East and

West of the perils to be guarded against, and the amount of effort needed to achieve consistency.

Punctuation. Copyediting in general is an art, not an exact science, but this is especially true in the case of punctuation. There are some kinds of punctuation that are directly related to good grammar, but for the most part the questions of punctuation relate more to taste and style than to right and wrong. The copyeditor's responsibility is to see that when the manuscript goes to the printer, it is punctuated in a way that will help the reader understand what the author wanted to say, and that the punctuation is reasonably consistent according to some acceptable system. A test often used for the placement of commas is to read the sentence aloud and see where natural pauses occur.

Abbreviations. As in the case of punctuation, most of the issues related to abbreviations are not matters of right or wrong but merely of consistency as to whether abbreviations will be used, and in which of the several accepted forms—for instance, "Major General Ahmed" versus "Maj. Gen. Ahmed" or "5 feet 9 inches" versus "5 ft. 9 in."

Alternate forms. The problem of alternate forms faces the copyeditor in many different ways, of which we will mention only one as an example: whether geographical names shall be used in their local or their internationalized forms (Firenze or Florence, Falastin or Palestine, Köln or Cologne, Takhte Djamshid or Persepolis).

Uniform style for auxiliary material. A major job for the copyeditor, especially in scientific or scholarly books, is to give consistency to the form of presentation of such auxiliary material as tables, footnotes, mathematical or chemical formulas, and legends under illustrations.

Other problems. There are other troublesome items in the list of things the copyeditor may have to do in trying to give consistency to a manuscript. Most happily for the Asian copyeditor, however, some of these additional problems do not arise in many of the Asian languages using scripts without capital letters or italic type. But in languages using roman letters these are big problems: *Capitalization*: whether to use capital letters in cases such as "the federal government of Nigeria" versus "the Federal Government of Nigeria." *Compound words*: for example, "textbooks" versus "text-books" versus "text books." *Syllable division*: when a word is broken from one printer's line to the next. *Use of italics*: for example, "La Prensa" versus *La Prensa*. *Units of measurement*: especially in dealing with metric and nonmetric systems.

Grammar

One of the copyeditor's jobs is to make sure that the grammar is correct in the manuscript as it finally goes to the printer. It is not easy, however, to say what *is* correct, even in one language, let alone in the many of interest to the readers of this book. In addition to questions of individual taste, there are almost philosophical differences about grammar in some languages; and the tendency to such differences of opinion is probably greater with respect to some Asian languages than to those of Europe.

All we can suggest as a rule is that the grammar generally accepted by people of good taste in the educated community is what the publisher wants in the firm's books. That does not really answer the question, of course, because the copyeditor must decide each case as it arises. One of the biggest challenges the copyeditor faces is to improve the grammar in the manuscript without changing the basic style or the ideas the author wants to express.

Clarity and Style

The delicacy of the copyeditor's job in dealing with grammar, as just mentioned, is slight compared with what he has to do in making the author's meaning clear when the author has not done so. If there is nothing actually incorrect in what the manuscript says, the author may be indignant about any changes unless the reason for the change is patiently explained.

As to style of writing, authors are, quite understandably, even more sensitive. Authors, and indeed many publishers, tend to feel that the style is so basic a part of the author's work that a manuscript should not be accepted unless the style can be accepted along with it; and that is even more surely the case in creative literature than in books of information.

Books of factual information are most frequently written by authors having special knowledge of the subject matter in the particular field; but they are rarely professional writers, and are not necessarily even experienced writers. It is in this kind of book, with this kind of author, that there is the widest opportunity for the copyeditor to help the author—and the reader—through clearer presentation of what the author was obviously trying to say.

But the copyeditor has to establish confidence if the author is to accept changes in grammar or style. The copyeditor must be a diplomat as well as a master of language to do this part of the job, and most important of all must feel strongly that the sole purpose of this work is to help express more clearly what the author wanted to say in the first place.

Factual Accuracy

This part of the copyeditor's job is another of those for which it is most difficult to draw rules. Obviously a copyeditor does not have time to check every fact in any book; but the copyeditor who is widely read and has broad knowledge on many subjects will note things that are wrong in reading the manuscript. And the really good copyeditor has an imaginative "sixth sense" that suggests checking statements that seem suspicious.

If the manuscript says that Mount Aconcagua in Argentina is 22,835 meters high, the copyeditor who is lucky enough to know that even Mount Everest is less than 9,000 meters will look it up; and a geography book will show that the altitude of Mount Aconcagua is 22,835 *feet* instead of meters. Or if, in a discussion of Asian languages, there is reference to "Sudanese," the copyeditor's general knowledge will identify that as an African rather than an Asian word; and further checking will confirm that the author meant to refer to the Indonesian "Sundanese." Or a reference to Emperor Jahangir doing something in A.D. 1720 (almost a century after Jahangir's death) may jump off the page and lead to checking whether the author's mistake was in the date or in the name of the emperor.

The service rendered in this way can be almost endless, and the copyeditor must have self-imposed rules on how far to go. If error after error appears in the factual statements that are checked, the copyeditor may finally decide that the manuscript as a whole is so unsound that it must be sent back to the author or handed over for complete revision to a specialist on the subject matter of the book.

Legality and Propriety

Many of the questions about legality and propriety of a manuscript will have been considered and answered before a manuscript is accepted for publication. But the copyeditor is responsible to the publisher for watching *in detail* for anything in the manuscript that might be contrary to the laws of the country or contrary to the policy of the publishing house as to decency and propriety.

The copyeditor will probably decide small issues alone, or in consultation with the author, but on major issues such as possible libel suits from people criticized, or major offense against the accepted standards of public decency, will undoubtedly wish to consult the high command of the publishing house. Standards vary widely, of course, not only from country to country but even from one period to another within a single country. Rules for solving the large issues cannot be stated in general. Each problem must be decided by itself in the light of all the circumstances at the particular time and place. And conscience is as important as intelligence in making each decision.

One special part of the copyeditor's work that may or may not be part of the legal problem is to make sure that the author is not violating the literary property rights of other authors or publishers. There is some discussion of this in Chapter 18. It may be noted here, however, that a country's lack of membership in an international copyright agreement does not relieve the publisher or the copyeditor of all responsibility. For one thing, in some countries there are local copyright laws, or laws that somehow prevent the theft of *local* literary property rights, even if the country has not signed an agreement protecting foreign authors and assuring its own authors of protection abroad. In addition, it is in the joint interest of all authors and publishers as a group to respect the rights of others, whether or not the country has reached the point of having formal laws on the subject.

Production Details

Although production details are not in all ways the responsibility of the copyeditor if there is a separate production department, the copyeditor still has an important job in relation to production.

For one thing, the copyeditor is the person who has to make sure that the manuscript is really 100 percent complete (which very few manuscripts in all history ever have been when first received from the author), including title page, table of contents, preface, footnotes, illustrations, legends for illustrations, maps or charts, chapter headings, bibliography, glossary, tables, and so forth; and, as the last step, usually after the rest of the book is in pages of type, the index.

The copyeditor, as coordinator of the work of the author, illustrator, designer, and printer, is the go-between who represents both the publisher and the author in relations with the other parties.

One of the copyeditor's important jobs may be the marking of instructions to the printer as to size and kind of type, length of type line, spacing between lines, and other matters of design. If there is a designer for the book, that person may do the actual marking of specifications for the printer, in consultation with the copyeditor. But in a small publishing house, without a designer or perhaps even a production department, the copyeditor discusses design directly with the printer. Having agreed with the printer about a plan, the copyeditor marks each place in the manuscript where it is necessary for the printer to have special instructions. (As an example: the copyeditor of the manuscript of this book, or the designer after discussion with the copyeditor, marked the beginning of the manuscript to show the printer what kind and size of type to use for the basic text, but then gave special instructions for indentions, sub-heads, the use of smaller type for footnotes, and so forth, on the pages where they occurred. The typesetter could then continue using the basic type size and page width except where such special instructions were noted.)

Tools of the Copyeditor's Trade

Few of the "tools" required in book publishing are physical objects. The really important things are the minds and imaginations of the staff members, and that is true of the copyeditors as well as of everyone else. A good general education, intellectual curiosity, a love of reading on a wide variety of subjects, a sensitive feeling for language—these are the most important items of equipment for a copyeditor.

But in addition there are a few physical things that the copyeditor needs: pencils, preferably in a distinctive color so that the copyeditor's markings are clearly different from the author's; scissors and paste or transparent adhesive tape (*not* any clips, which tend to come loose or to pick up additional sheets); and (in a publishing house of any size) a numbering stamp to give consecutive page numbers to the manuscript from beginning to end.

The copyeditor also needs reference books for checking spelling, facts, dates, and so forth. Whether or not the publishing house is large enough to have a general reference library, each individual copyeditor should have quick and easy access to a desk-size diction-ary and a desk-size encyclopedia (one in a foreign language the copyeditor can use if there is none in the local language). A general style book should be available, as well as whatever specialized manual is appropriate for the particular book. The general reference library, if there is one, includes multivolume encyclopedias in vari-ous languages, specialized dictionaries, atlases, and basic reference works of other kinds. But the copyeditor can get along, somehow, with the smaller works if necessary, and go to a public or university library for the things not available in the books in the publishing house.

Outside Copyeditors

Some publishers have most of the copyediting done by people outside the publishing house, working at home on some kind of fee basis. In one way this is an attractive method for a small publisher, because it makes it possible to engage people who have special knowledge of the subject matter of the particular manuscript; and it also saves the expense of carrying copyeditors on the payroll.

This system has the disadvantage, however, of entrusting the manuscript to someone out of contact with the publishing organization as a whole. The "outside" or freelance copyeditor may be less useful to the publisher than a full-time staff member when it comes to coordinating with illustrators, printers, and others, as mentioned above. And in connection with the job of proof handling, which we discuss in the next section, the publisher has to appoint someone else to do that work if the copyeditor is not a staff member in the publishing house itself.

On balance, it seems best, if the publisher can manage it, to have someone in charge of copyediting actually on the premises— whether or not there is use of "outsiders" for reasons of economy or in order to secure special talents—for some of the work of reading and marking manuscripts.

Handling Proof

Someone in the publishing house—usually it would be the copyeditor—receives the proof as it comes from the printer, sends it to the author, receives it back from the author with corrections, studies the author's correction marks to make sure they are clear and appropriate, adds any essential additional marks, and then sends the proof back to the printer.

One of the chief reasons for needless extra cost and for low typographic standards of book printing in many developing countries is the failure of the publisher to participate in proof handling. Too often the author is thrown on the mercy of the printer, and the publisher does not do anything at all about the book till the finished copies are delivered to the warehouse or godown. That is a costly method as well as an unprofessional one. The publisher should be in control throughout. Most publishers in countries where the quality of printers' proofreading is low have learned that they must read proof themselves if they want quality in their books. The authors and the printers cannot do it by themselves.

In developed countries, publishers have traditionally been able to depend on professionally qualified printers' proofreaders. In recent years, however, many printers have greatly reduced their proofreading in the interests of economy, and there has been a corresponding need for publishers to have proofs checked by an in-house or freelance proofreader.

If things go well, there are supposed to be just two proofs for the author and copyeditor to read: a *galley* the first time, in long strips and not yet in page form; and then *page proof*, after the type in the galleys has been corrected by the printer and divided up into pages, with page numbers in place. But, especially in countries in which printers tend to neglect their responsibilities in proofreading and in which the publishers themselves may not be very conscientious about the form in which they send manuscripts to the printer, one or more *revised proofs* may be needed in the galley or page proof stage.

Most authors are unfamiliar with the mechanics of book manufacture and may be thoughtless about the way they make corrections. The copyeditor can be helpful in guiding them toward economical methods. This is useful to the author, as well as an economy for the publisher, because the more lines of type that are changed, the greater the chance of *new* errors creeping in. Even a few words inserted at the beginning of a long paragraph may make it necessary to rearrange the type for the whole paragraph to the very end. In the page proof stage the changes are even more expensive: if insertion of a few words results in adding even one more line of type, then lines may have to be moved from one page to the next until the end of the chapter.

The same consideration applies to taking words out, as too much spacing between words is unpleasant to the eye, and it may be necessary for the typesetter to remake several lines in order to spread out inoffensively the extra spaces resulting from removal of words from a line. (This is another case, however, in which some Asian languages—for instance, Arabic and Persian—have advantage over those using roman letters because of the tradition of using long connecting lines between *letters* if necessary to eliminate extra space between words without need to reset many later lines.)

Author's Alterations

In most Western countries there is a well-established custom of charging the author for making more than a reasonable amount of change in the proof as a result of second thoughts or new ideas. That is, the printer is supposed to pay for the cost of correcting the actual errors by the typesetter; the publisher pays for a small amount of additional change that the author may wish beyond correction of printer's errors; and the author is usually obliged under contract to pay for any changes beyond that. Those additional changes to be charged to the author are called *author's alterations*, and they can of course be a subject of great argument.

In actual practice, few publishers are able to enforce the rule about "author's alterations" fully; but the rule is there for the publisher's protection if, as sometimes happens, an author gets into the mood of "rewriting in proof" and the result is a bill for corrections that is nearly as great as the cost of setting the type in the first place. Incidentally, the publisher's own editors sometimes think of "rewriting in proof" also, and this can be very costly.

The Hard Job and the High Challenge

The copyeditor has one of the most exacting jobs in the publishing profession. It requires intelligence, skill, and a high sense of diplomacy. It has many frustrations as well as many rewards.

There are times when copyeditors think that everybody is on the other side—that author, designer, printer, and others are against them. But the copyeditor also has the satisfaction of being the one person in touch with every aspect of the particular book. And one of the highest rewards comes from the privilege of closer association than anyone else in the publishing world with the author. Historic friendships have developed between famous authors and their copyeditors. There have been notable cases in which authors have refused to take new books to a different publishing house, in spite of the offer of higher royalties and other attractions, because they insisted on staying with copyeditors in whom they had confidence.

The copyeditor is the last person to deal with the manuscript before it goes to the people who will put it into physical form. Their work is considered in the next chapter.

6

Designing the Book

IN THE PRECEDING chapter we talked about preparation of the manuscript. When that job is done, the next thing is physical manufacture, to turn the manuscript into a book. It is of course the printer who does that, but there is another person, rarely thought of by the public, whose work comes first. That is the designer. In this chapter we shall speak about the designer's job before going on to book production itself.

The Designer

Just as a housebuilder may construct a dwelling from personally made designs, many books are made by printers who serve as their own designers. But every house and every book has a designer of some sort.

Whether or not the book designer is a specialist, *someone* in the printing plant, or in the publishing house, has to decide the way the book is to be made. The details include the size of the page, the kind and size of type, the width of margins and the position of the type on the page, the space between lines, the arrangement of chapter headings and page numbers, the plan for illustrations and tables, the kind of paper, the kind of binding, the kind and color of cloth or paper for the cover, and the thousand and one other details that affect the physical appearance of a book.

Most large publishing houses, bringing out a lot of new books each year, find it an economy to have a full-time designer as a member of the publishing staff. Small publishers are of course unable to afford that, and may either engage professional designers from outside on a fee basis, book by book, or develop a kind of part-time designer within the regular staff. In one-person firms, the publisher learns something about book manufacture as the work goes along, and book design in such cases is usually worked out informally between the publisher and the printer.

A book designer may or may not have additional artistic talents as an illustrator, calligrapher, mapmaker, and so forth. In fact, in many small publishing houses the decision to hire the person who later became the designer was made because of a particular large job for which an outside artist would otherwise have had to be engaged.

As suggested in the previous chapter, the copyeditor is a kind of coordinator of the work of author, illustrator, publisher, and printer; and in some cases it may be possible for the copyeditor in a small publishing house to develop an understanding of design problems and become, in effect, the publisher's "designer." In other cases in small firms the person who handles business relations with printers, paper merchants, and others may become a specialist in design at the same time. Or there may be some member of the staff who had previous experience in a printing plant and may be interested in becoming a part-time specialist in design for the publisher.

Whatever staff arrangement is used, it is absolutely essential that there be one person in the publishing house who is responsible for book design even if that means no more than consulting with the printer to make sure of approval, from the publisher's point of view, of the design the printer suggests using.

The person selected for the assignment must have some artistic taste, but also enough knowledge of book manufacture to understand what is physically possible. Most of the famous book designers in the world have had some direct connection with printing—as a hobby or for their own enjoyment if not in a professional way—and most of them have also had a talent for drawing letters. Those personal talents are not necessary, however, if the designer knows how such talents in other people can be employed.

The designer's purpose is to plan a book not only to look good but to present the author's and illustrator's ideas in the clearest and most intelligible way. A book can be a work of art in its physical form, and a designer can be a creative artist in as full a sense as the designer of Persepolis or Abu Simbel or the Taj Mahal. But, as in

those noble structures or any other artistic work, the first requirement is suitability of the art form to the purpose it is supposed to
serve. Prettiness would be the wrong appearance for an engineering
handbook, and a bold angular effect would be wrong for a book of
lyric poetry. The designer must understand a book's purpose before
deciding what form to give it; and the designer who thinks of artistic
beauty all by itself, without relation to the nature of the book, gives
poor service to the author, the reader, and the publisher.

But the designer thinks about more than just appearance. Expense must be kept constantly in mind, not only for the sake of the
publisher but also for the sake of the reading public. If the content of
a book has a natural appeal to a large reading public but the designer
specifies a method of production that will result in a selling price too
high for mass sales, that is a betrayal of both the publisher and the
reader. On the other hand, as we saw in the figures presented in
Chapter 3, there are kinds of manufacturing cost that are no higher
for a million copies than for one copy, while there are others (such
as the cost of paper) that increase in direct relation to the size of the
edition. The good designer keeps the distinction between these two
kinds of cost constantly in mind.

The designer must therefore have a sense of book publishing
economics as well as of artistic design, and must know something
about the size of the edition that is planned, how the book will be
sold, and other business considerations. Only a very wealthy publisher unconcerned with profits can afford the luxury of a designer
who plans books for personal satisfaction without thinking of the
interest of the author, reader, and publisher. It is, of course, obvious
that the designer must have up-to-date knowledge of the composition, printing, and binding technologies available in the country
where the work is to be done.

To sum up, in designing any book the designer tries to balance all
of these factors (some of which, of course, conflict with each other):
suitability of design to the subject matter, artistic attractiveness,
clarity and intelligibility for the reader, economy from the point of
view of the publisher and ultimate purchaser, and practical feasibil-
ity from the point of view of the printer. That is a heavy assignment,
and it is not surprising that some of the great book designers of the
modern world are better known and more highly honored, in the

book publishing profession and among specialists in the graphic arts, than the heads of publishing houses or the presidents of the printing firms for which they work.

It is of course impossible in this book dealing briefly with all the main aspects of book publishing to give a full description of the designer's work, let alone any question of telling how to do it. But the following sections touch on some of the main problems with which the designer deals.

Estimating the Size of the Book

The first practical step in designing a book is to find out how big it has to be for the purpose intended. This is like the architect's first questions to a new client: how many rooms must the house have, how big must each room be, and so on. When the architect knows those absolute requirements, various designs of different attractiveness and at different levels of cost can be considered.

In the case of a book, also, the designer wants to know first of all the absolute requirement in terms of the number of letters in the manuscript, and then can consider different designs using larger or smaller type, larger or smaller pages, wider or narrower margins, and more or less space between lines.

One way of estimating is to count the actual number of words in the manuscript, but that method is wasteful of time and is not very accurate anyway. The average number of letters per word varies greatly in writing on different subjects and among writers who use different styles, even when writing on the same subject.

The simplest method of estimating size is to select a page that looks as if it is about average for the whole manuscript, count the number of *characters* (individual letters *and* spaces between words) on that page, and multiply by the number of pages in the manuscript. This "character counting" is of course easiest if the manuscript is typewritten. But many handwritten manuscripts can be treated in the same way, especially in Asian languages in which there is a tradition of orderly as well as beautiful penmanship. Even if there is great variation, it is usually possible to pick what could be called a typical page and then, turning the pages of the manuscript, assign to each a value of some fraction of the typical page. Of course, in addition to the regular text pages, there must be allowance for tables, diagrams, front matter, index, and appendixes.

In any event, the designer starts with a "character count" showing how many letters and spaces there are in the manuscript. Then, from tables compiled in the past or available in printed form for most of the principal forms of type in the world, it can be calculated how many characters will go into one page of a printed book in the design planned. By dividing that figure into the character count of the manuscript, it becomes evident how many pages of the printed book will be needed for the basic manuscript. To that are added allowances for any illustrations, notes, tables, the title page and other front matter, the index and other back matter, and so forth.

We give this attention to the matter of estimating size because it is so basic to everything else in the physical book, not only in an artistic sense but in business terms as well. The cost of typesetting depends most on the number of characters, and does not vary greatly whether small type is used in a small number of pages or large type in a large number of pages. But the cost of paper and the cost of presswork (the work of the press in putting ink on paper) relate almost directly to the number of pages: presswork and paper for a 320-page book will usually cost just twice that of a 160-page book.

Making the Basic Design

Thinking only of attractiveness and convenience for the reader, the designer might plan a certain book in a way that would require 320 pages. But, thinking of economy and low selling prices, one might see that by using smaller type, longer type lines, and less space between lines, it *could* be compressed into 160 pages. But *too* much cramming together would be a false economy if the resulting appearance is so unattractive that no one buys the book, so compromise between the two extremes is likely.

The designer's greatest gift to the public is made by ingeniously finding a way of clear and readable and attractive presentation that is the least costly to the publisher and hence, in the long run, least costly to the purchaser.

No one part of the design can be considered in itself. We are accustomed, for instance, to read quite small type in a newspaper, and we do it easily because the lines are so short. But type of the same size on a book page of normal width would seem almost unreadable. Thus the book designer never thinks of type size by itself but always in relation to other factors.

The four decisions about type—kind of type, size of type, length of line, space between lines, all of which are governed by the need for legibility as well as attractiveness—have an effect on another big decision: design of the type page. That involves deciding the width of margins at the top and bottom and sides of the page and the placing of page numbers and (if they are used) the "running heads," giving the chapter title on each page or alternating with the title of the book. In books with chapters by several authors, the author's name may be in the left-hand running head, and the chapter title in the right-hand one.

In addition, the decision must be made—especially if typewriter or word-processor composition is to be used instead of printer's type—whether to use "justified" or "unjustified" lines, in other words whether the lines of type are to be of uniform length, so that the right-hand margin of the page is even but the space between the words varies, or whether the space between words is to be consistent, thus resulting in uneven line lengths. In typewriter or word-processor composition, more so than in conventional composition, justified lines can often result in such wide and uneven word spacing that legibility suffers, so it is important to have an operator who is skilled in hyphenation and has enough aesthetic sense to minimize the problem.

"Artwork"

If the book has illustrations or maps or charts or tables, the designer has a whole series of additional problems. The tables will require instructions to the typesetter about what type to use and how it should be arranged. And if the manuscript is already supplied with illustrations that the publisher has decided to use, the decisions may be limited to the method of printing and the position in the book, as discussed below. But if, as often happens, there are drawings or maps to be made—or to be remade because the workmanship was not good enough in the form submitted—the designer may have the extra job of engaging artists. In any event, the designer has to supervise the execution of this "artwork" so it fits in with the plan for the rest of the book.

The author is normally responsible for delivering artwork to the publisher, but if the author prefers not to do so—or is not qualified to do so—the publisher is usually authorized to have the work done and charge the cost to the author's royalty account.

Title Page and Cover Design

The part of book design in which most designers have the greatest interest, because it calls on their creative talents in the highest degree, are the *display items* such as title page, cover design, and the opening page of each chapter.

The cover design, and often part of the title page, may involve hand lettering or special type that would not generally be used in the main part of the book. For instance, a modern designer of a book in English might use lettering based on an Elizabethan form that would never be used today in an ordinary way. Or an Arab designer might turn to Kufic for display use, or an African might use decorated lettering suggesting motifs of African folk art, or an Asian might make a new adaptation of ancient forms of Sanscrit or Pali, or a Latin American publisher might make use of designs suggesting Inca or Aztec art. But such unusual treatment is not necessary, and in fact can be harmful if clear presentation is sacrificed to the whim of the designer. The requirement of striking and appropriate presentation can be met by an able designer through use of perfectly normal type or lettering in a tasteful and imaginative way.

The challenge in designing the cover of the book (whether a printed paper cover or a printed dust jacket to go over a cloth binding) is to create something eye-catching and inviting that will also be economically feasible. And the economic test of a cover design is not merely the cost of printing but its effectiveness as a "seller" of the book. No matter how fine a cover design may be as a work of art all by itself, it is not proper for a book unless it tells right away what kind of book it is and *makes you want to pick it up* when you see it in a bookshop or displayed on a rack.

All books should be self-selling, but it is especially important for mass-production books because they are on sale at many places other than bookshops, and with no clerks there to talk about them. The cover design can be the most important factor in deciding whether a book will be successful in mass distribution.

Choice of Equipment and Materials

In a country with lots of printing plants with different kinds of equipment, where it is easy to get any desired kind of paper or other bookmaking materials, the designer's problem of selection is quite different from what it is in a country less generously supplied. In the former case, for instance in a European country, the designer merely decides what will be best for the book and writes down those specifications, knowing that one printer or another, and one materials supplier or another, will be able to furnish what is wanted. But in a country with shortages—which is of course the case in many of the developing countries—things are the other way around. The designer knows, or must find out, what is available and has to limit the choice to those possibilities.

There are other elements involved in choosing a printer, related to quality of workmanship, business integrity, thoroughness in maintaining equipment, faithfulness in keeping to schedules, and, of course, the prices charged. And there are other economic factors such as how much cash the printer will need in advance, whether the printer will reduce the publisher's warehousing cost by providing free storage for some of the books after they are printed, and so forth.

Some of these questions do not concern the designer directly, but all are of concern to the publishing house as a whole, and the designer's wishes my have to give way to other considerations. For instance, the designer might think of a certain printing process for which the only equipment in the country is in a printing plant owned by someone of such low business honesty that the publisher has decided not to work with that printer. In that case, the designer has to plan the book in some other way. Similarly, the designer might have planned to use a certain kind of paper known to be available in the country, but the supplier of that paper, taking advantage of a monopoly, tries to charge an unreasonable price. Again, the designer's thinking must be readjusted.

For these reasons the designer's job is much more difficult in developing countries than in those with fuller supplies of equipment and materials. But the job is, for that very reason, an even greater challenge and should give higher satisfactions. To make a beautiful and practical book in spite of limited choices of printing processes and materials is a much greater achievement than if everything that might be desired is instantly available.

The designer can make a great contribution not only to future work but also to raising graphic art standards in the country by constant consultation with the head of the publishing house, and with the printers and materials suppliers with whom it works, about improvements for the future. A printer who is limping along with ancient equipment may be persuaded to modernize along lines useful to publishers if it is known that increased business will result. And a paper merchant may be able to order kinds of paper more suitable from the publisher's point of view if it is known that there will be a market for it.

We shall return, in the next chapter, to the matter of printing processes and materials, but it is useful to note here some of the ways in which those questions relate to the designer's work.

Printing Processes

The choices for the designer to make include: kind of composition (typesetting), kind of presswork (putting ink on the paper), kind of paper, and kind of binding. These subjects are discussed in more detail in the next chapter, and the reader previously unfamiliar with printing processes should not be disturbed if he does not understand, at this point, the differences among the processes. The important point is that the designer has choices to make, and that these must be made book by book, depending on the practical problems each book presents.

Typesetting. The choice affecting the first stage of the printing process is the method of setting type or arranging the letters (words) to be printed. Words to be printed can be prepared or "set" by mechanical or photographic methods, set in type by hand, typed on a typewriter or word processor, or drawn by hand.

The kind of material in the book makes a big difference in this decision. For instance, of the mechanical methods, Linotype or Intertype is generally thought to be cheaper for straight reading matter than Monotype; but for special kinds of composition (for instance if words from different scripts, say English and Hindi, are to be in the same line of type; or if the book has chemical formulas or many tables; or if there is to be full use of vowels in Arabic), Monotype would be cheaper as well as better, if indeed it is available in the particular country. It should be noted, incidentally, that those typesetting methods are increasingly being replaced, even in some of the developing countries, by photocomposition, which can be even better and cheaper.

Hand setting of type may be economically advisable in the developing stages of a printing industry, as suggested in the next chapter; but in addition there are possibilities of refinement in hand-set type not yet achieved, in many scripts, in mechanical typesetting.

For books to be printed in small quantities at low cost, it is wise, in countries where inexpensive forms of offset printing are available, to think of composition by typewriting or by hand calligraphy, without using type at all, for many kinds of books.

The ingenious designer does not hesitate to combine methods when there is a good reason for it. If there are only a few formulas in a book, most of the text may be composed by Linotype, but hand composition or Monotype used for the formulas.

Presswork.[3] If there are no illustrations in the book, the method of presswork—of applying ink to paper—can be decided on the basis

---

3. The word *printing* has two meanings. People outside the book industry use it for the whole process of composition, presswork, and binding. But in several countries

of the typesetting method that was used (Linotype, Monotype, and hand-set type may be printed either by letterpress or by photo offset from high quality reproduction proofs pulled from the type, while photocomposition and typewriting may require offset plates and presses), or on the simple basis of cost and quality and the equipment available.

If there are illustrations in the book, very careful planning is required as to the method of presswork and the kind or paper. It is in dealing with illustrations that the designer is most likely to think of combining methods of presswork. The best and cheapest form of presswork may be used for the text itself, but another method—more expensive but far better for illustrations—for separate printing of the illustrations.

As that last sentence implies, the *position* of the illustrations in the book has to be decided as part of the question about what sort of presswork to use. If it is all right for the illustrations to be gathered in a few sections, or to have separate illustration pages inserted between text pages, then separate printing of illustrations is possible. But if it is necessary for illustrations to be scattered throughout the book on the text pages themselves, the entire book would have to be printed by the higher quality, more expensive method.

Another part of the problem of presswork is the question of additional colors, besides black, in the printing. Here again, the designer considers whether it may be possible to arrange pages so that if additional colors are necessary they are confined to only some of the pages, and therefore it will not be necessary to put all the sheets through the press a second or third time to add the second or third color.

In countries supplied with presses able to print two or more colors at one time, use of such equipment naturally occurs to the designer if the edition is going to be large enough to justify its use.

Paper. The choice of paper depends partly on the method of presswork decided on. Quite aside from questions of quality, there are

---

people within the industry use the word to apply only to presswork—the process of putting ink on paper. In this book we usually say *presswork* for the latter restricted meaning, and *printing* when referring to the industry as a whole.

varieties of paper suitable for some kinds of presswork but not others, as will be discussed in the next chapter. It is worth stating here, however, that it is inexcusable for a designer to plan a book based on a certain kind of presswork unless paper for that presswork will surely be available.

In many developing countries there is often virtually no freedom of choice about paper: you have to use whatever is available. Where there is freedom, however, publishers can try to encourage paper merchants to stock the kinds of papers that will be needed for their books. Or, as will be discussed later, it may prove advisable for publishers to purchase paper directly from manufacturers who can make it to order. If they do that, the designer who is able to plan ahead can arrange for the publishing house to secure a stock of paper of exactly the sort needed for books coming along in the near future.

Binding. The major question about binding—whether the book will have a cloth or a paper cover (or both)—is usually made on commercial grounds, for reasons of manufacturing cost, selling price, marketing, and so on; and the designer follows whichever method is decided on.

If the book is to have a cloth binding, and if the designer is working in a country with a range of choice, there are a number of decisions to make. These include choosing the cloth and specifying the color and quality of the ink or foil with which it will be stamped, the quality and thickness of the binding boards, how or even whether the book is to be sewed, what kind of endpapers are to be applied, and other details.

In some developing countries, of course, these choices are not open to the designer, who just takes the best the printer and binder have to offer. But even in those circumstances the designer's attention to how the work is to be done can make a big difference in the appearance of the finished book.

If the book is to have a paper cover, and especially if the book is for mass distribution, so that low cost, sturdy binding, and attractive appearance are all important, the designer gives very close attention to the basic binding process. For example, it may be needlessly expensive to sew the folded sheets of a paperback book, as one would for a clothbound book. The methods of binding are discussed more fully in the next chapter.

Toward Better Design

Among the things designers can do to improve their own work are two of greatest importance: (1) learning as much as possible about printing processes, and especially about new methods that are introduced by local printers though without necessarily realizing all of the ways in which they can be used in book production; and (2) observing examples of good graphic art from as many sources as possible.

The designers as a group, or the overall book industry of a country, can make contributions toward improving design through joint study of common problems and through giving public recognition to good designs or ingenious new uses of printing processes.

Even if there are not enough full-time book designers in a given country to justify a professional association, it is possible to organize informal groups for joint study of the problems with which all are concerned. And, no matter how far a book industry may be from the full development desired, it is never too early to have annual exhibitions and prizes for the best books produced. Among the better known prizes and exhibits that already exist in certain parts of the world are the Leipzig "Best-designed Books from All Over the World," the American Institute of Graphic Arts "Fifty Books of the Year" in the United States, and, for children's books, the Noma Prizes in Asia, those of the Children's Book Trust in New Delhi, and those of the International Board on Books for Young People.

The chief message from such exhibits, and indeed from observing book production all over the world, is that a book does not have to be expensive to be beautiful. The really great achievement for a book designer is, within a tight budget, to create a work of art that will give pleasure to everyone into whose hands it comes.

7

Producing the Book:
Printing and Binding

THUS FAR WE HAVE been talking about things that are done chiefly by people on the publisher's own staff in developing and editing manuscripts and in designing books. From this point on, some of the things we talk about will be activities of other people or organizations, though they are under the publisher's leadership through some sort of business relationship.

The first such example is the work of the printer, who takes the manuscript and, following instructions from the designer, turns the manuscript into a printed book.

Printing is a separate industry from publishing. Book publishing firms may own printing plants, or a printing firm may own book publishing houses. But that does not remove the distinction between them, as noted in Chapter 2.

Printers are manufacturers, industrialists. They use machinery and raw materials to produce the miraculous physical object we call a book. The printer has no concern, at least theoretically, with what the book says, or indeed with whether anyone will want to buy it. Unless the customer, the publisher, goes bankrupt, printers get paid for their work whether or not a single copy is sold.

But of course the enlightened printer really *is* interested in the publisher's success in selling books, because a successful publisher will bring orders for printing more books in the future. And the publisher wants the printer to prosper, because modernization and improvement of the plant and of the printer's service depends on business success.

The publisher and printer are thus allies in a common effort—to make better books at lower prices and distribute them ever more widely, with profit for both of them. Each must have some understanding of the other's problems and aims.

Printing is technically the most intricate and difficult of all the branches of the book industry. It can be mastered only after years of experience, and a publisher cannot expect to have anything like the understanding of it possessed by actual printers.

Publishers *do* know, however, what they want printers to do, how they want the books to look, and what they can afford to pay for them. They owe it to themselves to learn something about the printing and binding processes and about what is and is not physically possible in a printing plant. The more they learn, the better they are able to protect themselves from careless and dishonest printers.

Even with printers who are completely conscientious, the publisher who is well informed will gain many benefits through intelligent cooperation. A good printer responds to, and goes to great lengths to serve, a publisher who uses the right technical terms and knows enough of the craft to demand only what is possible, and not ask the impossible. Such cooperation is important in any country, but more so in developing countries than in those with advanced book industries.

The purpose of this chapter is merely to suggest the main elements of book manufacture about which the publisher must know something, at least in broad outline, even though it is the professional printer who will do the work. There are three basic processes in manufacturing a book: (1) *Composition* is the process of producing and arranging the words that are to be reproduced on the printed page. Depending on the composition method that is used, this process will result in metal type or in sheets of paper (on which the text has been handwritten, typewritten, or "photocomposed"), referred to as *camera-ready copy*, which must be photographed in order to produce printing plates for the printing press. (2) *Presswork* is the process of applying ink to paper by use of a printing press and the metal type or plates. (3) *Binding* is the process of folding and assembling in proper order the printed sheets and then fastening them together in some way.

There are dozens of special processes within each of these main divisions, but everything in book manufacture is somehow included in one or another of the three. Although, as noted before, it is unrealistic to think one could learn book manufacture out of a book, brief comment on each of the main divisions may be helpful to the beginning publisher in seeing how they are related. It may be a useful guide to further study and observation.

Composition

Although a European, Gutenberg, is often thought of as the father of printing, type was invented by the Chinese long before him. And the Korean invention of movable type was the greatest typographic improvement until the nineteenth century.

The following sections discuss some ways of arranging letters for printing without the use of type, but type is probably still the most usual method, whether the printing is directly from the type itself or by some other process.

Typesetting by hand. In most developing countries, where labor is inexpensive, hand setting is the cheapest method; and it is easier to train a hand typesetter than the operator of a complicated machine. It is also possible for a skilled hand typesetter to achieve delicacy and accuracy impossible for a machine. In a plant using hand composition, production can be increased merely by hiring more people and getting more type, without the heavy capital investment needed for increasing capacity for composition by machine.

The disadvantages of hand composition include the slowness of the work, the expense of maintaining a large enough supply of type in a range of designs and sizes, and the poor printing quality that may result from varying amounts of wear on the type.

The type used for hand setting in the past was always foundry type, which is used over and over again. Although foundry type is made of very hard metal, it wears out a tiny bit with each impression. (An "impression" occurs each time the type comes in contact with the paper on the printing press; for 1,000 printed copies of a book, the type undergoes 1,000 impressions). Also, the printer has the extra expense of putting each piece of type back in its compartment of the type case after presswork (so it can be used again) as well as setting the type in the first place. Furthermore, few printers can afford enough foundry type to set a whole book at one time; they may do only 16 pages, print those, redistribute the type, set another 16 pages, and so on.

In spite of those disadvantages, hand composition from foundry type is still a widely used method in many developing countries and will continue to be so, especially for small printers in provincial areas.

But in recent years printers have developed a new method of composition making partial use of mechanical methods. This keeps the benefits of hand typesetting but avoids some of its disadvantages. Under this method the pieces of type are made by a Monotype caster (see section on Monotype below), and are of a type metal that can be melted down for recasting after each use. Because Monotype metal is much softer than foundry type and wears out quickly, constant melting down and recasting are necessary.

A printer with a plant of some size may have a caster for making the type to be used by hand compositions; or a small printer may buy type thus produced by a larger printer, and sell back the melted-up metal, after the type has been used. In larger cities, there may be firms specializing entirely in casting separate types (called sorts) to sell to small printers. The type made by a Monotype caster is crisp and clear and new every time it is used; and the printer can shift holdings of type—to different designs or different sizes or even different scripts— as needs develop and change.

This ingenious combining of traditional hand typesetting with use of modern machinery has great promise for developing countries even in mass-production plants in which full mechanization is right for the other main divisions of book production, presswork, and binding.

Monotype. This is a method of mechanical typesetting that uses separate pieces of metal for each letter, and in this respect is something like hand composition. There are two pieces of Monotype equipment: the keyboard which punches holes in a paper tape, and the caster which actually casts the letters in metal and arranges them in the desired form, controlled by the position of the holes the keyboard made in the tape. The paper tape can be stored for later reuse, the type being cast over again from the same tape without repeating the keyboard operation. The caster can also be used for casting types to be used for hand typesetting as mentioned above.

For normal typesetting of straight reading matter, without special complications, Monotype composition is often more expensive than the line casting methods mentioned in the next section. Of the mechanical methods of setting type, however, Monotype is the more flexible, and it therefore has special advantages for setting advantages for setting scientific formulas, complicated tables, letters with special accents, Arabic with a full system of vowels, and other difficult parts of a book.

Linotype and Intertype. These two machines, commercially competitive with each other, set *lines* of type instead of separate letters. The general method is called linecasting. It is necessary to reset a whole line in order to correct an error, and new errors may occur when that is done. These machines are not able to deal with certain scripts used in some developing countries, and they do not have as much flexibility as Monotype for some purposes. These linecasting systems are, however, the least expensive and most widely used methods of mechanical typesetting for usual composition.

Those methods of setting type (Monotype and linecasting) traditionally involve printing directly from the metal type on letterpress presses (although, alternatively, good quality proofs from the type can be photographed and the resulting film used to make plates for an offset press). The *following* three methods of "typesetting" do not produce metal type at all, but rather an image of the typeface is reproduced on paper or film, which is in turn either photographed or exposed to produce a printing plate.

Photocomposition. There are several commercially competitive machines on the market. The forms of the letters are reproduced photographically or electronically in the desired arrangement, and the machine produces a film or photographic print carrying that image. The film (or film made from the photographic print) is generally used for making a plate for offset printing (as noted under Presswork below), but it can also be used for making a plate for letterpress printing. There are more and more photocomposing units in operation in developing countries, and this method can be of great value in the future. Forward-looking printers in developing countries, and the book publishers who are their customers, should keep careful watch on developments in this field in coming years.

Another, very recent, development, however, may one day overtake all other methods of composition. This is a phenomenon called desktop publishing.

Desktop publishing. In the mid-1980s the development of desktop publishing in the Western world harnessed old typographic concepts to new computer technology, making possible the relatively inexpensive composition of magazines, newsletters, promotional material, and perhaps even entire books by publishers themselves rather than separate typesetters. As with much new technology, the new methods are easier to learn and cheaper in materials than other composition systems (with the exception of those discussed in the next section, on other methods of composition).

Desktop publishing combines a microcomputer (for instance the Apple Macintosh or the IBM AT), computer programs (software) for word processing and page makeup, and a laser printer to produce pages of composition on paper (camera-ready copy), which can be photographed to produce printing plates for an offset press. A limited, but widening, range of typefaces borrowed from traditional systems is available in the roman alphabet, and other alphabets are also becoming available. Illustrations can be easily accommodated into the page makeup.

This newest revolution in composition offers the developing world publisher or printer a relatively inexpensive way to produce composition of very close to typeset quality. The cost of a minimum system, which would vary depending upon import and customs costs, is in the neighborhood of $10,000 to $15,000, far less than the cost of the equipment required for a photocomposition system. New and exciting developments in this field appear almost weekly, but the publisher/printer may wish to settle for the next-to-newest and take advantage of the continuing lowering of prices as the newer models appear.

Other methods of composition. Typewriting, handwriting, and line drawings can be reproduced on plates for the printing press. Especially in South Asia, and especially for printing in Urdu, there is still quite a bit of hand calligraphy instead of typesetting, even for newspapers.

Typewriting, since it is very inexpensive, is often used, even in the most advanced countries, when the formality of a book produced with printer's type is not required, but it will probably be replaced more and more by desktop systems.

Black-and-white illustrations. Although illustrations do not involve problems of typesetting, they are treated as part of the process of composition because they, like the type letters, have a form that is to be reproduced by the succeeding process of presswork.

It is clearest to start off by thinking of two main types of illustrations: pictures in *line*, that is, pure black or pure white at any one point in the picture; and pictures in *continuous tone*, which may have a gradation of black through grays to white. A simple drawing with solid lines is a typical example of line, and a photograph is a typical example of continuous tone.

Since most printing is done with only one color of ink, usually black, a special process is required to print a continuous tone photograph, which has gradations of black to shades of gray to white. The continuous tone illustration is photographed through a cross-ruled screen in a special camera. The type of screen used depends on the quality of the paper to be used and the quality of printing desired. The resulting film (and therefore the printing plate) is broken up into various sizes of dots, all of which will be printed in black ink. Where dots are large and close together, the printed picture will look dark gray; where the dots are very tiny with a great deal of space around them, the picture will look almost white; and so forth. Thus the printed picture (*halftone*) gives the illusion of continuous tone.

To obtain extra quality, the illustration can be screened twice from slightly different angles and printed twice in black or in black and a second color. This is called a *duotone*. (It should not be confused with two-color printing, which simply lays a solid or screened color over or under a black-and-white photograph.)

Color illustrations. The same principles of line and continuous tone apply in color printing. For line printing, areas of different solid colors can be printed successively. For color photographs, or reproductions of color art, the illustration again has to be broken up into halftone dots. In the case of color this is usually done four times, at slightly different angles, because *full-color printing* (sometimes called *process printing*) is usually done with only four inks: a light blue called "cyan," magenta, yellow, and black.

The breaking up of a color illustration into four separate plates is called *color separation*. This can be done either with a special camera similar to the one mentioned above for black-and-white halftones, but using color filters, or by an electronic scanner—the newest and most sophisticated means of color separation. When the four halftone plates are printed successively (one in each of the four colors), the printed dots blend together into a pattern that gives the illusion of the full color of the original. (The black can be omitted, but the quality suffers, or special extra colors can be added for the finest quality, but this is very expensive.)

The operation of these cameras or scanners for black-and-white, duotone, and full-color printing requires a great deal of skill and judgment.

If the presswork for a book is to be by offset (see below), the publisher does not have to worry too much about whether the illustrations are to be in line or in halftone, because offset can handle either without great difference in cost between them. But if the presswork is to be by letterpress, the publisher will want to make the most careful calculation of cost. The blocks (also called cuts or clichés) for line illustrations are comparatively cheap and can be printed on almost any kind of paper. But the blocks for halftone illustrations are expensive and require the right kind of paper of good results.

The best surface for the printing of halftones by either letterpress or offset printing is coated paper or, as it is called in many countries, art paper. Such paper is expensive. So when possible the publisher plans to use that paper only for the pages carrying illustrations. For some kinds of books, especially textbooks in which halftone illustrations will be scattered through many pages, the publisher may use machine finish paper—also called English finish, or process-coated paper—which avoids the expensiveness of coated paper but gives fairly good reproduction of halftone pictures.

Presswork

Presswork is the process of putting ink on paper. The different kinds of presswork most widely used for book manufacture are discussed below.

Letterpress printing. This is the traditional kind of presswork used for centuries in many parts of the world. Ink is applied to the raised surface of the type, paper is pressed against it, and the forms of the letters are thus copied on the paper. In modern times, in addition to printing directly from the type, plates can be cast from molds made from the original type and used for printing instead of the type itself. The plate is a thin shell (traditionally of metal but recently sometimes of hard rubber or plastic) that does not wear out as quickly as type metal. It can be easily stored for use in possible later reprintings.

Many books all over the world are still printed directly from type, but lots of publishers use plates for most of their books. They cannot tell ahead of time which books will need to be reprinted, but they hope to save enough on the books that *do* go into reprinting to pay for plating all of them. An additional advantage of using plates is the speed with which a book can be reprinted, without having to go through the composition process again. A disadvantage is that when type has not been stored, any corrections that must be made will require resetting of all the pages on a plate, and a new plate must be made.

An alternative to plating is to store the type, hoping that the likelihood of a reprinting can be learned from early sales of the book before the cost of storage has used up too much of the saving that will be gained by avoiding recomposition. But a printer who uses foundry type for hand composition, cannot afford to let the type remain idle; and even if the type is made of type metal, it is costly (because of the interest on the investment) to delay melting it down for reuse. The printer therefore has to charge the publisher if, at the latter's request, he holds the type more than a few days after presswork.

With the spread of offset printing throughout the world, it has become increasingly economical to reprint books by offset, even when the first edition was printed by letterpress. Offset plates are made, in such cases, by photographing a copy of the original letterpress printed edition.

Planographic printing. This kind of presswork is called plano-graphic because, instead of using raised type, or plates with raised surfaces, the printing is from a smooth plate, a plane. The image of the letters is copied on the smooth plate; it is treated in such a way that the ink adheres to those parts of the plate but not to the rest. When the paper in pressed against a *blanket cylinder* in the press, the ink is transferred to the blanket and is then offset to the paper.

Modern offset printing is the most familiar form of planographic presswork, and is the most important for book production. It might be noted, however, that the kind of presswork called litho in South Asia, which is closely related to old-fashioned lithographing on stone, is another form of planographic printing.

The planographic class includes a whole group of processes using small machines such as Davidson, Multilith, and others, often thought of only as office copiers or for printing circulars and other small items rather than books. But this small equipment can in fact be used for book production, sometimes with great economy compared with printing by more formal means. One of the chief disadvantages of these easy-to-operate machines is the small size of the forms they produce (perhaps only four pages on a sheet), causing extra hand work in assembling the sections for binding. In many developing countries, however, hand labor is one of the cheapest commodities, so that small "office presses" in such areas do not have the drawback that limits their usefulness for book work in countries where labor is expensive.

Offset printing has revolutionized book production in many parts of the world. Among its advantages are that composition can be combined by the printer with drawings, photographs, handwriting, and so forth, in one operation. The last stage before the plate is made is production of a film carrying all of the images, and that film can be saved for reuse if it does not seem worthwhile to save the plate itself.

Offset presswork is especially significant in international cooperation among publishers interested in bringing out different editions—often in different languages—of books with expensive color illustrations. A duplicate set of films for the color illustrations can be made by the originating publisher and, because films are easily shipped, can be sold or leased to a publisher in another country, thus reducing costs for both of them.

Pressureless printing. New methods of presswork, using electrostatic image techniques, of which Xerox is the best known, seem certain to revolutionize the production of small editions. Use of xerography can make possible the printing of very small quantities (for instance, experimental editions of new textbooks or copies of out-of-print books for libraries or research scholars), without the prohibitive per-copy cost normal for small editions. In combination with microfilm, which can store large amounts of information in little space and at low cost per page, xerography makes possible publication, on demand, of books that have high value (medicine, science, technology, etc.) but a limited market. This process holds great promise, even though the problems of reproducing halftones and color have not been fully solved. As more production units come into operation in developing countries, the possibilities of xerography will deserve the most careful study of book publishers. Because this technique makes it so easy and inexpensive to copy the printed page, however, publishers should make certain that any required permissions or licensing fees are taken care of so that no infringement of copyright is involved.

Screen process. This is one of the simplest forms of presswork. It is commonly called silkscreen, though nowadays the screen may be of nylon, cotton, metal mesh, or some other material. It is used for many special operations, such as printing wallpaper. It is not feasible for whole books, but it is very useful for making posters or for single pages in color when the quantity is too small for normal commercial methods. For instance, for a book in a small edition in which it is desired to include a few color illustrations, ordinary methods may be too expensive, but an artist who does silkscreen printing may be able to produce the few pages needed in the small quantity at a reasonable price.

Special presses. There are many special kinds of presses for both letterpress and offset printing, but they are merely adaptations of the basic processes. Perfecting presses print both sides of a sheet at once. Web presses print from a continuous roll of paper, as newspaper presses do. Multicolor presses do two, three, four, or even more colors successively.

Although these advanced pieces of equipment are enormously expensive, they are economical for book work if the quantities to be printed are large enough. More and more of the large book printers and their book publishing customers in developing countries are thinking about ways in which such equipment will let them achieve—in the future if not right away—the economy of mass production for the great new mass distribution market they know is coming.

Binding

When the sheets have been printed, they come off the press in a large size with perhaps 8 or 16 or 32 or 64 book pages printed on each sheet. The process of binding involves folding the sheets in the proper way and gathering the folded sheets so the pages of the book will be in the right order, fastening the pages together in some way, trimming the edges, and applying a cover of some kind.

Folding *can* be entirely by hand, and in many printing plants in developing countries it still is, because labor is cheap and machinery expensive. Most book-manufacturing plants of any size, however, have at least some folding machines. There is an enormous variety of folders adapted for different purposes, different size sheets, different speeds of operation, and so on.

The next step after folding is *gathering* or *collating* the folded sheets in the order in which they are to appear in the book. Although most such operations are performed by hand in many parts of the world, there are ways of speeding up that work by the use of "rubber fingers" and different kinds of racks, revolving tables, and so on. In areas where labor rates are low, gathering machines are not usually economical except for very large quantities.

After the sheets have been folded and gathered, the next thing is to fasten them together. The simplest way of doing that is with wire staples. Sewing with thread is quite a bit more expensive, but for any book of much thickness it gives better results and permits the pages to turn more easily.

If a hardcover binding is to be used, the stitched sheets are trimmed on three sides before the binding is put on. If there is to be a paper cover, the trimming is done after the cover is applied so that the cover will be trimmed evenly with the text pages. If the binding is to be of the sort called "perfect," as described below, there is no stitching, and the sheets are trimmed on all four sides.

Perfect binding. So-called *perfect binding* has been a key to development of the paperback book industry in Western countries, and it is making rapid progress in developing countries also. The sheets, trimmed on all four sides, are set in the cover with a special adhesive. When it was first introduced, the only perfect-binding equipment was large and very expensive, and the results were often disastrous: pages tended to come loose, and the binding cracked in cold weather and deteriorated or attracted vermin in the tropics. New adhesives have been developed, however, that stand up well in all climates, and perfect-binding equipment has been produced in small units, some of which can be operated entirely by hand. There is a great future for use of perfect-binding methods in developing countries.

Burst binding. In recent years, a method of binding called *burst* or *notch binding* has been developed, which is a compromise between the expense of sewing with thread and the impermanence of adhesive binding. The folded sheets are trimmed on three sides only, and into the remaining (folded) side holes are punched, into which glue is forced in order to hold all the pages together. Since it produces a book that is more durable and easier to open than an adhesive-bound book, but less expensive than a sewn book, this method is especially appropriate for textbooks, which should be low priced but which, because they receive hard use, need something sturdier than perfect binding.

Printing the covers. Although cover printing is a presswork operation, it is so closely associated with the binding of books that it is convenient to mention it here. Covers that are inexpensive to produce, yet are effective "sellers" of the books inside them, need careful planning of the materials as well as of the design and the printing itself. Especially if shiny covers are desired (useful because they shed dust besides being eye-catching), the effect can be achieved in a number of ways. A shiny cover paper can be printed with high-gloss inks; or regular paper can be printed with regular ink and then varnished; or a method of lamination can be used, in which plastic is bonded to the surface after presswork. (This latter method gives the best appearance and the most protection to the cover, but it is also the most expensive.)

Because the printing of covers, often in four colors, is an expensive operation, it is wise, when possible, to print the covers for several books at one time, thus reducing the cost of presswork.

Paper

The publisher *must* learn something about book papers or accept whatever the printer offers, at whatever the printer feels like charging, whether or not the paper is exactly right for the particular book. There is an almost infinite variety of papers possible for use in books, from groundwood sheets like newsprint to the finest and most expensive art papers coated with talc and clay and other substances to give a beautiful printing surface. The publisher does not have to become a paper technician and learn all the details but needs to understand the principal kinds of paper, the kinds of printing for which they are needed, and how to distinguish them. Among the qualities that the publisher learns to recognize, beside the basic question of the size of the sheet (which must be suitable for the size of the press on which the book is to be printed), are: (1) ingredients (kinds of pulp, such as groundwood, woodfree, or rag; degree of acidity; coating agents; etc.); (2) weight (which will influence freight costs if books have to be shipped any distance); (3) opacity (the amount of "show through" of ink from one side of the sheet to the other); (4) bulk (number of pages per inch); (5) surface (suitable for halftones? for offset?); (6) color (bright white, blue white, cream, etc.) and tendency to change color with time; (7) direction of grain (important in the binding process); (8) folding quality; and (9) tear strength.

The wise publisher learns to weigh these various characteristics so as to choose the paper that is the most appropriate for a particular book and also the most economical. Some compromises must usually be made even under the best of circumstances.

If a publisher is in a provincial area where there is no good paper merchant available, there may not be much choice; and in many developing countries that have a shortage of foreign exchange, even the wisest book people sometimes have to change paper in the middle of a book. But any publisher in a large city with a variety of paper merchants is able to choose, within limits, what is wanted. A wise publisher will seek as much advice as possible from printers. But, on the other hand, it is extremely shortsighted for the publisher simply to leave it to the printer to decide. Advance planning about paper is one of the easiest ways for a publisher to increase the margin of profit.

Conclusion

This chapter has given only the barest outline and simplest statement of the process of book production. The simplification has perhaps led to some inaccuracy in description. But the purpose will have been served if it inspires publishers to learn more. This can be done in part by further reading, but chiefly it must be by constant observation in printing plants and by continuing discussion of common problems with other publishers, with printers, and, when possible, with suppliers of equipment and materials.

The publisher interested in building for the future must have some understanding of the printing industry. And the publisher must help the printers to see what the needs will be in the coming period, so that additional or improved or entirely different equipment—as required—will be included in the printer's long-range development plans.

8

Selling the Book

AFTER ALL THE PRELIMINARY work by the author, illustrator, editor, designer, and printer, finished books at last become available—printed and bound and waiting for readers. That is when the real test comes.

Throughout this chapter we talk about selling books and the sales department that performs each function. But the ideas presented here are just as valid for a research agency or some other nonprofit institution that may not actually sell its books but must somehow get them into the hands of readers in order to achieve its nonprofit purpose. So the "sales department" might be better called the "dissemination department," and it plays a crucial role in every kind of publishing house, whether to bring in money for paying the bills or to broadcast knowledge or ideas. The work of that department must be looked at with respect, not only from the point of view of the publisher's bank account, but also from the point of view of society; unless people read the books there is no public justification for the book industry.

So the constant challenge to the sales department is not merely to produce income but also to distribute books ever more widely. If the books are good ones, the publisher's interest and the public interest go hand in hand. As noted in the economic studies in Chapter 3, the easiest way to reduce the selling price of books is to lower the manufacturing cost per copy by printing more copies at one time; but it is pointless to print more books unless they can be sold.

The sales department holds one of the important keys to the publisher's business success and ability to serve the public. And, as always in this book, we emphasize that the reference to a "sales department" should not discourage small publishers who have no "departments" at all. The principles given here are just as applicable to the selling of books by a very small publishing house in which one or two people do all the work.

Ways of Selling Books

The many different ways of selling books can be divided most simply into four main groups according to who is the actual customer who will pay the publisher's bill: (1) individual consumers, (2) institutions, (3) retailers, and (4) wholesalers.

Individual consumers. Direct sale is made by the publisher to the final purchaser of the book. Among the methods for these direct sales are: (1) direct mail promotion and sale (see Chapter 9); (2) the publisher's own bookshop, if there is one (see Chapter 20); (3) the publisher's own mass distribution system, if there is one (see Chapter 13); (4) the publisher's own book club, if there is one (see Chapter 14); and (5) the publisher's own subscription-selling system, if there is one (see Chapter 14).

Institutions. The most important customers, of course, are school systems, libraries, literacy campaigns, and rural-development agencies. The techniques of selling to such institutions naturally vary greatly from country to country and from time to time. Special methods may also be necessary for the different kinds of books, such as textbooks (see Chapter 11), reference books (see Chapter 10), children's books (see Chapter 12), and literacy teaching books and reading material for new literates (see Chapter 16).

Some institutional sales can be made centrally, for instance through adoption of a school textbook by the ministry of education, which may place one order for the entire school system. But many institutional sales require that the publisher maintain a system of travelers who will visit institutions in different parts of the country, either as salaried members of the publisher's staff or as agents receiving commission according to the amount of their sales.

It should also be noted that direct mail promotion can be a powerful supporter of institutional selling, even though the sale is finally made in another way. The direct mail promotion may stimulate the sale if it gets into the hands of a librarian, for instance; but in addition,it informs potential readers of the existence of a book, and their inquiries put pressure on the librarian to order it.

Retailers. These are the merchants, of many different sorts, who sell books—most frequently one by one—to the actual users. The retailer normally handles a wide variety of books, not merely those of one publisher. Among the publisher's customers in this category of retailers are regular retail bookshops (see Chapter 20), mass distribution companies (see Chapter 13), book clubs (see Chapter 14), sale-by-mail retailers (see Chapter 9), subscription-selling companies (see Chapter 14), and peddlers and other mobile booksellers who carry books by foot, bicycle, automobile, and so forth.

Wholesalers. These people, who may be called either wholesalers or jobbers, stand between the publishers and the retailers who, in their turn, make the sales to the actual users of the books. The wholesaler does not, in theory, sell directly to consumers but in practice does often make the final sale, especially to institutions. Library wholesalers provide the main channel from developing countries into the libraries of Europe and North America.

The extra discount that the wholesaler receives from the publisher (on the theory that the selling is only to retailers) makes the wholesaler's retail sales a form of "unfair competition" with actual retailers. Action by wholesalers in undercutting the prices charged by retailers is forbidden by law in some countries and by business agreements imposed by publishers (as a condition of the extra discount) in many others.

A good system of wholesaling can make a very important contribution both to book publishing development and to the retail book trade in any country. If there *is* good wholesaling, then retailers, especially small retailers, have the advantage of being able to get the books of many different publishers from one wholesaler. And the publishers are able to make bulk sales to the wholesalers instead of having to deal separately with each retailer on each sale.

In countries that are large geographically, there is an additional advantage: the wholesaler may have regional depositories or godowns from which books that are in stock can be supplied more quickly than if the retailer has to order separately each time from the publisher in a remote city.

Of course a publisher who leaves everything to the wholesaler, without direct contact with important retailers, will lose out in the end. But a good wholesaler can be helpful in enabling the publisher to reach provincial areas or the market offered by small booksellers in remote locations. Not even the largest publisher can afford to maintain regular contact with every small bookseller throughout the country, but the wholesaler carrying a general line of books from many different publishing houses can do that.

The concept of wholesaling is especially attractive for the future of developing countries in which education (hence interest in books) has spread throughout the country, but effective distribution of books is still largely confined to principal cities. Much remains to be done, however, as very few of the developing countries have set up good wholesaling systems.

Export

All the methods listed above may be involved in export selling, so that in one sense export selling is no different from any other kind. In fact, however, there is a whole family of special problems. This is so whether the publisher's relations are directly with individual consumers (almost impossible in many countries) or with institutions, retailers, or wholesalers in the importing country, or with export jobbers in the exporting country. The headaches of foreign selling are so great that many publishers attempt practically no foreign operations of their own, and leave everything to the export jobbers who can afford the travel and other special expenses because of representing many different publishers.

Below are a few of the many factors that may affect development of the export market.

Language. The users of a book must understand the language in which it is written, and this restricts the export business for the publishers in many developing countries. Some languages in Asia,

Africa, and Latin America, however, have very wide use in more than one country.

English is the most widely used language, not only for intercommunication among developing countries but also for contact with the Western world. English-language publishers in such countries as India, Pakistan, Nigeria, Ghana, Kenya, Uganda, Tanzania, Malaysia, and Singapore have a real opportunity for future development of an export business—with each other and with the West.

French is also useful for interchange among certain developing countries and with Europe. The prospects seem especially promising for French-language publishers in the West African countries using the language; and there are possibilities in Morocco, Algeria, Tunisia, Lebanon, Syria, Malagasy, and other countries in which French is used along with one or more other languages.

Spanish, the language of most of Latin America, has obvious possibilities for book export, both within the area and for interchange with Spain. Mexico and Argentina are already large exporters to other Latin American countries.

Portuguese, the language of Brazil, the largest country of Latin America, is extensively used now only within that country and in Portugal, but it will become more important as the Portuguese-speaking areas of Africa develop economically and educationally.

Chinese is an important language, not only for the People's Republic of China, but also for the entire Overseas Chinese community. Significant export already takes place from the People's Republic to politically allied areas, and from Taiwan and Hong Kong to various Overseas Chinese centers.

Arabic is a language in which heavy export of books already takes place, not only among Arab countries but also from Arab publishing centers to other parts of the Islamic world. For Egypt and Lebanon, the principal publishers of books in Arabic, export has been the economic mainstay of the business in the past.

Urdu and Bengali are languages used by many millions of people in India and its neighbors, Pakistan for Urdu and Bangladesh for Bengali; from time to time, political difficulties prevent development of the common market, but the potential is very great.

Swahili has the largest potential for exchange of books in East Africa of any purely African language.

Persian is shared by Iran, Afghanistan, Tajikstan, and some other parts of the USSR, and the possibilities for export among them seem substantial.

Other languages such as Tamil, Punjabi, Pashto, Malay and Indonesian, Russian, German, and Dutch have more limited export possibilities in developing countries because they are shared with only one or two other areas or are minority languages restricted to particular communities.

Political obstacles. The free flow of books is often obstructed for political reasons by either the exporting or the importing country. Ingenious book-trade people are often able to find legal ways around these obstructions, not to mention the illegal means that are sometimes employed. Use of a third country as the intermediary between the exporter and importer is a method frequently used. In the past, Lebanon was an outstanding example of a country serving that third-country function, even when relations between two other Arab countries have been such that no direct trade between them was possible.

Censorship. Prohibition by censors of particular books or of particular kinds of books—for political, religious, or moral reasons—may also be an obstacle, although in overall terms it is usually more an inconvenience than an actual obstruction to the export trade as a whole.

Economic factors. This category of problems presents the greatest difficulty to the international book trade. It includes the troubles caused by systems of import licenses, the difficulty in securing foreign exchange, the levying of import duties and other taxes, differences in exchange rates resulting in increased selling prices, the expense of shipment and insurance to foreign customers, the difficulty in collecting money from foreign debtors, and the extraordinary amount of time between the retailer's placing of an order and receipt of the book.

Yet in spite of all these difficulties—which the government of the exporting or importing country may try to increase or reduce for various reasons of education, economics, politics, or propaganda—

the export business is well worth the trouble. For some countries, such as the United Kingdom for English-language publishing, Egypt for Arabic, or Argentina and Mexico for Spanish, export has been so large a part of the total book business that the full development of their book publishing would have been impossible without it.

Especially for publishers who have not had much export business in the past, every book sold abroad can be looked at as a "plus sale," hence one for which the publisher should be prepared to incur a little extra trouble or expense, because, aside from the extra cost, the book represents a net addition to the sales volume that would be otherwise possible.

The Process of Selling Books

The process of bookselling can be divided into three major divisions: (1) promotion, (2) getting the orders, and (3) filling the orders and delivering the books.

Promotion. This is the process of letting people know that the book exists, and of persuading them to buy it. It is so important to book publishing success, and is so special in its techniques, that it is treated separately in the next chapter.

Getting the orders. This is the process of following up the promotion campaign and actually getting people to place orders. If orders come in by mail, this may be merely an extension of the promotion department's work. But the more familiar part of the work of getting orders involves sales representatives who travel about to show new books to booksellers, schools, and libraries and take orders for them; and also to check stock of older books the bookseller has been handling and see if reorders can be secured.

The sales representatives who travel for publishers may be on a straight salary or they may receive a percentage commission on the orders they actually get. The two methods are often combined, with the sales representatives having small salaries and expecting to get most of their income from commissions.

A system called *ledger accounts* gives the sales representatives a commission on all orders coming from the assigned territory, whether or not the representative brings in the actual order. This is on the theory that it is the effective representation of the publishing house and its list of books, the careful cultivation of the booksellers, and the supervision of promotion in the area that produced the business.

The department responsible for getting the orders may have a number of subdivisions in a large house. These special sections may specialize in textbook sales, in library sales, in sales of special parts of the publisher's list (for instance, medical books or law books), in export sales, and so on; and there are almost always special sections when the publisher has a book club, a subscription book plan, a mass distribution system, or a large direct mail operation.

Filling the orders and delivering the books. This involves packing and shipping the books and making out the bills. That sounds simple but is actually the biggest "housekeeping" job in book publishing. Quite aside from the enormous clerical job of applying the right discount, keeping track of shipping charges, and maintaining records so the bill can eventually be collected (or the name and address of the customer can be kept for use in later promotion, even if the order itself was paid for in cash), the physical job of handling the accounts is a big one.

Storage is a constant source of trouble. In order to give good service to the customers, the publisher wants to have a stock of all books on hand at all times; yet the space available for the shipping room and storeroom is nearly always limited, especially if the publishing office is in an area where land is expensive. Publishers try to meet the problem in a number of ways. One method is for the printer to agree to store part of the stock and make deliveries—daily if necessary—to the publisher's own storeroom. Another method, quite widely used nowadays in Western countries, is to have the storage and shipping space in a separate location, in an area of cheap land, possibly outside the city but accessible by truck to some shipping point.

An obvious complication in book storage is the danger of damage to the stock from various perils. If damage is superficial, a new dust jacket is sometimes an inexpensive way of making the books salable once again, but large losses can be incurred if more serious harm occurs. Because so many of the developing countries are in the tropics, with heat and monsoons and book-hungry insects and other dangers, protection of book stock is essential, expensive though it may be. Water is clearly the greatest enemy, whether in moisture-laden air or in floods that invade godowns. For a book that will sell its whole edition quickly, there is of course no problem. But, as we noted earlier, the printing of books for more than just today and tomorrow is a key to sound economics in book publishing.

Closely related to the question of books damaged while in storage is that of damaged *returns*—that is, books that booksellers may be permitted to send back, after a time, because they cannot sell them. Comment on the publisher's policy in permitting returns is given below. Everything possible should be done to make the jackets and covers dust-shedding, the bindings firm, and the paper and binding cloth free from a tendency to discolor.

Another of the big and annoying problems in filling orders is that of planning routes of shipment. In a country with a comprehensive and efficient postal system, the only problem is to decide between use of the mail and (for large orders) separate shipment by rail or by commercial lorries. In areas where the postal system does not work well throughout the country, however, the publisher must use genuine ingenuity. Instead of just ignoring the problem, the publisher tries to find ways of delivering the books to the customer at lowest cost and with greatest speed, sometimes making use of distribution channels already established for newspapers and magazines, or making arrangements with bus companies that handle some freight as a sideline. In one way or another, however, the forward-looking publisher must be constantly alert to find ways of improving the delivery of books, which, in the long run, will increase the volume of business.

International Standard Book Number. A great convenience for publishers, booksellers, and librarians is the International Standard Book Number (ISBN), which gives positive identification of a book. The ISBN consists of ten digits, of which the first shows the language of the book (for instance, "0" for English) and the others the publisher and book title.

Most publishers secure an ISBN for each book they publish, and print the number on the page following the title page and on the cover of the book. Some agency in each country is in charge of assigning ISBNs to publishers in that country. In many countries it is the national library or some branch of the ministry of education. If it is difficult to find out locally where the national ISBN office is, write to the international headquarters: International Standard Book Number, Stats Bibliothek, Kultur Besitz, Potsdamer Strasse 33, 1000 Berlin 30, Federal Republic of Germany.

Collecting the bills. It is impossible for a person in another country to give useful advice about bill collecting to a publisher, because so much depends on local conditions in general and, even more, on personal relationships, the laws about business obligations in that country, and many other factors. Attention can be drawn, however, to the comments below about credit as a factor in sales, and the wisdom of patience with a good customer who is known by the publisher to be sound in the long run, whatever the present financial difficulties.

Of course orders will be received, under any circumstances and in any country, from customers of whom the publisher is suspicious; and there are other orders from booksellers who were trusted once but have since proved that they must be dealt with on a *cash-with-order* basis. Or, in countries with a *collect-on-delivery* system in the postal service, that device may be used when the customer's credit standing is unknown. For some orders that are large enough to make it worth while, a *sight draft* paid through a bank may be used. In a number of countries, national airlines have a collect-on-delivery system (called "contrareembolso" in Spanish and Portuguese) that can be useful.

But all these methods are at best merely alternatives, involving extra cost and delays, to an orderly extension of credit to customers who have proved worthy of it.

In this connection attention is also called to the discussion in Chapter 17 of cooperation among publishers in investigating booksellers' credit standing, and in joint efforts not only at avoiding losses through bad debts but also in helping good booksellers to survive in spite of temporary shortage of cash.

Factors Influencing Sales

In addition to the values given to a particular book by people outside the sales department—the quality of the book, the prestige of the author's name, the timeliness of the subject, the attractiveness of the design—there are seven business factors that are of top importance: (1) selling price, (2) discount, (3) credit, (4) return privileges, (5) promotion, (6) service, and (7) timing.

Selling price. Each book is a business problem in itself, and no outsider can give a publisher really useful advice about the pricing policy to follow in each case. Some books will sell no more copies at §1 than they would at §5, while other books may double their sale if the selling price is reduced merely from §2.50 to §1.50.

One element in the publisher's decision about whether reducing selling price will increase sales is the judgment of the *basic necessity* of the book for the potential customers. An engineering handbook may be an absolutely essential professional tool so that, within reason, the customers will pay whatever may be necessary in order to get it. On the other hand, a novel is not, except for students of literature, an essential tool, and there may be great difference in its sales performance at a low price and a high price. The prices of any books with which the publisher is competing must also be taken into account.

Publishers normally have guidelines in their minds as to the relation of selling price to manufacturing cost. In some countries, and for some kinds of books, they may use a factor as high as six—making the selling price six times the manufacturing cost. In other countries, and for other kinds of books, it may be as low as three or three and a half times the manufacturing cost.

Another method is to look at the price per page that can usually be charged, with the rate for scientific and technical books being up to three times as much per page as for other nonfiction, and maybe four to five times as much as for popular fiction. This is a good way of comparing one's own prices with what is being charged by other publishers.

Selling price cannot, in any event, be considered apart from other factors, of which the manufacturing cost is the most important but by no means the only one. The method of marketing may limit the highest a price can go. For instance, it would be futile to try mass distribution of a book with a very high selling price; but, with ingenuity on the part of the designer and manufacturer, and vision on the part of the sales representatives, it may be possible (depending on the subject matter) to convert a small-edition, high-price book into one suitable for mass distribution at a very low price, using the principles we examined in Chapter 3.

Relation of price to discount. Selling price is also related to the question of discount mentioned under that heading below. For instance, a bookseller may expect a profit of §5 on a §25 book, even though the publisher allows only a 20 percent discount. But the same book if selling at §10, though carrying a 40 percent discount, will give a profit of only §4. Or, looking at it the other way around, the publisher will have to charge more for a given book if a decision is made to allow a larger discount in order to interest booksellers.

Break-even point. Still another factor entering into the decision about selling price is the probability of selling out the edition or—from the unhappier point of view—the likelihood that the publisher will be left with a lot of unsold books. As we saw in Chapter 3, the publisher can figure out ahead of time the *break-even point* for recovering manufacturing cost, and that may have considerable influence on the decision about selling price.

Low price and high profits. Although a publisher's courage is best and most usefully shown in the decision to price a book low and hope that the public response will be strong enough to bring more total profit—though less on each copy—it is useless and foolhardy to do that unless all the other factors are right, or can be made right. But if the other things can be properly handled, especially the method of marketing, the publisher who wants the business to expand and prosper is extremely shortsighted to keep on in the same old tradition of high prices and small editions. Both the bank account and the feeling of serving the country will benefit from wise application of a low-price policy.

Price fixing. This discussion of selling prices should end with something on the subject of price fixing, which is an effort by the publisher to make retailers charge the individual customers just the price established by the publisher—no more and no less.

Especially in remote areas where necessary books (for instance, required textbooks) are hard to get, booksellers have been known to hide their stock and sell books one by one at a big markup over the established price. Or, in contrast, booksellers in big cities may *cut* the price in order to get business from their rivals.

On the latter point of price cutting, there is some difference of opinion among economists, and even among people in the book trade, about whether the practice is bad. But there is no uncertainty about marking up; everyone agrees that it is bad for the book business and certainly a tragedy for a child who *must* have a particular textbook.

In some countries there are laws to prevent price cutting, but—oddly enough—practically no legal rules against marking up. The publisher can help prevent overcharging by (1) widespread publicity giving the established price, and clear printing of the price in each copy; (2) assurance of delivery of books in adequate quantity to each region to prevent any *actual* shortage, though this cannot prevent an artificially created shortage by a selfish conspiracy of the booksellers in a community; (3) allowance of enough discount to booksellers so they can make a fair profit by selling books at the established price; (4) discipline of booksellers who are overcharging by refusing to sell them books in the future; and (5) in really bad situations, in which all the existing booksellers in a community are overcharging, help and encouragement in establishing new retail outlets that *will* treat customers fairly.

Discount. The bookseller's profit comes from the difference between what is paid in buying the books from the publisher and what the retail customer pays in the bookshop. If a book has an established selling price of §3.00 and the publisher allows retailers a discount of 33 1/3 percent, the retailer pays the publisher §2.00 for the book and has leeway of §1.00 for paying expenses and making a profit.

It is the system of discounts that gives the publisher the advantage of a huge distribution system, far larger than could be maintained by the publisher alone. The discount persuades other businessmen, for their own profit interests, to help the publisher sell the books published.

In general, discounts tend to be higher in countries with advanced book industries, perhaps in part because the more experienced have a livelier sense of the advantage of getting other people to help them sell books. Publishers in developing countries sometimes start off with an idea of selling all the books themselves, thus saving the cost of discount. As the possibilities of a broader market appear, however, they see more and more clearly that—even if they have their own bookshops—it is in their interest to take advantage of as many other outlets as possible.

Just to emphasize the publisher's interest in having a thriving retail book trade all over the country, it might be mentioned that publishers sometimes take the position that all the bookselling business in a given area belongs to the retailers in that area. If an order for 500 copies of a book comes direct to the publisher from an institution, the publisher may refer the order to a retailer in the area from which the order came. Some of the profit on that particular sale is lost (because of the discount given to the bookseller), but the publisher benefits in the long run through strengthening the book trade. And of course the publisher acquires a friend for life in the person of the bookseller who has received this surprising piece of business.

Besides the discounts the publisher gives to retailers, a somewhat larger discount is given to wholesalers who distribute to retailers. In order to pay expenses and still have a profit, the wholesaler must of course have a larger discount from the publisher than is allowed in turn to the bookseller.

Publishers may also allow discounts for certain special kinds of purchasers (libraries, educators, school systems), and for any purchaser buying a large number of books at one time.

There is the widest variety of discount scales around the world, with differences not only from country to country and among publishers within a country, but also from one time to another. And there are important variations among different kinds of books, even within the list of one publisher. In some countries there is an informal understanding, or even formal agreement, among publishers on what discounts to allow; although in at least one country (the United States) such agreement is forbidden by law, with the idea of protecting the booksellers (hence the consumers) from a price-fixing conspiracy by the publishers.

Most publishers in the United States try, in their discount scales, to distinguish between the kind of book (for instance, a textbook) that has an automatic sale, so there is less need for encouraging or rewarding the bookseller, and the kind of book whose sale is less certain and on which the bookseller is taking a greater risk. For these riskier books, such as novels, there will probably be a greater total sale if stocked and displayed by booksellers in general.

The *full trade discount* for the latter kind of book may vary from 25 to 40 percent for small quantities or up to 48 percent or even more for very large quantities. But the *short-discount book* (with textbooks as an example) may have a top discount of only 20 or 25 percent for retailers, whatever the quantity ordered. The wholesaler may get 5 percent or more in addition. Some publishers have no different scale for wholesalers and retailers in the high quantity, recognizing that in the very large quantities only the wholesalers are likely to place such orders.

For export sales to retailers in another country, the publisher may allow additional discount, and something in addition for export jobbers.

For the publisher's direct sales to individuals or institutions, an *educational discount* may be allowed, perhaps 10 or 15 percent to libraries and teachers; and there may be other special categories. Some publisher's discount schedules are so complicated that it takes two or three pages to print them, though such complexity is not recommended. It is necessary to hold to whatever discount schedules are established. Once purchasers learn that discounts can be changed by arguing, there can be no end to such effort at gaining concessions.

Each publisher has many special things to think about in drawing up the discount schedule, but the general considerations for all of them are: (1) sufficient discount to give incentive to the bookseller, and more incentive for the book that does not have an automatic sale than for one that sells itself; and (2) fairness of treatment as between two booksellers who are competing with each other for a given sale, and both of whom the publisher wants to keep as friends.

Credit. In addition to selling price and discount, already discussed, another big factor influencing sales is credit. This is the question of how much time the publisher will allow purchasers, especially retailers and wholesalers, for paying the bill after they have received the books.

Credit has advantages for the publisher as well as for the booksellers. It increases sales because: (1) it permits the bookseller who is working on a narrow margin of cash to order books with the knowledge that some of them will have been sold and will have brought in money before the publisher's bill has to be paid; (2) it permits the bookseller at a distant point, to which shipment of books may take weeks or months, to buy books without tying up capital for that extra amount of time; (3) it encourages the booksellers to have books in stock even though it will be a long time before they may sell them to individuals from their bookshops. On that last point, publishers frequently allow some additional discount on "assorted orders for stock" as well as allowing some credit arrangement permitting extra time for payment.

The publisher's calculation of the cost of the credit system becomes more and more accurate as time goes on; and that cost is of course included in estimates of the overall publishing cost when selling prices are established. Three items of expense are involved: (1) the interest cost of the working capital that is tied up while the publisher waits for payment of bills, (2) actual losses through uncollectable debts, and (3) the clerical and accounting and debt-collecting cost as a result of permitting delayed payments. But the cost is well worth it if the credit system is a sound one. It must be recognized, however, that the cost of extending credit to individuals is so great—in administration, quite aside from uncollectable bills—that many publishers in Europe and North America have a firm *cash with order* rule for individuals. Of course credit card systems—in those countries that have them—are almost as good as cash, though subject to some abuse.

Conditions will vary greatly in different countries, and in some areas any credit plan is highly dangerous. As the book trade becomes more experienced, however, and as booksellers come to recognize their own loss if they take unfair advantage of the publisher's trust, a credit system becomes more feasible. The final step comes when, as in many Western countries, the publishers cooperate in the field along lines suggested in Chapter 17.

Return privileges. The bookseller has an enormous investment in the books bought from the publisher but not yet sold. Especially if the bank balance is low, the bookseller may feel that the investment is that inventory of old books prevents buying new books. The bookseller would therefore *like* to be able to return unsold books to the publisher. The publisher, on the other hand, would *like* to regard all sales as final and never have to take back any books at all. In most book industries, some kind of compromise is worked out between these two positions. Sometimes the amount of return permitted is fixed as a percentage of the amount of business the bookseller has given the publisher in the last year.

A plan permitting more or less unlimited returns raises serious problems for the publisher and cannot be recommended. The greatest difficulty is in connection with new books: the bookseller who thinks any number of unsold copies are returnable may tend to become reckless in ordering, even though transportation in both directions must be paid. If a lot of booksellers do that at the same time, the publisher may *think* an edition has sold out and order a reprinting—only to have thousands of the first printing flood back as returns a few weeks later. The problem is especially serious in mass market publishing, where the returns for some titles may run as high as 50 percent.

There is one kind of return, however, that a wise publisher will always permit: return of outdated textbooks when the publisher is bringing out a revised edition. And most publishers will allow return of extra books ordered specifically for an impressive window display.

Promotion. The vigor of the publisher's promotion campaign—and the bookseller's confidence that the publisher will really do as much promotion as was promised—will play a big part in the bookseller's decision about how many books to order. Promotion is one of the critical factors influencing sales, both directly and through its influence on booksellers. The subject is treated separately in the next chapter.

Service. The bookseller's faith in the service the publisher gives customers can play a big part also. The term "service" includes such things as the speed and accuracy with which orders are filled, the care with which the books are packed to avoid damage, the courtesy and promptness with which errors in billings or shipments are corrected, the thoroughness with which the bookseller is kept informed of new books and new editions and major promotion campaigns, and a general feeling on the part of the bookseller that the publisher understands the problems and has the bookseller's interest at heart.

Timing. The time schedule for a book is important in its effect on sales. This is not merely a question of the time of year at which a book is published but also of the time of availability of finished copies for promotional use before publication, the timing of promotion campaigns in relation to the publishing date, and other factors. This is dealt with below in discussion of cooperation between the manufacturing and sales departments.

Cooperation with Other Departments

A good sales department cooperates very closely with every other department in the publishing house. The people who handle sales have a direct interest in what all the other departments do, and work with them as closely as possible. These are some examples:

Editorial. Unless the editorial people turn out books that will appeal to the public, the sales representatives will have an impossible job trying to sell them. In the field of textbooks, the representatives' regular contact with schools and libraries and officials of the ministry of education gives them a clear view of what kinds of books are needed. Through the years, many of the best ideas for editorial development of textbooks have been brought to publishing houses by sales representatives. In fact the representatives make up a kind of mobile unit of the editorial department, keeping in touch with changes in the curriculum, new teaching methods, and trends in thinking about new kinds of textbooks.

Wise editors are always interested not only in getting ideas from sales representatives but also in giving them, in turn, a clear idea of what is in the books they will sell, the kinds of purchasers most likely to be interested in them, and so on.

In a small publishing house, the exchange of ideas between the two departments is easily taken care of quite informally. Large houses, however, have to take special steps to make this exchange possible, especially because many of the sales representatives travel extensively or even live in the regions they serve rather than in the city where the publishing office is situated.

One of the methods of exchange frequently used is a "sales conference." For this occasion, which may be held two or more times a year and lasts several days each time, all the sales representatives are called in from their posts, and foreign travelers plan their home visits for those times. At these meetings the editors present the new books to the sales staff, trying to stir up the enthusiasm of the representatives, explaining the special characteristics of the books and the kinds of readers to whom they will appeal, and the special opportunities for sales or promotion that the editor has learned of through close knowledge of the manuscript. In the sales conference it is the editor who must "sell" the idea of the book to the publisher's sales staff.

Design and manufacture. The interest of the sales department in the work of the designer and manufacturer has been mentioned in the last two chapters. The physical appearance of the book can be a large factor in its salability, and the selling price resulting from the manufacturing cost can be even more important. The ingenuity of the designer and printer therefore creates the physical and economic conditions within which the sales representative has to work with a book.

The designer and manufacturer, in their turn, depend on the sales department to make possible the things they want to do. Not only is everyone in a publishing house dependent on the income produced by the sales department, but the designer and manufacturer have a special kind of interest. As suggested earlier, a printing process that the designer would like to use may be quite impossible in economic terms unless the sales department can find some imaginative way of reaching a large market to justify a large edition of the book.

Finally, one of the biggest points of common interest between the sales representatives and the people who produce the books is the time schedule of production. A textbook intended to be used in a given school year will lose all its potential business to rival books if manufacture is delayed beyond the start of the year; or a biography of a politician standing for election will lose much of its sale after election, especially if the candidate loses the election; or a book about an improved farming method needs to fit into the crop season; and many other examples could be mentioned.

Timing is important not only as to publication date but, especially, as to the amount of time the sales department and the promotion department will have *before publication* for getting orders from bookstores, delivering the books, printing promotion circulars, arranging for radio programs, and doing all the other things necessary for proper launching of a new book.

The timing of reprintings may be almost as important, from the standpoint of profitable book publishing, as the timing of the original publication. If a promotion campaign is successful and a book starts "running away" with heavy sales and much public discussion and word-of-mouth publicity, it is heartbreaking if delay in reprinting prevents the sales department from filling the orders everyone has worked so hard to produce.

Promotion. This work is, in most publishing houses, treated as part of the sales department, with the head of the promotion division being responsible to the general sales manager. In the cases in which promotion is a department by itself, it is necessary to have the closest and most friendly relations between that department and the salespeople who depend on it so heavily. The need for this close cooperation will become clearer in the next chapter.

Accounting. The accounting department is always interested in the sales department, because the sales representatives are the people who produce the income that pays the expenses. The sales representatives are dependent on the accountants, in turn, because the accounting department maintains the records that guide the representatives in collecting their bills and in planning sales campaigns, and the records on which their commissions are based.

Market research through records of sales. An accounting department can really be turned into an "intelligence agency" for the sales
representatives. It can show details not only about total sale, income, expense, and so forth, for each book, but also about the sales
trends regarding books in particular areas, the performance of
regional sales representatives, the growth or decline of business of
particular retailers, and other matters.

For most of the publishing firms in developed countries it is now
becoming possible to use electronic equipment not only to speed up
the handling of orders but also—the point we are interested in
here—to produce the market research information for guiding later
policy. For many publishers in developing countries it would not at
present be economical to consider electronic equipment, but there
are hand methods, or ways of using very modest equipment, that
can give the sales department, and editors also, information of
highest value for future planning.

This subject is too big to treat in detail here, but one example
might be given of a simple hand method that can be used without
waiting for the time when electronic machines are everywhere
available. If an extra carbon copy (or photocopy) is made of every
bill, those extra copies can be given to the sales department for hand
sorting in many different ways—geographically, by subject matter
of books, by retailers, by sales representatives, by institutions, and
so forth.

And it might be worth while to cite an example of how a sales
department can use this very elementary kind of market research to
multiply its sales. Suppose a Malaysian publisher has brought out a
work on monsoons, intended by the author to serve weather experts
and other scientists, but including facts about the nature and extent
of property damage from monsoons. The sales department might
note, from its study of the duplicate copies of orders, that insurance
companies and lawyers handling monsoon damage suits against
such companies were beginning to show an interest in the book.
And that might suggest, in turn, that a campaign of direct mail
promotion should be directed to insurance firms and lawyers. It is
that getting of the "plus" business, perhaps not even thought of
ahead of time, that can be so helpful to a publisher's profit; and a
careful examination of the orders that come in is the best way of
getting ideas for securing those "plus" sales.

Teamwork in the Publishing House

Teamwork in the staff of a very small publishing house is easy. But the larger and more successful the house becomes, and the more separate departments that come into existence, the more difficult— yet at the same time more important—it becomes to keep up effective working relations among them. And it is the sales department that suffers the most if there is a breakdown of the cooperative spirit or an overlooking of the joint interest of all.

The greatest danger to sound thinking in the sales department, hence to its ability to get cooperation from the others, is a tendency to regard its job as the only important one, because it is the only one that brings in the money. It is true, of course, that the others could not survive without sales; but it is healthy for the sales people to keep vividly in mind at all times that there could not be any sales without the indispensable work of all the other members of the team.

Regular meetings of departmental managers are especially useful in large houses, as well as daily circulation of correspondence files. In many houses there is also daily circulation of the order file, letting the rest of the organization see what is being achieved in distribution of the books.

In every way, therefore, it is of greatest importance to have a spirit of friendly cooperation. Together the departments can achieve business success; in opposition they can bring disaster to the publishing house.

9

Promotion: Making People Want to Buy the Book

THE TERM *promotion* includes all the methods used by a publisher to let the world know that a book exists, and to make people want to buy it. Promotion is the field of book publishing in which imagination and alertness bring the quickest and biggest rewards. An editor may need years to develop a manuscript growing out of some creative idea, but the book promotion person may see in weeks, or even in days, the pleasing results of some new thought about a way of advertising a book to the public.

Promotion of *some* kind is an obligation on the publisher for every single book brought out. If the publisher is not going to take vigorous steps to tell the world about the book, and to help the appropriate readers for that kind of book understand why they should buy it, the book might just as well have been published by the author.

Each book's promotion needs are different from those of every other. No one can say the exact combination of promotion methods that ought to be used for all books. The promotion budget is rarely able to include all the things that might be done, or even as much for each of the selected items as one might like. The promotion manager has to decide, for each book, how the available promotion money will be best spent. Incidentally, it is usual to set up a budget for initial promotion (perhaps 10 percent of the expected sales income for the first edition) and not spend more until there is evidence that the book has really "caught on" and that sales will go beyond the first edition.

We describe in this chapter several kinds of promotion that are most often used by book publisher in various countries. Each of these methods *may* be useful for a particular book. Some of them, though valuable for some kinds of books, will be of no use at all for others. There are, however, six items of promotion that every publisher is likely to use for every book: (1) the jacket or printed cover of the book itself, (2) review copies for newspapers and magazines, (3) presentation copies for selected individuals, (4) announcements to the book trade, (5) sales representatives' calls on bookshops, schools, and so forth, and (6) printed advertising of *some* sort.

Comment on these and other promotion methods follows, but the reader will undoubtedly think of other possibilities especially suited for the particular country or kind of publishing.

Jacket or Printed Cover

The jacket or printed cover of a book may be no more than the "eye-catcher." But the customer whose interest has been caught wants to learn more about what kind of book it is, who the author is, what opinion has been expressed about the book by qualified critics, and so forth. It is to give information of that sort that the wording of the jacket description (the *blurb* as it is called in the United States) makes its important contribution to sales.

There was a time, which some people fear is not entirely over yet, when some publishers thought it proper to make extreme statements on their jackets, using the most colorful adjectives and making the most extravagant claims for the book and its author. In general, however, simple, accurate, and responsible statements are best for use on jackets.

The same thing can be said in general about artwork. Though the purpose is to draw attention to the book, this is not necessarily achieved by using large and vulgar lettering or garish colors. The artwork should give an honest suggestion of the kind of book it is, just as the wording on the jacket should describe it honestly.

Review Copies

Wise use of review copies can be one of the best and least expensive forms of promotion. The review copies may be sent to newspapers, magazines, newspaper columnists (if they comment on books regularly or if they have special interest in the subject matter of the particular book), and to radio and television reviewers.

The list of people to receive copies is of course carefully drawn up long in advance, using the knowledge not only of the sales department but also (for special angles related to the book itself) of the editorial department and of the author. The list is retained and, sometime after publication, is checked to see which publications actually published reviews. No reviewer can be expected to publish comment on every book received, but if book after book is sent without any review appearing, that reviewer will be cut off the list for the future.

One of the forms of cooperation among publishers mentioned in Chapter 17 is joint effort at persuading publishers of newspapers and managers of radio and television stations to give more space or more time to book reviewing, or to establish book-reviewing departments if they do not have them already.

The number of copies sent out for review depends on many factors, including the size of the country and its language pattern, number of reviewing media in the country, the kind of book, the size of the edition, and so on. In a very large country such as India, with many publications and a huge population to be reached, the number of review copies of a book published in English would be quite large, because the language is so widely used by book readers throughout the country. The same would be true for a Portuguese book in Brazil. On the other hand, the number of review copies of a book brought out by an Indian publisher in the Gujerati language could be much smaller. It is hard to imagine any book for which fewer than a dozen review copies would be needed in any language, and the normal expectation would be anywhere from 25 to 200.

A word might be added here about how publishers' accountants charge the cost of review copies to the promotion departments. Under one method there is no charge at all: the number of copies to be used for review is decided ahead of time and that number deducted from the total edition when the sales department figures how many copies it has to sell and what income will be received if they are all sold. If 100 free and review copies are to be used of a book printed in a 5,000-copy edition, the income figures are based on an assumed sale of only 4,900. Under the other method of charging the cost of review copies, the promotion department is charged with the actual manufacturing cost per copy.

Presentation Copies

This promotion method, very much like that of review copies, is a way of getting free promotion through the interest of prominent individuals whose opinions carry weight with the public. The presentation copies are usually sent along with a personal note from the author or publisher, and often with a request for a comment on the book. The recipients can be of many sorts, such as: (1) leaders of public opinion in either civic or intellectual life; (2) special authorities on the subject matter of the particular book; (3) lecturers or other public speakers whose references to the book will influence others; (4) important figures in education, library work, and so on, whose good opinion of a book may influence officials who make selections for textbook adoption, library purchase, and so forth; (5) chief booksellers who will be good customers for the book if they like it; and (6) newspaper editors who may decide to publish editorials on the subject matter of the book.

Even more than the list for review copies, the list for presentation copies has to be carefully prepared in order not to waste copies. Special care has to be taken about the suggestions offered by the author. The proposals can be of great value, but sometimes may be more reflective of friendship and personal obligations than of the proposed recipient's ability to help sales.

The charging of the cost of presentation copies is handled as described for review copies above. The number of copies assigned for presentation varies more widely than review copies. For some few books there may be virtually no presentation copies; for some few other books there may be justification for literally hundreds. In a large country with many bookshops, publishers have been known to use 1,000 copies for reading samples for booksellers when they felt that the book had possibilities for tremendous eventual sale if the booksellers would really get behind it and push.

Copies of textbooks are presented under rules quite different from all other kinds of books because of the usefulness of free *examination copies* for teachers who will consider them for class adoption. This matter is considered further in Chapter 11.

Trade Announcements

Trade announcements are not so much items of promotion as "notices posted on a bulletin board," telling the book trade that a certain book is to be published on a certain date at a certain price and at a certain discount. For alert booksellers, this basic information is in fact a kind of promotion because they will react by placing orders. But the basic information to the trade is also useful for later reference, for reordering books when stock has been sold out, and for answering questions when customers ask about a book without having full information about it.

Most publishers in most countries get out a *trade list* at least twice a year, giving the basic information about all their forthcoming books, and the list is broadcast to the entire book trade. The next step beyond that is a *seasonal announcement* (called seasonal because, depending on the custom in the particular country, the announcement is timed for the spring, fall, winter, etc.). It is a small catalogue in the form of a circular, frequently with illustrations, not only listing but also describing and actively promoting the books that are to be published. Unlike the trade list, which goes only to the book trade, the seasonal announcement is also used widely for direct mail advertising (see that section below). This kind of catalogue is most useful if it lists new books at the front, followed by a selection of the most active books from previous seasons or years. There should also be clear statement of the terms of sale (for instance whether cash must accompany orders from individuals).

In addition to the sheets or circulars giving information on the whole list of books, publishers usually get out some kind of separate announcement about the individual books at the time of publication, or a few weeks before that.

A most important supplement to the printed pieces sent out by the publisher is the trade journal—in a country lucky enough to have one—which carries the basic listing of new books of *all* publishers. That is a special convenience to booksellers, who need look in only one place to get information about any new book. And in some countries, there may be a library journal as well as book trade journals. Here, again, the kind of cooperation mentioned in Chapter 17 might include joint efforts at establishing a book trade journal or a library journal if there is none already.

Sales Representatives' Calls

No matter how well other promotional means are used, there is no adequate substitute for personal calls by the publisher's representative on booksellers, schools, and libraries. This might reasonably be looked at as part of the selling job described in the previous chapter, rather than promotion; but it is a kind of promotion in itself. In addition, the sales representative is a carrier of the printed promotion pieces which are put in the customer's hands.

A special reason for having printed promotion pieces available well in advance is so that the sales representatives can have them when they make the calls. Most useful, of course, is a finished copy of the whole book. But the sheer bulk of sample copies of all the new books in a given season may be too much for the sales representative to carry. If the printing of circulars and jackets or covers is properly planned, however, the representative can carry those.

Also, because the sales representative may be the only member of the publisher's staff visiting outlying regions, those trips can be most helpful in bringing back information useful in guiding later phases of the promotion campaign, either in general or in relation to the particular area. The representative will also discuss with the bookseller any ideas for *cooperative promotion* (see that section below), suggestions of places where advertising might be placed, public appearances that might be arranged for the author, and other local parts of the promotion campaign.

Space Advertising

Space advertising is so called because it involves purchase of space in a newspaper or magazine for running advertisements about a book. Not every book gets a response from space advertising, and there are some books for which a publisher, in all good conscience, may decide to do no space advertising at all, but rather to devote the whole advertising budget to direct mail or some other method.

Conditions differ widely among countries, not only as to the number, kind, and quality of widely read publications, but also as to the kind of people who read them. No outsider can suggest general rules. It might be pointed out, however, that a policy of using advertising space from time to time is one way of encouraging publishers of newspapers and magazines to install or enlarge book review departments. It would be improper, of course, to use advertising as pressure on the publication to review a particular publisher's books; but a general practice of at least occasional advertising by *all* book publishers helps the publication to sustain, through advertising income, the editorial cost of a book section.

Large publishers have an advertising department that makes arrangements for all its advertising directly, or places it through an independent advertising agency. The design and layout of the advertisements may be by the advertising agency, by the publisher's advertising department, or by artists and layout people who are also the publisher's book designers.

Coupons. Advertising that carries a coupon to be filled out and sent in by the customer requires special mention. Booksellers do not approve of coupons in publishers' advertising, of course, because it means that the publisher is competing with them for retail sales. But coupons have value for the publisher's market research because they show the kinds of customers who are responding, and also something about the drawing power of different kinds of advertising. The coupons can be keyed with a letter or other symbol showing the publication from which the coupon was clipped.

There is one other point to be mentioned about coupons in space advertising. Sometimes, when the publication urges a book publisher to take advertising space but the publisher is not sure it would be worth the cost, it is possible to make a special arrangement. The book publisher agrees to pay a certain amount *for each coupon returned*, so the cost is very slight if the advertising fails to draw many orders, yet the publication carrying the advertising gets perhaps even higher income than normal if the return is very good.

(Under this plan the coupons are addressed back to the newspaper or magazine, and are then turned over to the book publisher after they have been counted.) Still another form of the same kind of business arrangement is a method of having the newspaper or magazine serve as a bookseller. That is, the book publisher pays nothing at all for the advertising space itself but gives the publication a good discount on the copies of the books which the publication buys to fill orders it gets back through coupons.

Direct Mail Advertising

This method of advertising, direct by mail to the customers, is increasingly used in developing countries, but is still not as common as in Europe and North America. That is partly because some of the postal systems are inefficient, and also because of the difficulty and expense of transmitting money by mail. Even at present, the method has possibilities, and it holds very great promise for the future.

As techniques get better, this method can be used to some extent for books of wide popular appeal. But the most natural use of the direct mail method is in connection with books for special audiences for which it would be wasteful to do indiscriminate general advertising.

The difference between direct mail and space advertising is sometimes emphasized by saying that a direct mail circular sent to carefully selected address lists is like a rifle shot, direct to the target; but that space advertising is like a scattergun, which is not too accurately aimed but covers so wide a field of fire that some hits will be made anyway. Two examples: a specialized medical handbook would surely benefit most from the rifle shot method, though a novel of possible interest to any literate person would need the scattergun.

The two great elements of a direct mail campaign are (1) the circular or other printed piece that is to be mailed, and (2) the list of names to which it is to be sent. The two things must be planned in relation to each other. Not only the kind of list but also its size may affect the design of the circular. In fact, if a list is very small and the book being advertised is just right for the special audience making up the list, it may even prove economical to use a personal letter instead of a printed circular, or perhaps in addition to it.

Name lists. Imagination in compiling the list of names can be very rewarding. Among the sources that can be used for the names and addresses are: (1) previous customers of the publishing house (especially if, as suggested in Chapter 8, the names have been sorted to show the kinds of books in which they are interested); (2) teachers, professors, and other professionals who work in the field with which the book deals; (3) librarians, school principals, ministry officers, and others interested in a wide range of books; (4) membership lists of societies, professional associations, and others, in the field of the book; (5) subscription lists of magazines and journals or (not so valuable but more likely to be rentable from the magazines) lists of former subscribers; and (6) special lists compiled by the author.

Coupons. Direct mail circulars usually include a coupon for the customer to clip and send back to the publisher, ordering a copy of the book. Booksellers' disapproval of coupons (mentioned above in connection with space advertising) is only partly eased by including in each circular some wording such as "Order from your bookstore, or if none is available use the coupon below." What booksellers really like is to have the name of the bookstore instead of the publisher for the return address; and this can be arranged, at least for large bookstores, under the plan of *cooperative promotion* described below.

Credit. One of the factors that has made direct mail advertising so useful and so effective in countries such as United States is the development of a tradition of widespread sellling by mail without requiring cash in advance. There is a modification of the full-credit plan, however. Even though cash may be required in advance, the sale can be *on approval,* with a promise of "prompt refund if you are not fully satisfied."

Direct mail advertising has possibilities in any event, but it would be unreasonable to expect full results in a country in which—

because the tradition of ordering by mail on credit has not yet developed—the customer has to find some way of sending the advance payment before ordering a book.

A major factor in direct mail selling in Europe and North America is the widespread use of credit cards. Now that the credit card practice is becoming more familiar in developing countries also, it holds great promise for the future.

Indirect effect of direct mail advertising. The original idea of direct mail advertising was the actual selling of books by mail, and for many kinds of books that is still the publisher's main purpose when sending out circulars: orders come directly to the publisher. And because the publisher does not usually have to allow any discount on those individual orders, that can be a profitable business. Many publishers figure that if 2 or 3 percent of the people getting circulars order books, they will more than pay for the cost of the mailing, and anything above that represents a really good profit.

But it must not be overlooked that for some kinds of books and for some kinds of markets, direct mail advertising is effective even though most of the purchasers go to bookshops instead of ordering by mail from the publisher. (The point is especially important, of course, in connection with the comment above about the reduced effectiveness of direct mail selling when the tradition of sending books on credit or on approval to individuals has not been established.) Some people are natural bookstore customers and rarely if ever buy books by mail; yet a good circular may stimulate them to go to the bookstore and buy the book advertised, with eventual increased orders for that book from the bookshops.

In any event direct mail advertising is one of the best ways of causing *talk* about a book, and it is generally agreed that word-of-mouth publicity is one of the strongest kinds of book promotion.

Radio and Television

Lecturers, commentators, and broadcast book reviewers can be helpful both in making the listeners and viewers wish to buy the book and in adding to the word-of-mouth promotion.

Radio and television can also be used for actual paid advertising, in countries in which advertising on the broadcasting system is permitted. But not nearly enough is known about whether such advertising actually sells books.

At one time, publishers in Western countries tended to think that radio and TV advertising, though good for other commodities, was not a good way to promote books. The reason for this was not fully understood, though lots of theories were offered, usually related in some way to the fact that the broadcast audience includes a large number of people who may be quite uninterested in books, even if they are not actual illiterates.

In a country with a low literacy rate the proportion of illiterates would of course be especially high, and much of the cost of radio advertising would have to be regarded as wasteful. What is not yet known is whether the cost of radio advertising is justified for literates who *are* reached through that medium.

Posters

Printed posters, often using an adaptation of the design of the jacket or cover or circular of the book, are sometimes given to bookstores, as well as being put up in other locations. The poster cannot be too large because most bookshops lack space. On the other hand, if a poster is small it may not be any more effective than a pile of copies of the book itself. Most publishers seem to feel that posters, if justified at all, can be economically used in only a few promotion campaigns. The poster is certainly not one of the items automatically planned for every book.

Exhibits

Exhibits are a great nuisance to plan and conduct—far more nuisance than anyone outside the book field can imagine—but most publishers think they represent an important kind of promotion for groups of books. Only in the most unusual circumstances is it economical to have an exhibit for just one book. But if the exhibit deals with a lot of books, the cost and the nuisance are easier to justify.

One of the discouraging aspects of exhibits is the difficulty of measuring their promotion value in exact terms. Everyone agrees that exhibits are useful, though no one can say *how* useful.

There are exhibits of many different kinds. The greatest book exhibit in the world is the mammoth Frankfurt Book Fair in Germany at which publishers from many countries make annual displays of their wares; but there are many other kinds, down to small local occasions such as a meeting of teachers or librarians or doctors or engineers in one section of a country. The kinds of books selected for display are of course varied according to the people expected to view them. For very large exhibits, it will often be worthwhile to print a small leaflet listing the books and including an order form.

One of the "housekeeping" aspects of exhibiting concerns such items as display racks and cases. Any publisher or group of publishers constantly engaging in exhibiting will find it an economy to build substantial equipment that can be "knocked down" or folded up for shipment so it can be used over and over again, without need for new construction each time.

Another of the housekeeping problems is the collection of the books after the exhibit is over and packing them up for shipment home. One way of meeting this problem is to make an agreement, before the show, with a bookseller who will take the entire stock of exhibit books at the end, at perhaps 60 percent discount, thus saving the publisher the cost of packing and shipping those presumably soiled copies, as well as the trouble of handling those operations in a city that may be remote from the publisher's office.

It is also the custom at some exhibits (the Frankfurt Book Fair is one of them) to let individuals buy books on the spot at half price during the last day of the exhibit. Incidentally, some exhibits regularly combine sales with exhibiting, though this is forbidden by some exhibit sponsors. Orders may usually be taken, however, and it is usual to give a special discount to the purchaser. An incidental benefit of taking orders it to have some measure of the success of the exhibit.

Publicity

No matter what other kinds of promotion may be planned, every new book should be studied for possible stories for newspapers, television, radio, and magazines. If the news is interesting enough, the publisher may get a lot of useful free promotion. The news story may relate to the subject of the book, biographical facts about the author or—most useful of all—some surprising fact contained in the book but never before known by the public.

Many publishing houses have the rule that *every* new book published must have its own publicity release, which is usually a reproduction of a simple typewritten sheet that is sent to newspapers, magazines, book reviewers, and bookshops.

Newspapers and magazines that have large book sections, including "book notes" as well as formal book reviews, may be able to use items from news releases, whether or not they also carry a regular review later on.

Prizes

Some books benefit from the promotion resulting from prizes awarded to them by other organizations, such as the Nobel Prize, the Adamjee Prizes in Pakistan, the Noma African Publishing Award, the National Book Award in the United States, and Unesco prizes in various countries. In some countries there are hundreds of book prizes each year, and the alert publisher will try to keep track of them, making sure that all of the books of appropriate sorts are considered, and then being ready to make good promotional use of the award in advertising if the books win.

But there is another kind of promotional use that publishers make of prizes. Prizes may be offered by the publisher, for instance, for an essay by schoolchildren on the subject of the book, or some other prize system attracting the interest of people who have to know about the book in order to compete for the prize.

Prizes are also offered by publishers to the authors of unpublished manuscripts as suggested in Chapter 4, though this is more often a device for encouraging promising authors to submit their books than actual promotion of the books finally selected.

Magazine Publication

Parts of a book, especially a nonfiction book, can be used as magazine articles or newspaper features before book publication. Especially if the author insists that a note identify the article as part of a forthcoming book (with a listing of the actual title and the publisher), this can be quite helpful. There was a time when publishers disliked prepublication use of parts of their books, but the general opinion now seems to be that, if the practice is not overdone, attention can be called to the forthcoming book in circles where normal publicity might never reach.

The magazine or newspaper publisher is expected to pay for use of the material from the book, whether the use is before or after publication; and the use is of course only by permission, at least in countries where literary property rights are protected by law. The sharing of any fee paid by a magazine or newspaper for use of parts of a book between the author and publisher is in some way fixed by their contract, as discussed in Chapter 18.

Personal Appearances by the Author

If the author is someone with a national reputation, appearances as lecturer or radio speaker or as guest of honor at a dinner or reception can be of great value. The personal appearance may not sell books directly, but it can be a most useful supporter of other kinds of promotion, especially newspaper and word-of-mouth publicity.

Personal appearance of an author at an *autographing party* sponsored by a bookseller is one of the forms of cooperative promotion discussed below.

A special kind of personal appearance that is almost certain to have wide newspaper coverage is one made by the author in calling to present a copy of a new book to the prime minister or other leading public figure.

Promotion of Groups of Books

When a publishing house is young and the number of books it has brought out is relatively small, it is easy (though expensive) for promotion to deal separately with all the books published. But once the list begins to grow, it is useful to think of group promotion of special kinds of books. Thus there may be space advertising listing perhaps a dozen books on one subject such as medicine or law, a special circular showing all the books for children's supplementary reading, and so forth. The cost for any one book is fairly small because the total cost is divided among them all, yet the impact on the potential purchaser with an interest in that field can be very strong. (Such group promotion has editorial value, also, as it calls attention to the publishing house as one with special interest in the given field, and therefore one to which new authors in that field should consider submitting their manuscripts.)

One item of group promotion that is expensive and that is not a "selling tool" in itself is nevertheless necessary every once in a while if not every year. That is a *general catalogue* listing all books published by the house that are still in print. This is of great value to librarians and bookshops, and the cost may be justified as part of the publisher's service to those good customers, even if the general catalogue does not actually create new sales in itself. And it is of course a way of helping to maintain sales of older books on the backlist as mentioned in Chapter 4.

In countries where *graded reading lists* (classifying books according to the age or reading level) are issued, teachers and librarians seem to think that is the most useful kind of general catalogue.

Cooperative Promotion

Cooperation between publishers and booksellers in promoting a book can be rewarding in many ways. For one thing, the sharing of their joint interests and their joint profit in a project they have carried out together can lead to especially warm friendships and pleasant business relations in the future. But, quite beyond that, the process can produce book sales.

Booksellers and publishers may cooperate as to space advertising in newspapers or magazines serving the bookseller's market area. Under this plan the publisher agrees to pay perhaps half the cost of space advertising placed by the bookseller. The advertising appears over the name of the bookseller but is limited to books of the particular publisher. Normally there is an agreement of the maximum amount to be spent in this way by each partner.

Another form of cooperative promotion involves direct mail. The publisher agrees to print up copies of direct mail circulars *with the bookseller's name and address for the return coupon.* The publisher supplies the circulars printed in that way, and the booksellers mail the circulars to their own customer list as well as to libraries and other possible institutional purchasers in the area. Actual printing of the bookseller's name and address is feasible, of course, only if the number of circulars to be used is fairly large. But in order to help small booksellers, the publishers often print a certain number of circulars with a space left blank for the address, and small booksellers can then rubber stamp their names. Publishers sometimes make a token charge per thousand circulars supplied, simply to guard against irresponsible requests by the booksellers.

Cooperation with booksellers is also extremely useful in planning personal appearances of authors, in arranging radio programs or public lectures, and in many other ways. The bookseller's knowledge of the market area is a valuable supplement to the book publisher's more general knowledge and connections.

Creative Imagination and a Sense of Timing

Many people think that promotion is more fun than any other part of the book publishing business because there is such a variety of methods and such satisfaction in discovering new opportunities and then in alertly taking advantage of them.

This chapter has listed some of the most familiar forms of book promotion, but there are many others that have been tried in the past in different countries. The imaginative promotion manager can invent still others, such as signs on tramways and buses, slides projected on cinema screens, displays in theater lobbies, giveaway scorecards or programs at cricket and football matches, and so on. A promotion manager once had twelve beautiful and strikingly dressed fashion models simply walk about in places of public gathering, each carrying a copy of a new novel with the title prominently displayed. That stunt may have been more useful for public entertainment than for selling books, but it at least started word-of-mouth publicity.

Whatever the method, the general rule of book promotion is the military principle of "supporting the divisions that are advancing." That is, if several books have been given a chance to show their sales strength through initial promotion, and only some of them respond with good sales, those are the books that the publisher feels deserve a larger piece of the budget for future promotion; and there may have to be a regretful decision to spend no more promotion money on the books that failed to move. The key to success for a promotion manager is a kind of sixth sense that tells when a book is about to "run away" and become a best seller. When one knows that—or thinks one knows that—the decision may be made to gamble on the future by spending much more for promotion than the sales just up to that point could support.

The two qualities that a promotion manager must have, besides enjoying hard work, are creative imagination and a sense of timing. Both are needed in order to see openings that occur and then make immediate use of them. The need for imagination is obvious, but a sense of timing is just as important. Not only must the first promotion campaign be perfectly scheduled, but the follow-up of the "advancing divisions" must be vigorous and prompt. The promotion manager has a calendar constantly in mind, and must always be aware not only of what is happening in the world but also of scheduled events and of possible trends of future public interest.

The methods used must be right for the particular book. The wrong sort of promotion, if seeming to fool the public about what kind of book is being advertised, can be harmful to the publisher's reputation and in the long run not of much help even to the book promoted. But if the promotion is of the right sort and at the right time and carried out in the right way, the rewards can be very great.

In trying to make the promotion right for the particular book, the promotion manager will find that the author can be the most useful partner. Many publishers have a questionnaire in which they ask the author to suggest review media, organizations whose membership might be circularized, publications that would be the most useful for advertising, and so forth. In fact, a continuing friendly cooperation between author and promotion manager can benefit a book in innumerable ways.

And the promotion manager should be aware of serving the public as well as the bank account of the publisher. In telling the world that a good new book has come into existence, the promoter is supplying a critical link in the chain that stretches from the author's writing table to the reader with a book in hand.

III

Kinds of Book Publishing

10

Trade Books and Other Kinds of Publishing

THE PURPOSE OF this brief chapter is merely to give a kind of checklist of some of the chief kinds of publishing. Later chapters give more information about some of them.

Some of the types of publishing differ from the others according to the kinds of books with which they deal—for instance, law books or medical books. Others use special publishing methods—for instance, book club or subscription publishing. And of course some use special publishing methods *because* of the special subject matter—with textbooks being the clearest example of that kind of publishing.

The father of all is *trade publishing*, which is to say the publication of books for general reading intended to be sold primarily through the retail book trade. We do not include a separate chapter on this major subject because this book as a whole deals with it.

Quite a number of the special kinds of books may be handled at the beginning as regular trade books and only later may have special departments of their own. We therefore list as subdivisions of "trade" the kinds of books that may eventually have separate departments in some large publishing houses but are usually treated as trade books by many publishers.

Kinds of Publishing

A partial list of kinds of book publishing might include the divisions shown below. And we repeat the comment made several times before in this book, that the reference to "departments" should be no discouragement to a small publisher who has no departments.

We intend merely to show the different ways of looking at the different kinds of publishing, even in a one-person publishing house.

Trade publishing. This is the category of general books of the sort most naturally handled by the retail book trade, including literature, biography, and all nonfiction books for general reading. Books on special subjects but normally handled as trade books are also included. The fields covered might be poetry, religion, business, art, music, picture books, how-to-do-it books, and so forth. One of the major fields of coming importance in developing countries—children's books for recreational reading—may be approached at first as trade books and then later become a separate department. Or, because of the use of such books for supplementary reading in school, the trade department and the textbook department may work on them together, both in editorial development and in distribution.

Textbooks. See Chapter 11.

Children's books (aside from textbooks). See Chapter 12, and note comment in the section on trade publishing above.

Mass distribution books. See Chapter 13. These are the books, usually paperbacks and always low in price, which have their major sale other than in bookstores, through use of wire racks and other small displays wherever people gather.

Book clubs and subscription books. See Chapter 14. Note that these are *methods of publishing* which may be used for books on almost any subject. Book club books were at first of the sort we call trade books, but in later years many specialized book clubs developed—history, science, mystery, and so forth. Subscription books are most frequently in the reference category or are sets of books on one subject.

Reference books. This category includes dictionaries, encyclopedias, atlases, and similar books, usually involving a long and expensive project of editorial development.

Technical and scientific books. Although the books in this category may sometimes be used as textbooks in universities—and such sales may represent a major item of income for the publisher—the field is far wider than that. It includes all the books in which scientists, engineers, and technicians share their knowledge with other professional workers in the field. The books may therefore be research reports, handbooks, or original contributions to knowledge. In many of the developing countries there has been a tradition of using books in English or French, rather than in the national language, for work in these fields, but there is pressure for change in some countries. Of course for many subjects and in many of the developing countries, advanced technical and scientific books simply do not exist.

Vocational and professional books. In many ways these are similar to the technical and scientific group, but there are special problems and opportunities for marketing.

Scholarly publishing. This term is often used to describe the broad field of books by scholars and scientists, including the technical and scientific category mentioned above. This is the kind of publishing typified in Western countries by the work of university presses but very incompletely represented in the developing countries which for the most part have not responded adequately to the possibilities of scholarly publishing about their areas and by their scholars. For example, the best books on French-speaking West Africa or by French-speaking West Africans are still published in Paris, rather than in Dakar or Abidjan. In some countries research institutes, government agencies, and academic departments of universities have been the major publishers of this kind of material for decades before the establishment of university presses in those countries.

Law books. The situation varies widely from country to country. The language of instruction used in law schools is one factor, but there are additional questions related to whether an English or Napoleonic or Ottoman or some other foreign code is used as the basis, what the status is of civil versus religious laws, the interplay of community law with legal statutes, and so forth. For several developing countries there are clear possibilities, not yet realized, for producing law books to serve the specific needs of those countries in a way that foreign books cannot possibly do.

Medical books. European languages (English, Spanish, French, Portuguese) are used as the languages of instruction in most of the medical schools of the developing countries. Because the practicing physicians were trained in those languages, they tend to want books in those same languages for keeping up in their fields. But there are some few medical schools using national non-European languages for instruction, and there are many training schools for auxiliary services, such as nursing, public health extension work, and school health instruction, in which books in a non-European language are essential.

Furthermore, there are two special opportunities for medical publishing in developing countries. One results from the fact that most of the medical books in the world issue from countries in the temperate zone, while many of the special medical problems of the developing countries are peculiar to the tropics. The other special opportunity relates to what is called the *paramedical field*—that is, to preparation of instruction books and handbooks for people who have less than full professional training as doctors yet try as best they can, especially in outlying areas, to help people in need of medical attention when no doctor is available. Books on first aid, on infant care, and on the kinds of subjects suggested by the book title *What to Do Till the Doctor Comes* can be useful in all countries. And in those countries that have formally adopted a plan of paramedical service for provincial areas there are even wider possibilities.

Mixture of Publishing Methods

The above listing of the kinds of book publishing is of course far from complete. In any event, the lines of division between the different kinds are hazy. The sole purpose of the listing here is to suggest to the beginning publisher the variety of possibilities. One does not have to worry about whether a certain project falls into one category or another. The book referred to above, *What to Do Till the*

Doctor Comes, might be handled as a trade book for sale through bookshops; or it might be issued in a cheap edition for mass distribution; or it might be developed specifically for sale to the ministry of health's paramedical service.

The important thing is to have a book that will serve the public in some way, and then find ways of letting the public know about it and of making it available for purchase everywhere that customers may be found. In doing that the ingenious publisher does not think about an outline of departments, but just considers what is best for each book.

11

Textbooks

TEXTBOOKS DESERVE special attention in any thinking about book publishing in developing countries. The first steps toward local book publishing in any country are likely to be in the field of schoolbooks, and the textbook publisher is part of the country's educational system as surely as the teacher. There is a *necessity*, understood by everyone, about textbooks more than about any other kind of book.

That necessity, combined with the large number of children in school, gives economic possibilities to textbook publishing that are not found in any other branch of the business. But there are also some economic risks and business disadvantages greater than in other fields.

In quite a few developing countries—including several that do not follow socialist methods in other aspects of their national life—there is virtually no private textbook industry. Textbooks in those countries are either produced by the state itself or under such direct state control that there is no room for private initiative. This book is not the place to argue the merits of one system or the other, but the general principles expressed here are of equal validity whether the publishing auspices are public or private.

The publisher who wants to produce a *good* textbook must make a larger financial investment in editorial preparation than is the case for trade publishing, and must maintain that investment over a longer period. Also, the textbook business is highly seasonal in character, with perhaps two-thirds of the sales being made in a three-month period. And the publisher may do all that work and spend all that money without knowing for sure that sales will result.

A novel that is only fairly good will always have some sale; whereas a textbook, even if seemingly the best one available, may prove to have no sale at all if the educational authorities—in many cases government ministries—follow the system of "adopting" a single textbook in that subject and at that level, and do not happen to pick the particular one.

We shall comment at the end of this chapter on the general problem of competition for "adoptions." Even at the start of this consideration, however, it must be stressed that the greatest economic difference between textbook publishing and most other kinds is the highly competitive nature of the textbook business. A person who reads one novel is likely to read another, whereas the parents who buy a fifth-grade arithmetic for their children cannot be imagined as customers for another fifth-grade arithmetic.

That leads to a comment on the differences in educational publishing at different levels of school. There are economic differences of the sort just mentioned—that is, in the degree of competitiveness—but there are also differences in the need to have the books rooted in the particular culture, hence differences in the acceptability of foreign books.

There is a continuous scale from primary school through university, and the higher one goes in the scale the easier it is, especially in certain subjects, to use works of foreign origin. In the case of schoolbooks, although the general educational principles followed may be the same in both foreign and local books, the *content* must grow out of the local culture and have meaning in terms of the life experience of the children using them. In contrast, a university level textbook in chemistry, for instance, may be just as useful (if the original language can be understood or if a proper translation is made) in Britain or Burma or Bolivia, whatever the country or origin.

Even in the sciences there is a great need for textbooks dealing with local agriculture, mineralogy, fauna and flora, forestry, and other special fields. And in the social sciences and humanities there is a vast area seldom touched upon by foreign authors—music, dance, linguistics, art, sociology and anthropology, and many aspects of economic development.

The greatest possibilities for publication of original textbooks are, however, at the primary level in most countries, next greatest at the level of secondary and specialized schools, and least at the university level.

We have spoken several times in this book about the function of the publisher as the director of the grand strategy in book publishing and the responsibility in organizing and coordinating the work of the various partners. In no other kind of publishing are the needs for that kind of leadership greater than in the textbook field. The publisher's talents as diplomat, educator, and businessman are all required. Most important of all is an understanding of the educational needs and then the ability to lead the team of editor, author, illustrator, and printer in producing a book that will satisfy those needs.

In many ways, of course, textbook publishing is like any other kind, and many of the general ideas presented in earlier chapters are fully applicable to schoolbooks. This special chapter is included, however, to discuss some of the differences both in editorial preparation and in promotion and sales.

Once in a while the whole process of producing a textbook may start with submission to the publisher of a manuscript that is found to be acceptable. Although that will not happen very often, examination of manuscripts that are submitted may be very useful. Even if the manuscripts are themselves quite hopeless in publishing terms, they may lead to related ideas for different kinds of books, or open up avenues to new writers.

Assuming that the unusual does not occur, and that the publisher must take the initiative for creating a manuscript that does not yet exist, the steps described below are the ones usually followed in preparing, producing, and distributing a new textbook.

Selection of the Subject

A successful schoolbook publisher, besides being a good businessman, must also be an educator, qualified by background and dedication to better teaching. If the publisher does not have an educational background, there must be a chief editor or some other highly placed staff member who is given virtually full authority to make the decisions relating to the educational aspects of the books.

In order to know what textbook market is waiting to be filled, the publisher obviously must know about the country's educational system. It is not enough merely to see what is being done at the moment. One must also know trends in thinking, changes of curriculum that are being planned, new teaching methods being considered, and so forth. There would be no point in preparing a new first-grade reader in French for Moroccan schools, for instance, if a new educational plan provided for a shift to Arabic as the language of instruction in that grade in the following year.

Selecting the "Team" to Prepare the Manuscript

If the publisher's editor happens to have been a teacher in a particular subject—such as history or mathematics—before going into publishing, it will be natural for that editor to serve as editor for those books. If not, the publisher will wish to consult specialists, even during the first stage of deciding what manuscripts should be prepared. After that decision is made, selection of the editor to supervise preparation and production of the book is the most important act in textbook publishing.

The editor may be a full-time employee of the publishing house or may be engaged on a part-time basis for this one purpose, receiving a fee for the work or sometimes a royalty based on eventual sale of the book. Teachers are the kind of people most frequently engaged for that purpose. They have clear advantages because of their closeness to the educational process. They must also have—or be given by the publisher—an understanding of the publishing process, including at least the fundamentals of book publishing economics.

The editor's role is crucial as "captain of the team" that is creating the textbook. The editor, in turn, selects the authors for their writing ability and knowledge of the subject, and makes an agreement with them about compensation, usually on a royalty basis according to sales. The editor will also be likely to name consultants who are normally paid fees based on the amount of time they give. They may be officers from the inspectorate of the ministry of education, reading specialists from a teacher training college, or active teachers in the field of the particular book.

Next, the editor will appoint an illustrator who may also (see Chapter 6) be the designer, usually paid on a fee basis. If the illustrator is not going to serve also as designer, and if the publishing house is a small one without a regular designer on its staff, the editor will probably wish, even at this early stage, to decide on the probable printer of the book. In that way, the printer's knowledge of technical problems can be available to the rest of the team during the planning stage. That is important, of course, not only for the sake of the appearance of the book but also in considering questions of cost that will constantly arise as decisions are being made about production details.

By this time the publisher will have assembled quite a large team with specialized knowledge and skills, all of which can be drawn on for turning out the best possible textbook. A warning must be given, however, about the disadvantage of "committee decisions." There is danger that individual abilities will be lost in a group. The final result, in that case, may be an uninspired performance, following standard formulas to which no one in the committee can object but which prevent the emergence of really fresh and challenging new ideas. In many countries with highly advanced book industries a clear reaction has set in against unexciting "formula" books. There is an attempt nowadays to put the individual author back in the center of the stage, so the genius for awakening young minds can be given full freedom.

The wise editor, in other words, though filling the role as "captain of the team" with authority to make final decisions, will allow full scope to the imaginative authors picked to do the writing.

Drawing Guidelines for the Book

After the members of the team have been chosen, but before the writing begins, agreement must be reached on a wide range of questions. If a series is planned, there must be agreement on the number of volumes and the content and size of each—always in relation to the official syllabus and likely revisions in the future. Then authors are assigned to each volume. One of the biggest decisions in economic terms, and also important educationally, relates to the illustrations: how many, using what art medium, reproduced by what printing process in how many colors, how positioned in the book, and so forth.

A schedule must be agreed on, to make sure that the publisher's capital is tied up during this preparatory phase for the shortest possible time.

In drawing the guidelines for design and production, the selling price of the book is of course one of the biggest factors to keep in mind. In many countries the purchase of schoolbooks is in the hands of the ministry of education, and ministry budgets are always under great pressure. In other countries, though the ministry or the schools may select the books, parents are expected to buy them for their children and they can do so only at great sacrifice. The ministry's or the school's choice will always be based, at least in part, on the selling price, whether because of their own budgets or because they know the low income level of the average parent.

Thus the editorial team's ideas for producing interesting and attractive books always have to be judged not only according to their own merit but also in terms of cost. A novel or some other trade book that seems too expensive will lose some of its sales; but a textbook that is too expensive may be refused approval by the ministry and get no sales at all!

The following three examples are issues that might be faced by the team in weighing attractiveness and educational effectiveness, on the one hand, against cost on the other.

1. The team decides that, ideally, the book should use both line blocks and halftones for the illustrations. But the publisher knows that §0.25 per copy in a 5,000-copy printing can be saved by using a certain paper that is available. Halftones printed on that paper, however, would be muddy and disappointing. After long discussion with the editorial team, the editor sees that every concept needing illustration can be presented through line drawings, without need for halftones. So the publisher decides in favor of the cheaper paper, without halftones, and a lower selling price for the book.

2. The team may decide that the new textbook must be accompanied by a teacher's manual, giving chapter-by- chapter suggestions about how to use the book, classroom activities that will make

the instruction more valuable, and (if there are school libraries in the country) supplementary reading that will be interesting for the children as well as educationally useful. The authors have agreed to prepare the manual without extra compensation, and the publisher has agreed to present a free copy of the manual to each teacher who uses the book as a classroom text. The production cost of the manual may be recovered from the sales income from the textbook. The cost of the manual, therefore, must be held to the minimum to avoid having to increase the selling price of the textbook. After discussion with the team, the publisher decides that physical attractiveness of the printing is not as important for teachers as for child readers; and that the manual can be typewritten and cheaply reproduced, perhaps by mimeograph or photocopying.

3. The team may decide that two-color printing would be advisable. Imported books were inspected, some using as many as four colors; and educators in the field testified to the inspirational effect of colors in stirring the interest of young readers. But the use of a second color might increase the selling price by 25 percent or more, and the publisher fears that such an increase might kill the book's sale. The publisher therefore urges the team to reconsider, and see if there are not other means, besides color, to capture the interest of the learner. The team responds to this challenge by suggesting more attention to the kind of black-and-white drawings that will be used, inclusion of vivid examples and interesting problems in the writing, and use of visual variety in the arrangement of text and illustrations on the page. So the decision is made to do without the second color, except for the introductory first-year book. This was to be almost entirely a picture book anyway, and color was considered essential. Even so, a 25 percent price increase seemed unthinkable. To take care of the extra cost in that first book in the series, the publisher might decide to reduce the size from 96 to 64 pages.

Preliminary Manuscript and Preliminary Edition

When the guidelines have been set, responsibility shifts temporarily to the authors. There are a few—very few—textbook authors who put full time on that work; most of them combine it with other jobs (though often they derive more income from the textbooks than from other sources). On evenings or weekends or whenever they can find a block of time for writing, the authors set to work transforming the guidelines into actual pages of a manuscript. The creative writing process has begun.

The editor is in close touch with the authors during this period, keeping the writing moving forward and helping the authors overcome feelings of discouragement and insecurity. Consultants may be asked to clear up uncertainties in the guidelines, and conferences will be scheduled with each author and the illustrator. Finally sections of the manuscript, usually isolated chapters, will begin to appear in the publishing office. Some will be brilliant, but others will present problems calling for all the editor's tact and imagination in working with the authors and consultants to revise the material. In some cases it may be necessary to change writing assignments, or even to bring in new authors.

Eventually, the preliminary manuscript and illustrations will be complete. Criticisms by consultants and other readers will have been considered, and changes will have been made, where justified, because of those comments. The wording of the text will have been carefully examined, and the illustrator's preliminary drawings will have been studied by the authors and consultants. The manuscripts will at last reach the point where it seems to be as good as the entire editorial team can make it. But the most important critic—the child—has not yet been consulted.

The publisher's investment in preparation of the book is so great, and the cost of producing the book in a large edition will add so much to the risk, that a preliminary edition for test use can be crucial for textbooks, especially at the primary level. The extra cost will often prove to have saved money in the end. It is surprising how many sections of a manuscript cannot be understood by children, and how many sections that seemed interesting to adults produce only boredom in young readers.

Final Edition

Unless the testing of the preliminary edition shows that things are so wrong that extensive rewriting and another preliminary edition will be necessary, the manuscript is now reaching the end of its long road. Minor revisions are made in the text as a result of the class-room trial, and the artwork is put in final form by the illustrator.

The steps in design and production discussed in Chapters 6 and 7 are followed with even more care for textbooks than for other books. The illustrator-designer will prepare a *dummy* of the complete book, in order to show the printer, page by page, exactly how the type and illustrations are to be arranged. And for no kind of book is it as important as for a textbook to make sure that proof is read carefully not only by the printers but by the editors and authors.

When the time comes for the start of presswork, the illustrator-designer will probably be at the printing plant to check the exact position of illustrations, the evenness of black in the printing, and other details. This is a critical moment when the publisher can insist on the same high level of performance from the printer that has been demanded from the editorial team all the way through. In fact, it is not uncommon in some countries for a representative of the publisher to stand by during the entire press run.

Promotion and Sales

One of the advantages of textbook publishing over other kinds is that the people controlling the market are easy to identify and reach. Ministry of education officials, school principals, individual teachers—these are the people who buy schoolbooks or select or approve them, thereby causing others to buy them. Those people who influence the sale of textbooks are relatively few in number and the channels to them are wide open. Furthermore, as professional educators they should be greatly interested in learning about new teaching tools.

The techniques used in telling these sales influencers about a new book are more or less the same in most countries:

Review copies. These are sent to appropriate educational journals, national and international.

Advertising in professional journals. Publishers disagree about the value of this kind of advertising, but it does permit announcement of the book in such journals long before the appearance of a review; in fact, if desired, such advertisements may appear even before publication.

Mail announcements. These go to education officials, school principals, and others. In addition to special announcements of each new book to these names on the publisher's mailing list, there will usually be an annual mailing of a catalogue including a complete list of schoolbooks.

Exhibits. These are shown at professional meetings.

Presentation copies. Although some publishers tend to be overcautious about giving away free copies for promotion purposes—and the process is indeed an expensive one—the majority of experienced textbook people think this is the most important of all forms of promotion. This puts in the hands of a potential customer a copy of the book itself.

Sales representatives' calls. Representatives of the publisher (full-time or part-time, salaried or on a commission basis) call on educators personally, showing the book and explaining its merits. Even a small textbook publisher may have to use this method, especially in reaching schools in outlying regions, if selection of books is school-by-school rather than through a central ministry. If adoption *is* central, the head of the publishing house will usually conduct the dealings with the ministry directly. If there is approval of more than one book, however, then each publisher will wish to have the best representation possible throughout the country, in the hope that both schools and booksellers will know about the book and be sure of having it available.

Although, as we noted at the beginning of the chapter, school textbooks have to be nationally oriented, and the domestic market is therefore the chief concern of a textbook publisher, there are some export possibilities. Such possibilities are especially good, of course, when the national languages are the same and there are basic similarities in the national economies and basic cultures. Another kind of textbook that "travels" well is a science textbook, especially in the pure sciences.

If the export market is a small one, it will be served through sale of copies of the originating publisher's edition. If it is large, however, the originating publisher may authorize a publisher in another country to bring out a separate edition of the same book, perhaps with some adaptation to make the book more acceptable in the new country. This licensing of foreign editions, usually with payment on a royalty basis, may well be part of a *two-way* flow. A network of such cooperating publishers could perhaps bring about a practical approach to regional publishing which offers enormous economies and long-term opportunities for progress in publishing. The method is especially attractive if the books have multiple-color pages which can be produced at low cost in one place for different publishers' editions, even though the rest of the book is locally manufactured in each case.

Textbook Adoptions

The textbook publisher considering a heavy investment in a new book or series of books would naturally like to have *assurance* from school authorities that the book will be officially approved or adopted if that risk is taken.

The publisher's desire for monopoly is understandable because of the hope of minimizing risk and increasing profit, but a case can be made that such exclusive selection may also be in the national interest. It can be pointed out that there may be both educational and financial advantages through concentration on a single book or series, rather than wasting resources on several. It can also be argued that there can be great savings of cost through production of large editions of a few books, rather than small printings of many. Those are valid arguments, deserving serious consideration.

Yet at the same time the individual publisher will realize that if the principle of exclusive adoption is followed, and if one's own book does not happen to be selected, then one will be completely shut out from the market. Also, the publisher's professional educational interest will show the advantage of competition in excellence among books. If official approval is granted to only one book and a large number of copies are put in circulation, there will be great resistance to change, regardless of the need for revision or availability of a better book.

For these reasons there is a continuing search for some middle ground. There is need for a method that will avoid the deadening effects of single book approval, yet will also avoid the financial waste of excessive publication of directly competing works. One of the compromise methods involves multiple approval (but in a limited number, perhaps four or five books) by a central authority, with freedom to individual schools or districts to make *their* single book adoption from among the titles on the centrally approved list. This method is especially promising when there is a large number of separate school systems, as is the case within each state of the United States; or in the separate government, church, and private school systems in many African countries.

As part of any such plan there should be a clear understanding that any approval, at whatever level, is for a stated period, normally four or five years. That agreement about the length of time during which approval will be valid has advantages both ways: it assures the publisher of a basic market for a reasonable length of time, but it also establishes an end to the monopoly so that better books can be considered for substitution after that time.

The important thing is that the publisher, both as a businessman and as an educator, has a stake in keeping textbook publishing as open as possible. Both publishing and teaching will benefit if publishers are constantly encouraged to produce better, and ever better, books.

12

Children's Books

BOOKS FOR CHILDREN are in many ways the most important books in the world. This is true not only of textbooks for formal classroom training but also of books children read for their own pleasure. Textbooks are not enough for a country with a rising literacy rate and a lack of good teachers. Books that young people can read for personal enjoyment and profit are needed in every country, but nowhere as desperately as in developing countries.

The practical value of children's books aside from textbooks has not always been recognized. In the past too many educational administrators have considered children's books as "luxuries" that only wealthy countries could afford. However, there is growing recognition that encouragement of publication of books for supplementary and general reading can be *an economy* from the national point of view.

A children's storybook, or a book of factual information that really catches children's interest and leads them on in their reading, can be one of the least expensive and most effective educational tools. And it can be the means of saving the huge educational investment the country has made in teaching its children to read. If there are books on which they can practice the art of reading for their own reasons, education can continue in some measure, in spite of poor teachers or even a child's withdrawal from school.

Although the value of books for children's general reading is now more widely recognized, very little had been done about it as yet in most developing countries. Dozens of these countries boldly spend large fractions of their total national budget on other facilities for education, but hold back from committing the small additional amount needed to supply this critical element.

The Reasons for Emphasizing Children's Books

As we shall see when discussing the economics of children's books below, neither publishers nor educators nor librarians can do what is needed by themselves. They have to work together. If they do not, little if anything will happen. But the incentives for joint interest in children's books are almost overwhelming.

The reading habit. Young readers are at precisely the age when lifelong habits are formed. If they are able to get books that reward them, they may become book readers for life; if not, even the art of reading may be lost.

Numbers. Because the number of children in school was so small in the early history of many developing countries (7 percent in Indonesia at the time of independence), the number of literates among the older people is relatively small. Thanks to the wonderful expansion of education in recent years, the number capable of book reading is far greater among young people.

Relation to education. No textbook can appeal successfully to all tastes, nor can it provide enough reading matter to satisfy the youngster who has learned the fun of reading. Furthermore, even if the classroom textbook is a good one, it cannot have the appeal to a young reader of a book read for its own sake.

Ideals and national unity. The right kinds of children's books can implant ideals and contribute to a sense of unity with people living in other parts of the country—and can do those things in ways acceptable to a young reader who would resent and resist direct "preaching."

Influence on the household. One literate child in a household can have great influence not only on brothers and sisters, by inspiring them to want to acquire the art of reading, but also on illiterate parents who are proud to have their children read to them. This is especially useful in national terms as a vehicle for transmitting information on health, agriculture, and other matters.

Language for Children's Books

The largest number of books for children will of course be needed in the national language, whether that is an indigenous language, as Thai in Thailand, or a foreign language that has been adopted as the national language, such as English in Ghana, French in Guinea, or Spanish in Chile. Although mastery of the national language is the ultimate goal, consideration must be given to the question of children's books *for beginning reading* in mother tongues, if those tongues have a written form and are used by large numbers of people.

There in not complete agreement on this question. Some observers believe that the national welfare is best served if the students are taught the national language from the beginning, without providing any literacy instruction in the mother tongues. Other observers feel quite strongly the other way. Learning to read, they say, is not at all difficult *if the language is already known through the ear*. What is extremely difficult is to learn a new language and to learn the art of reading at the same time.

People who accept the latter argument think that the child's knowledge of a mother tongue, an asset with which the child arrives at school, is a priceless educational tool which should not be thrown away. Rather, the child should be taught to read in that language and, having learned, should have the chance to read interesting books in order to discover the enjoyment of reading from the beginning. (This argument in favor of giving children reading matter in their mother tongues has a second part: the teaching of the *oral* form of the national language should start from the first day of school so the new language is already known when the reading of that language is taught two or three years later.)

Although, as noted, not all authorities agree on this matter, there are many developing countries in which the quality of teaching in the national language is so low (especially if the national language is of foreign origin) that children do not learn to read in that language for quite some years after the start of school. Even in the many English-speaking countries of Africa in which instruction starts in mother tongues and theoretically shifts to English in the third year, there are not enough teachers with adequate English for the purpose; the reading of English may be postponed to the fourth, fifth, or even sixth year.

The practical issue, quite aside from theories about teaching methods, is whether those children are to be deprived of reading matter during all that time, or whether supplementary reading books in their mother tongues are not greatly needed.

The point is made especially clear when one considers the high percentage of children who drop out of school after learning to read their mother tongues but before learning English, French, or other national languages.

Typographic Presentation

The type of script in which children's reading material is presented raises another question on which there is disagreement on many points. Everyone grants that the type should be large and well spaced, and that the printing must be clear. But in certain languages there are some special problems. For example, should children's books in Arabic have full vowel markings, or should the printing be without vowels, as will be the case with most of the books (except the Koran and poetry) that the young people will read when they grow up? In Persian, should children's books be hand calligraphed in Nastaliq script, the traditional form for Persian, or should the children become accustomed from the beginning to the Nashkh type (much easier for the modern printer) that they will read in most books, newspapers, and magazines as adults?

These and other typographic questions, like the ones relating to languages, have to be considered by the publishers in each country in consultation with the educational authorities.

Content of Children's Books

Everyone who has tried writing for children agrees it is one of the most difficult tasks a writer can face. Great litterateurs are not necessarily as good at it as less famous writers who have devoted themselves to this special form of composition. Interest, movement, and action must be kept alive, and the language must be simple and

direct. Only a relatively small number of words unknown to children of that age can be used; and when an unknown word is
introduced, its meaning should be made clear by its context in the
sentence. (Not "There was a visor on his hat," which would be
meaningless to anyone not knowing the word *visor*; but "The visor
on his hat shaded his face from the sun.")

Of course the age level of the intended readers must be carefully
considered, not only as to the words used but also as to the basic
subject matter.

A criticism properly brought against the American and European
children's books often suggested for reading in developing countries is that they do not deal with facts, objects, and situations that
are meaningful to the children of Asia and Africa and Latin America.
One of the strongest arguments for developing juvenile book industries in those areas is to make sure that children's books *will* be
responsive to the interests of the child who reads them.

Care should be taken, however, against going too far in "localiz-
ing" the subject matter. The foreign aspect of the books in the past
was, of course, wrong. But it would be tragic if, in the process of
correcting that error, the book publishers in developing countries
should make their books narrowly nationalistic.

Books must be *understandable and interesting* to the children who
read them, but they should also open wide horizons. The wheat-
eating children of Pakistan should know something about life in a
rice-eating village of India or Bangladesh; the cotton-growing areas
of a country that also has textile mills should know something about
the lives of the people who tend the spindles. All of them should
get, through books that are fun to read, some view of the rest of the
world. It is a satisfaction to most Americans that among juvenile
fiction characters well known to children in the United States, many
are from other countries and other cultures.

Another word of caution can perhaps be offered: because of the
popularity of books of factual information, and the obvious educational value they have, there is danger that both educators and
publishers may overlook the need to provide the stories and folktales and other works of the imagination that feed the spirit as well
as the mind. Without these, a children's library cannot be consid-

ered complete from an educational standpoint, or satisfactory from the point of view of the young readers using it.

Designer and Illustrator and Printer

For many kinds of books the illustrations are merely decoration. For children's books, however, the illustrations may be at the very heart of reader interest, and so essential to the book's purpose that it would be unthinkable to publish the book without them.

The illustrator's role is so important that many of the great children's books have been prepared jointly by author and illustrator or—in those happy cases where both talents are found in one person—by an author-illustrator who conceives and carries out the writing and illustrating of the book as one operation.

The designer and printer also have major parts to play. In fact, the ideal way to prepare a children's book is through close collaboration of author, illustrator, designer, and printer. The illustrator's consultation with the designer and printer should, if possible, come at the very beginning of the work, at the stage when the pictures have been planned but not yet executed. With the designer's advice, the illustrator may be able to employ methods which, without sacrificing the interest of the juvenile readers, can considerably reduce the cost of the book.

Economics of Children's Books

Few children's books are bought directly by children. Often they are bought by parents. But in countries with low per capita income and an already heavy burden of family expense for the purchase of required textbooks, there is not much leeway. There is some market for children's books in every country, no matter how low the average income, if the books are reasonably priced in terms of that economy. But, as we saw in Chapter 3, it is necessary to print in large quantities in order to get low prices. In many of the emerging nations there is not yet a large enough sale to individuals to make possible, by itself, the large quantities and hence the low prices those individuals require.

The biggest natural market for children's books, in both developed and developing countries, is schools and libraries. If the market can be reached, *then* the quantities printed can be large enough to justify the low prices that individuals can afford. In the United States it is said that 75 percent of the sales income for all normal kinds of children's books is from sales to institutions, chiefly schools and libraries. Without that solid economic foundation for the juvenile book industry, the publication of children's books in America in anything like their present number, or at their present prices, would be impossible.

When ministers of education urge publishers to bring out more children's books, the publishers are quite justified in asking the minister when the policy of regular purchase of books for school libraries will begin. School libraries—and village libraries and other kinds of public libraries—have their own rich usefulness in educational terms. But they also have the power, through their book purchases, of giving juvenile book publishing the economic base without which it cannot survive.

The libraries themselves cannot exist unless the right kinds of books are published to stock them. And the publishers cannot afford to publish such books unless a market is assured. The publisher has to take chances, of course, on each book. But one needs to know that there is a school and library market in general for children's books that are well written, well illustrated, well printed, and offered at reasonable prices.

This interdependence of libraries and book publishing is discussed further in Chapter 16.

Economies in Production

Because illustrations can represent so large a part of the total cost of producing children's books, most of the major economies to be considered relate in some way to the pictures. For one thing, as suggested above, early consultation with the illustrator may make it possible to avoid needlessly expensive printing processes, or use of extra colors on more pages than necessary, or duplicate cuts or clichés for title page and cover if one set would serve both purposes.

There are also wonderful opportunities for major economies through collaboration of publishers working in different languages. Publishers can undertake joint production, for all of their editions, of the color pictures, leaving blank space for the text which can be imprinted later in the different languages. In large countries which publish in many languages—such as India—there may be that kind of collaboration even within the country. There can also be international cooperation among different Asian or African or Latin American countries, as there is among European countries and between Europe and the United States.

In some countries (such as Indonesia) there are legal restrictions on the import of books printed in the national language, but there is no obstacle to importing sheets of pictures. In fact, in many countries there is an import duty on unprinted paper but not on printed books; one therefore encounters the curious situation that the local publisher's portion of a jointly produced edition, printed in another country, can enter more cheaply than the same weight of unprinted paper.

Economies in the cost of films for offset printing can be gained even if joint printing does not prove possible. Even duplicates of offset films are extremely expensive, but one set of films can be routed, successively, to different publishers in the same country, or even in different countries.

Although international cooperation in joint production can be carried out, if necessary, on opposite sides of the world, the regional approach is of course the most promising, not only because of ease of communication and transport but also because of general suitability of illustrations throughout a region. Although East African societies, for instance, differ significantly from area to area, there are some general similarities among them that can make illustrations acceptable in all, or at least more acceptable than illustrations intended for European or American children.

13

Mass Distribution

THE DEVELOPING COUNTRIES of the world are extending education to their whole populations—rich and poor, farmers and factory workers, villagers and city people. The chief emphasis, naturally, is on young people, but adult education is also receiving attention. The expansion of education in Asia, Africa, and Latin America in past decades—and the further expansion planned for the coming decade—are without historical precedent.

But although education is being taken to every section and level of society, book publishing has not kept up with that sensational educational movement. Millions of people who are potential book readers and book buyers are being produced by school systems and adult literacy campaigns. Yet the book publishing industries of the countries concerned have done little to exploit the business opportunity or to give their societies the books they need.

The publishers have tended, in general, to concentrate on the relatively easy job of selling books at high prices to the small section of the population that is well educated, fairly prosperous, and easy to reach. They should not be blamed for this in view of the difficulties they have faced, especially the high cost and frequent unavailability of finance capital as explained in Chapter 3. But that ignoring of the major part of the possible book market is no longer acceptable in view of the developing countries' national goals.

If the publishers wish to respond to the opportunity—in many ways the most remarkable opportunity yet opened to the book publishers of the world—they have to take the leadership. They must *want* to start an entirely new kind of publishing enterprise, with low prices and large quantities and problems of organization and distribution such as they have never faced before. If they do

want this, it is in the national interest for others, especially development banks and other providers of capital, to help them achieve it.

The three elements a country needs for an educated citizenry are
(1) a school system, (2) a system of libraries, and (3) a system of
nationwide distribution and sale of inexpensive books. The second
and third elements are upholders, supporters, and intensifiers of
the first. In fact, for many people, libraries and cheap books can be a
kind of substitute for school when the individuals have to drop out.

Everyone in the world seems to understand the need for schools,
and most countries are prepared to spend huge amounts to make
them available. Libraries are also highly valued, even though there
is not yet a very large expenditure on them. But mass sale of books,
the third element of national education, is widely ignored. In too
many quarters it is regarded as "just a business" rather than a basic
part of a country's education system.

Mass distribution *is* a business, of course, and the people who
conduct it are seeking a profit, which they are entitled to have if they
do a good job of serving educational needs. We are now going to
look at some of the special characteristics of mass distribution. They
are different, in a number of ways, from the usual kind of publishing.

Many people, not understanding the facts of book publishing,
think of paper covers as being the whole basis of mass distribution
of low-cost books. A paper cover is indeed somewhat cheaper than a
hard cover, but a paper cover has no magic in itself, as we can see
from looking at publishing in many of the developing countries
where almost all books are bound in paper, yet without ever gaining
mass distribution. And we know in Chapter 3 that it is production in
large quantities that holds the real secret of low-priced books.

The whole point of a mass distribution plan is that really cheap
books are made available everywhere, not merely in cities and not
merely in bookshops of the normal sort. It is the combination of
those two factors—low selling price and widespread availability—
that has made possible the revolution in paperback distribution in
Western countries and that holds such exciting promise for all the
developing countries. In order to achieve mass sales, the basic needs
are:

1. *Equipment for book manufacture* that will bring *great* economies in

mass production, following the principles of high quantity and low cost that we examined in Chapter 3. (As noted earlier, a publisher does not have to own this equipment, but the printers with whom publishers work must have it if low-priced books are to be possible.)

2. *Equipment for distribution*, such as small trucks, or scooters, for taking the books from central depots to the hundreds or thousands of points of retail sale.

3. *Equipment for display* at points of retail sale, chiefly racks of wood, plastic, sheet metal, wire, or other material. (The existence of such equipment leads to at least some standardization of the size of books to fit into it.)

4. *A system* or organizational plan for moving books from the point of manufacture to regional centers, and from there to the points of retail sale; and for regular checking of the stock of books at the selling points in order to replace books that have been sold, take back books that are not moving, and collect money from the retailer for the books that have been sold.

5. *Capital* for the distribution equipment and display equipment mentioned above, the initial costs of setting up and operating the system until income starts balancing that expense, and the cost of manufacturing the books that are to be sold. (That last part of the capital requirement—for the books themselves—may be met through business arrangements with cooperating publishers under some of the plans described below.)

6. *A small editorial and production staff.*

Advantages of a Reprint Program

Although there are some outstanding examples of mass distribution plans that have been based largely on original books, such as Penguin Books in the United Kingdom and the *Que sais-je?* series in France, most of the successful mass market plans in the world have been based on *re*prints of books originally brought out in the normal way for bookstore sale.

Among the advantages of using reprints instead of original books are (1) the testing of public reaction that books receive in their normal editions, (2) the avoidance of editorial development cost, (3) the ability to draw on all books published, instead of being confined to a small number of new books, and (4) in countries where good facilities are available, the economy of reprinting by photographing the pages of the previously printed book or by using existing plates, thus avoiding the heavy cost of typesetting.

It must be remembered, however, that if a mass distribution plan *does* depend on reprinting of normally published books, then it is essential that such normal publishing continue. Otherwise, after the most attractive of the previously published books have been used in a reprint program, there will be nothing further for the reprint program to "live on" in the future. The reprint publisher has a lively interest in seeing normal publishing prosper.

Kinds of Books for Mass Distribution

In the early period of the paperback revolution in Western countries, many people thought that the only kinds of books that would sell well by such methods were those dealing with sex, crime, and violence. For a long time it was actually true that the great majority of the titles displayed were of that sort. Little by little, however, publishers with vision and courage discovered the salability of many other kinds of books, including classics, how-to-do-it books, juveniles, history, literature, philosophy, psychology, and useful information. And with the development of the so-called *high-price paperback* (selling in the United States for $8 to $15, instead of perhaps $4 to $7 for a normal paperback or $20 to $30 for the hardbound original edition), there is now a wide range of books on almost every subject, especially books useful for supplementary reading in university courses. These high-price paperbacks have their largest sale in bookshops, especially in university communities, but some also appear on newsstands and at other mass market outlets.

In spite of the argument for a reprint program, as stated above, there will surely be many opportunities, in every developing country, for an imaginative publisher to plan books that will appeal to the particular market in that country. An example might be a cheap but authoritative book on baby care that recognizes the actual conditions in the country as to foods, family habits, methods of sanitation, and so forth.

Whether the books are new ones or selections from previously published titles, it is important that the editor of a mass distribution system give special attention to *market research*—studying what kinds of books the customers really want. As a matter of fact, such study is easier in a mass market project than for almost any other kind of publishing, because the *feedback of information* from the retail sales outlet is so regular and in such easily handled statistical form. No other kind of publisher can learn so quickly and so accurately what kinds of books the public likes.

"Advertising" Mass Distribution Books

Quotation marks are placed around the word "advertising" in the heading above because, in one sense, mass market books have no advertising at all. The margin between income and manufacturing cost is so narrow that no advertising of a normal sort can be afforded.

But in a broader sense, mass market books have the most effective advertising of any kind: they are constantly before the eyes of the possible customers, at bus stations, in food shops, and wherever people gather. The cover design of mass market books is therefore even more important that it is for other books. Although four-color printing of shiny covers is very costly, the mass market publisher is willing to accept that. One of the manufacturing economies is to do the color presswork for a group of books at one time, thus reducing the cost for each book.

Another form of valuable advertising that mass market books get, besides display at the point of sale, is display in schools and libraries that recognize the educational value of bringing the books to as wide an audience as possible. There are also some schools and libraries that actually sell mass market books as a means of encouraging reading development. Such sales are often handled by the students themselves, though usually under adult supervision.

Cost Factors in Mass Distribution

Aside from the cost of the books themselves, the mass distributor has to think of the cost of equipment (a capital cost) and the working capital required to set up and maintain a distribution system reaching all parts of the country. It is difficult to meet those overhead costs—even if the individual books show a good profit—unless the total volume of business is quite large. In other words, one cannot have a profitable mass distribution business for just a few books; there must be a large and continuing stream moving through the channels established.

That is one of the arguments, aside from the argument of giving a wide editorial selection, for basing a mass distribution plan on use of books from all publishers rather than from a single publishing house, unless that one publisher has an enormous list of previously published books.

To have a large volume of business is the first requirement for a profitable mass distribution plan. The next is to make use, to whatever extent possible, of decentralized existing organizations and distribution channels. If, in some region of a country, there is already a book distributor doing an effective job of taking books from the provincial capital to small retailers in the area, that firm might adapt its methods and acquire the equipment needed to service mass distribution retail outlets in the province. That would save the central mass distributing organization both the cost and the continuing responsibility for setting up a new system in that province. Or there may be an efficient motor freight line whose lorries could move books from the point of manufacture to the regional distributors, thus saving the cost of buying trucks for that purpose.

Another cost is the royalty or other payment to the author or (in the case of books previously issued by another publisher) to be divided between the author and the original publisher. Because the margin of profit on each book is so small, and because the common objective of all the partners in this kind of publishing is to sell very large quantities at necessarily low prices, most authors' contracts provide that the royalty paid on a copy of a mass market book will be lower than on a regular edition.

But of all the costs, the most basic is of course the one mentioned earlier: the manufacturing cost. The dramatic reduction of manufacturing cost per copy when quantities go up to big numbers is the basis of success in mass market book publishing.

Business Arrangements

Mass distribution projects can be set up in a wide variety of ways, of which only some are listed here: (1) A large publisher may set up a mass market plan for that publisher's own books. (2) A publisher may set up a plan using a selection of books from all publishers, making arrangements to pay the other publishers a royalty. (3) An independent operator, engaging in no other kind of publishing, may make mass market publishing the sole business, drawing on the books of all publishers and perhaps from time to time commissioning new books also. (4) A specialist in distribution, without becoming a publisher in the full sense, may merely take books to the provinces and service retail outlets. The publishers thus served do all the rest of the work, including production of the books, which are sold to the distributor at some very large discount. (5) A group of publishers may combine in setting up a jointly owned mass market publishing house, or a jointly owned distributing company as mentioned in item 4.

Long-Term Advantages in Mass Distribution

Mass distribution can be justified as a way of making profits—sometimes very large profits—in book publishing. And one of the most pleasing facts about this is that mass market sales do not seem to cut down the sale of regular editions through bookstores. There have been examples in Western countries of an *increase* in the sale of the expensive hardbound edition of a book after it has gone into a cheap paperback edition. In a broader sense, however, the two markets seem to be relatively independent of each other, because the huge audience to which mass market books are exposed includes only a tiny percentage of people who normally go into bookshops.

Although mass distribution has its own justification in terms of profit, the long-run advantages to a country's book publishing industry, and to its educational welfare, can be even more important. A mass market system develops book readers and book buyers throughout the country, giving a great expansion to the economic base on which a book industry rests, and carrying a nation closer to its goal of a literate and informed citizenry.

Publishers in developing countries have barely scratched the surface of their possible business. Even those houses that have been unusually successful have concentrated on the cities and on the elite. But, thanks to the spread of education to all areas and all classes, a truly nationwide market is now waiting for the publishers bold enough and imaginative enough to seek it through mass market methods.

14

Book Clubs
and Subscription Books

OF THE MANY special kinds of book publishing practiced in Western countries, few have aroused more interest in developing countries than book clubs. Because of this fact, and not because the book club idea is necessarily applicable in all developing countries, it is worth our attention here. And because there is some relationship between methods of book clubs and those of subscription book publishing, that operation is also discussed.

After the first success of general book clubs, such as the Literary Guild and the Book-of-the-Month Club in the United States, many other kinds of book clubs were developed to serve the interests of special kinds of readers: Scientific Book Club, Religious Book Club, the Junior Literary Guild, History Book Club, Engineers Book Club, and many others. Those specialized clubs have their own usefulness and methods, but it will be easiest to understand the problems and the techniques of book clubs if we start by thinking about book clubs that bring out general books that may appeal to literate people of any sort and living almost anywhere. Novels, biographies, and nonfiction books of general interest are the most natural kinds of books for such clubs.

Two basic thoughts lay behind the book club idea. The first was that if a publisher could be sure of a large sale of any book, the quantity printed could be increased and the selling price therefore lowered because of the saving in manufacturing cost per copy. The second, which was more important, at least in the United States before the development of mass distribution of paperbacks, was that there were many potential book readers not served by bookshops, and their business could be secured if some way could be found to send them books by mail and receive their payment by mail in return.

In later years it became evident that book clubs could also get business from city people, even though bookshops were available to them, because of the special inducements in the way of lower prices, free books, and so forth, that the book clubs offered. This raised serious problems as a result of the antagonism of booksellers, who saw some of their business slipping away.

And, quite aside from the booksellers' own feelings, any publishing plan that would drive retail bookstores out of business would clearly be bad for the publishers and bad for society. We shall return to this problem—not yet entirely solved—of the effect of book clubs on the welfare of retail bookselling. But it should be noted here that book clubs, although originally thought of as serving only a rural market, turned out to have possibilities in cities also.

The conditions essential for a successful book club seem to be: (1) a substantial number of literate people economically able to buy books, not necessarily with access to bookshops, who want or need guidance in selecting what books to buy, or who wish to take advantage of the saving in cost through book club purchase; (2) an efficient postal system for delivery of the books ordered; (3) a convenient means of transmitting small amounts of money, whether through an easily workable postal system of "collect on delivery" or postal money orders or wide prevalence of individual checking accounts or credit cards; (4) an aggressive method of promotion to enroll subscribers in the book club; and (5) available printing equipment for producing large printings at a much lower price per copy than in editions of normal size.

As to that last point, about facilities for printing, it must be said that in many cases new *thinking* is needed more than new equipment. There are plants in Asia, Africa, and Latin America that are physically able, at the present time, to give greatly lower per-copy costs for large editions, but the printers have so vague an understanding of costs that they go on performing operations in the same expensive ways they might use for small editions. Or, even if they gain economies, they may fail to pass them on to their customers, simply because they are unaware of them. The situation has not been unknown in the United States and other developed countries. This is an additional argument for publishers to learn all they can about printing costs.

Few developing countries are immediately able to satisfy all five of the above conditions, and a publisher thinking of going into this special kind of publishing should consider the extent to which failure to meet one or another of those requirements would be fatal.

There have been successful book clubs making use of original books which they have commissioned, but the largest number of successful book clubs (like the mass distribution reprint publishers we mentioned in the previous chapter) have depended on books that have been editorially developed by other publishers. Permission to reprint them in book club editions is secured under some business arrangement with the original publisher. In this way the book club publisher saves not only the cost of editorial development but usually also the cost of typesetting. Those savings, added to the economy of reprinting in large quantities, make it possible for the book club to sell at a lower price.

For small book clubs dealing with books in special fields, and therefore in small quantities, it may not be necessary to print books at all. They may simply buy finished copies of the book from the original publisher, of course at a very large discount. If the book club is able to make its selection before the publisher has gone to press with his book, the number of copies needed by the book club can be added to the number the publisher was going to print anyway, and the publisher's cost in producing those extra copies can be very low, as we saw in Chapter 3.

If, however, the book club is going to produce its own edition, the cheapest way is usually to rent the original publisher's plates if the book was plated for letterpress printing, or lease his films if the original book was printed by offset. A letterpress book that was not plated may be photographed and reprinted by offset. Sometimes, if the original book was in a very large format or had the type arranged lavishly with extra space between the lines, study may show it is actually cheaper to reset the type so the book can be issued in a smaller format or fewer pages for the book club edition.

The business arrangements under which the book clubs get permission of the original publishers for reissuing the books are usually on the basis of a per-copy fee, combining a percentage of the book club edition's list price (which royalty the original publisher divides with the author in some way, see Chapter 18) and a "plate rental" if the book club uses the publisher's plates.

Usually, in order to persuade the original publisher to grant the right of reprinting even though the exact number of copies is not yet known, the book clubs make an advance payment or "guarantee," which is the minimum to be paid to the original publisher. Additional amounts will be paid later as justified by the number of books actually sold.

How a Book Club Works

There are so many different book club plans that it would be impossible to name any one method that is common to all of them; and it would be hopeless to advise a publisher in a particular country which might be best. The following paragraphs may help to show, however, approaches that have been used. Some of them may suggest adaptions suitable for particular countries.

Agreement with the subscriber. The subscriber is notified by mail each time (in many plans once a month) that a new book is to be issued as a "book club selection." The subscriber has to tell the club by return postcard in a specified time (perhaps three weeks) whether that book is wanted. *If there is no reply, the book club is authorized to assume the subscriber wants the book.* (That "fail-safe" provision is regarded by many as the real secret of book club success.)

The subscriber does not have to order every book offered, but under most book club plans a certain number (perhaps four) in a year must be taken, and the bill is paid by mail, usually within thirty days; or, in a "collect-on-delivery" system, the postman is paid the amount the club charges, plus the small collection fee.

In most club plans, the subscriber may choose from books that have been offered previously instead of accepting the new selection. With a club that has been in business for some time, there is therefore a very wide field of choice.

Depending on the particular plan the club follows, there may be free books or other bonuses after a certain number of books have been bought by a subscriber. These are discussed under "special inducements" below. A typical subscriber's coupon might read: "Please enroll me as a trial member of your Book Club and send me *free* the encyclopedia of art which you have advertised. I agree to purchase at least four additional monthly selections during the first year I am a member. I have the right to cancel my membership at any time after buying these four books. If I continue after the trial, I am to receive additional free books of my choice for every four books I buy at the Club's special low prices. As my first monthly choice, please send and bill me for the following:. . . . "

The newsletter. The newsletter that is sent to all subscribers is of great importance in keeping up interest and in persuading subscribers to take more books than they would be likely to choose without this stimulus.

A typical newsletter may devote perhaps a fourth of its space to announcing the new selection, with biographical information about the author, prepublication reviews of the book, and estimates of its importance by authorities. The rest of the newsletter may be devoted to prominent listing of other highly recommended books that may (under some plans) be chosen by the subscriber instead of the main selection, and to a listing of the many previous selections from which a choice may be made. The newsletter are usually illustrated, at least with photographs of authors, and sometimes with illustrations or jacket designs from the books.

Selection committee. The names of the book club's "judges" or selection committee are perhaps of less importance now than when the book club idea was new and many of the potential subscribers were less able to judge for themselves. Even today, however, many clubs put great stress on the famous names of the judges: authors, scholars, or people in the public eye whose standing inspires confidence.

It is recognized, of course, that the judges cannot read all the books that might possibly be considered, but the judges of the well-established clubs really *do* make the final selection, and frequently provide statements for inclusion in the newsletter explaining their choice.

Promotion. Because no club has ever had a membership that is renewed 100 percent each year, some members are constantly dropping out, and the promotion department must be busy all the time in signing up replacements, even aside from the natural desire to increase the club's membership as much as possible.

The promotion campaign usually presents two arguments: (1) the "special inducements" in the way of low prices, free books, and so forth (discussed below); (2) the distinction of previous selections and the advantage of new selections (presumably of the same high quality) being offered to the subscriber each month.

Both space advertising in newspaper and magazines and direct mail advertising are used to attract new subscribers, usually with handsome illustrations of the books from which free selections can be made.

Special inducements. The most frequent special inducement offered to new subscribers is a free book, or several free books, given to the subscriber at the time of signing up, and requiring no payment at all but merely agreement to buy (for instance) four of the twelve monthly selections to be offered in the coming year.

Another inducement frequently offered is "one free book for every four purchased." Still another method involves no free books but a billing at very much less than the listed selling price for each book the subscriber takes. And some clubs combine elements of all these plans in some way.

Booksellers' complaints. It is those special inducements, of course, that arouse the booksellers' bitter protests. There have been times when an individual book club subscriber has been able to buy a given book at a price lower than a bookseller can purchase it from the publisher with a booksellers' discount.

The book clubs, and the publishers who cooperate with them, have tried to meet this criticism in various ways, including setting up plans under which the bookseller can take book club subscriptions and receive a commission on them. It is a fact, however, that booksellers will never be enthusiastic about book clubs. The best that can be hoped is that—as the book clubs claim, and as we mentioned in the previous chapter in connection with mass distribution books—the majority of book club subscribers would not be very good bookstore customers even if there were no book clubs at all.

And it is surely true that, in a number of Western countries, the major book clubs have helped to develop a regular reading habit among millions of people, some of whom will become bookshop customers, though they might not otherwise have had much to do with books.

The book club versus bookshop problem is not to be taken lightly. Every possible means should be used to protect the interests of the bookseller and the continuing survival of bookshops, no matter how strong the case may be for book clubs when considered by themselves.

School Book Clubs

A special kind of book club that has met with great success in the United States is the school book club, using a national school magazine as the basis. Under this plan the teacher, or a classroom committee appointed by the teacher, serves as collection agent and order taker. There are school book clubs for different ages of young people and for different kinds of books.

Subscription Books

Subscription book publishing is something like a book club operation, in that it does not greatly depend on bookshops but makes extensive use of space advertising and direct mail advertising. But subscription selling usually makes wide use of door-to-door sales representatives. The money value of the books sold tends to be quite large, so it is worth going to great lengths to get a subscriber.

The subscription method has been used for many different kinds of books, but the most familiar example is a multivolume encyclopedia. In general, subscription sales representatives try to handle books not regularly available in bookshops. Payment in installments is customary, sometimes on a volume-by-volume basis as the books are delivered over a period of time, or sometimes one-fourth or some other fraction of the total amount in each installment.

In some plans the whole series may be delivered at the outset (if the subscriber establishes a general credit standing), and sometimes there is a special incentive such as an additional volume or a case to hold the books as a reward for full payment in advance.

The subscription method has been used with great success in Latin America, not only for *colleciones* (sets of books) in various fields but also quite extensively for medical books.

The Lesson of the Book Clubs

Perhaps book club methods and subscription book methods will not be immediately useful in all developing countries. But the lesson those inventions in book publishing offer may be not so much the specific plan as the creative imagination which developed methods of reaching millions of people who were not buying books until the new device was created. No foreigner can tell exactly what plan will work in any contry, but publishers with active minds and a desire both to make a profit and to serve their fellow citizens may be able to find a way.

15

Translations: Windows on the World

TRANSLATIONS OPEN windows on the world, and make contributions to the mind and spirit that are not possible in any other way. No matter what stage of development a country has reached, it cannot get along without translated books. Yet translation projects have special difficulties and problems for the publisher, not only in editorial preparation but also at the business and economic level. This chapter will consider some of the ways in which publication of translations differs from other publishing.

Through the ages, translations have been among the most influential books. The Western world, especially, is in deep gratitude for the enrichment and stimulus which came through the translations made at the court of Haroun al-Rashid and Mamoun during the Golden Age of Baghdad. The translations from Greek classics to Arabic, and later from those translations and from original works by Arab and Persian scholars into European languages, made one of the most important contributions to the Western Enlightenment.

But one need not think of only one period to find examples of how translation has affected world thought. Plato, Aristotle, Al Razi, Montesquieu, Jefferson, Locke, Marx, Freud, Einstein, and Ortega come to mind as thinkers whose influence through translation has been greater than in the languages in which they wrote.

The usefulness of translations is not limited to exchange between countries or between ancient and modern times. In large countries using many languages, translations from one regional language to another, or from a regional language to the national language, can help create a spirit of brotherhood and understanding within the nation.

In developing countries there may be special justification for translations as a *temporary substitute for certain kinds of books* that, later on, will be written locally. That is merely a way of getting certain kinds of needed books quickly, before local writers and publishers are quite at the point of producing their own originals. But long after that temporary need has been filled by local books, there will still be a desire and need to keep open the "windows on the world" through translations from other countries, no matter how many books are being written locally.

One can observe in the United States, for example, that the more developed local writing has become, the larger the number of translations published. With the exception of the kinds of books (for instance, primary and secondary school textbooks) which will always be preferred in the original rather than a translated form, books are not competitive but actually support and encourage each other. Book publishing development is all in one piece, and the interest in translations continues permanently.

Western countries, and especially the United States, have been slow in recognizing the need for translation from Asian and African and Latin American sources, and have concentrated too heavily in the past on translations from one European language to another. But that fault is being corrected. Much still needs to be done, but in the United States there has probably been more publishing of translations from Asia, Africa, and Latin America in the last forty years than in all previous American history.

In this chapter we will consider the following aspects of translation projects from the publisher's point of view: (1) title selection, (2) the mechanics of the translation process, (3) the issues of adaption when translating into the new language, and (4) some of the economic problems.

Title Selection

Because foreign organizations are frequently involved in some way in translation projects, the first and most important thing to say on the subject of title selection is that *local people must pick the books*. The people making the selection, or advising the publisher about the books on which capital is to be risked, must have not only a superior command of the language from which the translation is to be made but—just as surely—an understanding of the needs and interests of the readers in the new language. Unless the selectors have both qualifications, the right books will not be picked.

One question that must always be in mind is whether the *additional* readers of a translated edition will be numerous enough to justify the cost. For instance, it would be ridiculous to incur the cost and labor of translating a British work in chemistry into one of the African languages of Ghana, where every reader intellectually competent to use the book was educated in the English language. On the other hand, translation of such a work into Portuguese might make the book available to thousands of Brazilian readers who could not conveniently use the original; or a translation into French would reach thousands of Africans to whom the work would otherwise be inaccessible; and there might be similar justification for translation into the national language in Indonesia, where the older generation was educated in Dutch and the younger one in Bahasa Indonesia.

There are certain kinds of books, of course, for which good translations are very difficult to make. Some people say flatly that "poetry cannot be translated." That may not be entirely true, but there is no doubt that a poet is needed as translator, and the result is more likely to be a new poem, using the original theme, than a literal translation. Certainly many students of Persian say that the famous English translation of Omar Khayyam by Fitzgerald "may be good literature, but it isn't Omar."

Poetry is merely the clearest example of the kind of literature in which the exact words in the original writing have color and overtones and subtle meanings that cannot be copied exactly in translation. But there are many other kinds of books with the same problems. This may be especially true in books for very young children involving rhyming sounds or other plays on words that cannot be the same in the new language. The people selecting the books to be translated have to judge the difficulty of such problems against the overall value of the book itself.

In general it can be said that the lower the level of literacy the more difficult it is to make a translation that is faithful to the original and yet has high interest for the reader. And, in contrast, the higher one goes in the literacy scale, the easier it is for a skilled writer to make an exact translation that is both accurate and readable (excepting, of course, translation of books dealing with modern technology for which the terms may not exist in the new language).

In the field of supplementary reading, translations can be especially useful in "opening windows" by giving impressions of how people live in other parts of the world. In spite of the difficulty of making good translations of children's books, as just noted, it is worth making the effort in order to broaden horizons for readers of the translated editions. Both translated books and original books dealing with foreign characters and foreign scenes have for many years been bestsellers in the American juvenile market. Ferdinand, Babar, Heidi, Ping, Ali Baba—from Spain, France, Switzerland, China, and Iraq—have long been among the most popular characters in children's books in the United States as in many other countries.

Supplementary reading books of an informational sort, such as popular science, can be adapted as described in a later section of this chapter; and they can be of highest value both in developing an interest in reading and in extending formal classroom teaching.

To summarize about choosing books, every book selected for translation should be judged not only on its own merit in the original edition but according to the likelihood that it can be made attractive, meaningful, and genuinely useful in translation. An additional question is whether adaptation of a proper sort will make a book right even if it would not be fully suitable in a direct and unadapted translation.

The Mechanics of the Translation Process

After selecting the book, the next most important act of the publisher in any translation project is the selection of the translator. Far too much translation has been done—in all ages and countries—by uninspired hack workers who have no true literary ability. Bad books will result if the translator has merely the patience to plod along, turn out more or less passable material, collect payment, and move on to another project. Even some of the ablest writers, with high literary standing for their own work, can slip into that hack-work attitude when doing translations. The need, obviously, is for people who have full knowledge of the original language, a good style in the language of the translation (which *must* be the translator's mother tongue), and a feeling that translation is a high challenge and a difficult but rewarding form of creative literary work.

But there is another requirement for translators besides the one relating to language. Especially in books of fact and information, the translator must understand the subject with which the book deals. Because there are many developing countries in which the number of people with high ability in both languages is very small, it is often impossible to find any one person who is both a good translator and a specialist in the subject of the book. In those cases the best solution may be a two-person team, with one of the two being an expert in the subject matter and the other having the special language skills. For a children's book on animals, for instance, the team might be composed of a zoologist and a writer with experience in writing for young people.

If it is not feasible to have a two-person team work on the translation, it is at least possible to pick as one of the *revisers* who checks the translation before printing someone who has the talent that the translator lacked. And *every* translation should have a reviser, no matter how able or how famous the translator. Even in the cases in which the translator is both an authority on the subject matter and a writer of great skill, a reviser will still be useful in preventing confusion for the reader, if not actual error in translation.

In many countries the tradition of using translator-cum-reviser as a team is so well established that both names customarily appear on the title page, and the translator considers it to be no indignity for the reviser to receive public recognition. In such countries there is even a well-understood scale of payments for the two partners, with the reviser receiving perhaps one-third of the amount per thousand words that is paid to the translator.

There is such a wide variety of problems, peculiar to each language, for translating into all of the languages of interest to the readers of this book that it would be useless to attempt any detailed discussion of them here. The greatest general problem, of course, arises from the lack of good bilingual dictionaries between the original languages and the languages of translation. Because of that lack, publishers who have had experience in translation work use various substitutes.

Among the substitutes for bilingual dictionaries, one of the most useful is a collection of the indexes and glossaries of previously published books on the same subject. They may not all have scholarly authority, but they at least show the translator what terms have been used by previous writers on the subject. Further, there are many partial collections of bilingual equivalents issued by such institutions as the Arab Academies in Cairo and elsewhere, the Dewan Bahasa dan Pustaka in Kuala Lumpur, and ministries of education in many countries.

In any work of scholarship, especially in scientific fields in which terms have not yet been fully established, it is useful for the translator to translate the index before any other part of the book. This method has special value when a team of several translators has to be used for a large work, with need for agreement on terminology from the beginning. And publishers who work consistently in a given field sometimes make a master index of *all* the indexes of the books they have published in that field.

When there is no generally accepted word to use in translation, a decision must be made between coining a new word or—the most frequent practice in most Western languages, at least in the sciences—attempting to adopt the international form of the word, perhaps with some minor variation of spelling.

Of course the one most difficult question in all translation work is whether the translation is to be literally accurate or is to convey the author's full meaning even if that cannot be done with a word-by-word translation. The question can never be answered in general terms. Each issue must be decided separately not only by the brain but also by the conscience of the translator. The one thing that is unforgivable is for a translator merely to skip difficult passages without consulting the publisher and gaining agreement to the omission.

As a final comment about translators' problems, it should be said that the rate of payment, on the basis of wordage, should be higher for children's books than for any other, because the number of words is small yet the literary requirement the most exacting.

Adaptation

Conscience as well as intelligence plays a major part in decisions about adaptation as well as about the question of literal translation just mentioned. Especially in a book on a controversial issue, it would clearly be dishonest to "adapt," even if only by selective omission of passages, in a way that would change the message the author was trying to give the world.

But wise adaptation can be one of the most effective ways of making a book in translation as valuable and as meaningful as it was in the original language. There are many degrees of adaptation, from small changes in words, conversion of measurements to familiar figures, and so on, to major changes involving omission or addition of whole chapters, substitution of entirely new artwork, or—at the extreme end of the scale—the writing of a virtually new work based on the original.

Something like adaptation is the commissioning of an introduction by a well-known local writer or a specialist in the subject matter of the book. This helps to make clear to the reader starting the book the local significance of the work from abroad which might otherwise seem "strange."

And in books of facts or information the text can be made much more understandable if examples cited are from the local culture rather than objects or customs from across the sea. It is impossible, or at least usually improper, to do this in works of fiction in which the foreign scene is part of the story and is one of the "window-opening" values of the book. It would be silly for Westerners to "adapt" *Hajji Baba of Isfahan*, for instance, and call the hero "Bob Evans of Liverpool" and wipe out all the Isfahani references that give the book its charm and special character.

Merely to suggest the kinds of adaptations that can be considered, here are some examples from the lists of publishers in various countries who cooperated with Franklin Book Programs in issuing translations:

1. In a book for young poeple about girls who became famous, the Indonesian edition omitted two of the less interesting chapters about Western women and added new ones on two famous Indonesian women, Kartini and Maria Ulfa Santoso.

2. In the Bengali edition of a children's book on the weather, examples of South Asian weather replaced the North American examples in the original.

3. In all of the Franklin-sponsored translations of the *Columbia-Viking Desk Encyclopedia*, the staff in each country discarded thousands of the entries of purely Western interest in the American book and wrote thousands of new entries dealing with Eastern religion, history, art, animals, plants, and so forth.

4. In the Arabic edition of a book quoting occasional passages from the Bible, the editor supplied footnotes giving parallel quotations from the Koran.

5. In hundreds of editions of informational books showing young people making experiments or having experiences demonstrating scientific facts, new drawings were made to show local faces, local dress, and familiar local objects instead of the foreign examples in the original books.

6. In the Urdu edition of an introduction to painting for young people, some of the original pictures that would have been offensive in a Muslim country were omitted, and new illustrations presented some of the works of the great Pakistani painter, Chughtai.

7. In all of the Franklin-sponsored editions of the book *This I Believe*, the statements of personal belief as published were drawn only in part from the original book; an equal number were newly written by famous people in the countries in which the translated editions were published.

8. In the Portuguese edition of a North American book, *A Parent's Guide to Children's Reading*, the Brazilian editor substituted examples of books in Portuguese for the English-language books cited in the original.

The Economics of Publishing Translations

From the publisher's point of view, the most basic economic fact about publishing translations is that there is frequently need for paying an extra amount for editorial preparation. Unless the publisher is a "pirate," or is publishing works no longer in copyright, something must be paid in royalty or some other fee to the original proprietor in the foreign country. In addition, a royalty or a flat fee must be paid to the translator and reviser in the country of the new publication. Also, the in-house copyediting cost of a translation is often at least 50 percent higher than for an original manuscript.

It is for that reason of double cost that publishers, when selling translation rights to a publisher in another country, usually recognize the justice of charging less than the royalty that would be normal for a book in their own language. There is an additional special problem when the levels of the economies in the two countries are quite different from each other. An amount that would seem fair from the point of view of the original publisher may be simply impossible when judged in terms of the local economy of the publisher who wants to issue the translation. In such cases the publisher who is selling the rights, if wise and experienced, will adjust the rates to the new conditions.

Another problem, partly related, arises in countries which impose so high a tax on royalties that are transmitted to the original publisher that the amount paid by the translating publisher may be cut nearly in half by the time the money arrives in the proprietor's country. In such cases, also, a rule of reason must prevail. The translating publisher must be prepared—if wishing to continue issuing translations and if there is no chance of changing the country's tax rules—to pay more for the translation rights than would otherwise seem to be justified.

An economic fact underlying everything about translations is that, in general, the foreign authors are not well known, and the publisher must frequently take special care, and perhaps incur special cost, in promotion to balance the lack of automatic interest. The name of the translator, the name of the author of the introduction, the new artwork, the cover design, the attractiveness of the title in the new language—all of these factors can be useful in promoting a translation. U Nu's sponsorship in the 1950s of a Burmese translation of an American book was undoubtedly the reason for its becoming the all-time best seller in Burma up to that time.

Conclusion

Because we have given so much attention to the special difficulties of translation work, we should emphasize that many of the most successful publishing projects in all history—successful in profit for the publisher as well as in influence and in literary value—have been translations. The American combined catalogue *Paperbound Books in Print*, listing the titles which were so successful that they went into large reprint editions in paperback, includes hundreds and hundreds of translations. According to Unesco, the number of books published annually in translation has been about 50,000. Although many of them were of course translations from European languages into the languages of developing countries, almost 70 percent of the total were published in the developed countries themselves. In fact, the more highly developed a country's book industry, the more likely it is to have an active list of translations from other languages.

Translations will continue to be published in all countries, whether developed or developing, and will continue to make contributions, as they have through history, not only in transmitting the thoughts of great thinkers to all nations but in giving all people a sense of participating in the lives of others throughout the world.

IV

Building for the Future

16

Libraries, Literacy, and Reading Development

BOOK PUBLISHERS who want to help their own future, in addition to helping the educational and economic advance of their countries, will do everything they can to aid development of libraries, the intelligent planning and carrying out of literacy campaigns, and improvement in the teaching of reading. These are the most effective ways of increasing the number of people reading books, and of increasing the number of books that book readers will want to buy.

All good citizens want to help bring these things about, but the book publisher has an additional economic incentive.

Libraries, literacy, reading development, and book publishing are all closely related, and improvement in any one element has an immediate helpful effect on the others. Libraries cannot exist unless a book publishing industry is producing the books the libraries need; and book publishing of the many kinds depending largely on sales to libraries (for instance, supplementary reading books for young people) cannot exist without libraries.

Literacy campaigns, by producing future book readers, are "manufacturing customers for publishers." However, the publishers must make available the right sort of reading material for new literates, or most of the people trained in literacy campaigns will sink right back into illiteracy.

The Enjoyment of Reading

The enjoyment of reading, once discovered by a new reader, makes possible education even without adequate teachers or further schooling, *provided* there is access to books that are enjoyable to read because they meet personal needs and interests. Encouragement of "reading development" of that sort, progressing from the lowest to steadily higher levels of reading, is clearly in the business interest of the book publishers. But unless the book publishers provide the sort of reading material that will appeal to new readers, the school systems and the libraries cannot do their jobs.

The statements above are obvious and familiar. But we repeat them because they are of such overwhelming importance to the publisher's long-term economic welfare. And the Western compilers of this book confess with shame that it took Western publishers some centuries to discover them. In the United States, to cite one example, it is only in the last fifty years that the relationships have been fully understood and American publishers have taken initiative in trying to help advance library and reading development.

There are many signs that the developing countries are moving directly toward objectives in many fields, without going the roundabout way of Europe and America. Perhaps that will be the case in this matter of publishers' support of and help for libraries and reading development. Nothing could be more hopeful for the economic prosperity—and the educational value—of book publishing in Asia, Africa, and Latin America than a determined effort by the publishers in those areas to mobilize public support for (1) a nationwide library system, (2) an effective follow-up of literacy campaigns by provision of reading material for new literates, and (3) improved methods of teaching reading (and of demonstrating the *enjoyment* of reading) in the schools.

We shall try in this chapter to set down some of the things publishers may wish to have in mind about libraries, literacy campaigns and reading development, and publishers' cooperation with libraries. These are extremely complicated subjects that have been deeply studied by professional specialists in many countries. We can do no more here than suggest some general considerations from the standpoint of national welfare and the publishers' business interests.

The Publisher's Best Friend

Libraries are book customers in themselves; the more libraries there are, the more such customers there will be. Libraries also develop the appetite for reading which will produce a horde of new individual customers in the coming period. The library is thus the publisher's best friend; and the wise publisher will become the library's best friend in return.

Every country needs a national library, equipped, staffed, and stocked to serve as the central depository of books in that country, and (depending on the library organization in the country) perhaps also to give guidance and direction and to provide cataloguing and purchasing and other central services for all the libraries in the country. The function of that kind of great central library is fairly well understood.

We prefer to emphasize here the smaller decentralized library units such as provincial libraries, public libraries in cities aside from the national capital, branch libraries in big cities, neighborhood reading rooms, book collections for workers in industrial plants, and—probably the most improtant kind of libraries in lasting effect on the mass of the population—school libraries and village libraries.

City libraries. Great cities may be too large for one library building to serve all the people. It is simply too difficult for everyone to come to one place. The obvious solution, used extensively in Western countries, is a system of small branch libraries in different sections. For instance, in the portion of New York City called Brooklyn, with a population of about three million, in addition to the large central library there are fifty-eight smaller libraries.

Because of their size, larger provincial and city libraries have the advantage of being able to support special services, such as preparation of reading lists, arrangement of exhibits, and possibly even maintenance of a library school or at least training courses for librarians. It is also obvious that a large library can afford to have specialists (for instance, a children's librarian) on its staff, while smaller libraries may have to get along with only one librarian, or with no really trained librarian at all.

Large libraries have many advantages, and the emphasis we give in this chapter to smaller libraries must not be thought of as an argument against the big libraries. They are absolutely essential. But almost every developing country has a national library or large public library of some sort, while the development of school and village libraries has had comparatively little attention. And because school and village libraries can extend into the most distant parts of a country, into regions from which the national capital may seem as distant as the farthest foreign country, their development should be the chief subject of attention in the next decade.

School libraries. We considered in Chapter 12 the basic and continuing need for supplementary reading books and observed that they are not frills but an essential part of education. The school library is the easiest, cheapest, and most natural way of making such books available to the children who cannot afford to buy them personally or at least have not yet learned the habit of reading for pleasure.

In a large school the library may also include a few reference books such as a dictionary, encyclopedia, or atlas; it may also include a few books intended not for the students but for the teachers. However, the main purpose of a school library is to offer the young reader a selection of books from which to choose.

Even a tiny collection of a dozen books is better than nothing, though of course a greater variety of tastes can be satisfied if there are more books. Especially at the beginning stages of a school library system, when the individual collections must be small, it is useful and sometimes possible to arrange for exchange of the collections among the schools every few months.

Different countries use different methods of financing school libraries. Sometimes there is central purchase of the books by the ministry of education, which then sends the books to the individual schools. Or sometimes the ministry gives each principal or headmaster a small sum, varying in size according to the number of students in the school, with which to buy the books. There are also a number of countries—Indonesia, for instance, and a number of Latin American countries—in which fathers' clubs or other private groups in local communities make voluntary contributions for buying books.

A variation of the school library idea is a plan for classroom libraries, which involves having a small group of supplementary reading books on open shelves actually in the classroom. This has advantages, of course, in inviting inspection of the books by the students, but administration is more difficult, and it is more expensive both in initial cost and in the cost of lost books than a central system under control of one teacher in the school. It seems probable that a system of classroom libraries, valuable though it can be, may be too difficult and expensive, except for special cases, in the early stages of a school library system.

Only the very largest schools would be able to afford a full-time librarian, but every school with a book collection needs to have *someone* in charge, not merely to care for the books but also to help guide the young people in their use. Usually the headmaster or principal appoints one teacher to have that part-time responsibility; and it is possible to give some training in a brief summer course of a few weeks to all the teachers thus appointed in an area. In addition, a pamphlet can be prepared showing the teacher how to administer the book collection and—much more important in educational terms—how to introduce young people to the use of books, and how supplementary reading can extend and support classroom education.

It should be mentioned, incidentally, that no school library system will work if the teachers are held financially responsible for books lost. Under any such rule, the teachers will naturally do everything possible to limit use of the books; they may even go to the point of storing the books away under lock and key. Some loss of books must be accepted as part of the cost of a school library. Efficient administration will reduce the loss, and that is of course a necessary objective to avoid deliberate encouragement of theft. But it must be recognized that even a stolen book *does* get read, which is the purpose of a book!

For the reasons outlined in Chapter 12, reading by young people is in many ways the most important kind of reading there is. School libraries offer the most efficient and cheapest way of getting young people to read, both for the sake of the books they choose and for forming the habit of book reading that will stay with them through their lives.

Village libraries. In some communities it is possible to have the school library serve also as a public library for the local community. This is especially easy to justify when voluntary local contributions have financed the purchase of books. In such conditions the school library may be open for lending books to outsiders during an evening hour or on holidays.

Usually, however, the need for student use of a school library is so great that it is not possible to permit outsiders to borrow the books. In any event, one of the greatest needs in a village library is different from school need: namely a collection of books interesting to adults.

Village libraries are sometimes established by prosperous individuals or by voluntary groups who wish to help their communities. But in many developing countries there is already an extensive system of village centers of some sort, going under such titles as Rural Reconstruction, Community Development, Basic Democracy, the Panchayat System, and so forth. Especially in Latin America, there is participation by Rotary Clubs, Chambers of Commerce, and private civic action groups. The local centers for such movements give the perfect base for a library, and frequently a staff for administering it.

Also, as noted in the next section, many countries have national literacy organizations with centers in different parts of the country, and these also can be used as bases for rural libraries.

When we speak about a village library, the reference is of course to a collection of books, not to the construction of a building. The collection may be kept in a school, at a community center such as just mentioned, at a district magistrate's office, at a gendarme post, or even in the private house of the headman of the village or someone appointed to take charge. In any centrally organized plan the books may be delivered in a wooden box which, when opened, becomes a library shelf; and there are some countries which have tried to arrange for a periodic exchange of the boxes among community centers in a given area.

The greatest obstacle to a system of village libraries does not seem to be a financial one, but the lack of suitable books. Too often the only books that are simple enough for newly literate readers are children's books, and they may not be interesting to adults. This is one of the clearest cases we can cite of the need for cooperation between publishers and the governmental or other authorities in charge of libraries. The publishers need advance assurance that there will be a market if they bring out such books; and the people thinking of setting up libraries need assurance that the right kinds of books will be available. A hand-in-hand advance is clearly necessary.

Although stories, folktales, and other books appealing to the imagination are also necessary, books of practical value are needed in village libraries—books giving useful information about health, agriculture, and child care, and how-to-do-it books of many kinds. One thinks naturally of the ministry of education as the unit of government most concerned with libraries, but it frequently happens that village libraries are of even greater interest to the ministry of health, ministry of agriculture, ministry of economic development, or another agency of government. Alert ministries of information or national guidance recognize the usefulness, from their special point of view, of having book collections throughout the country to help form a spirit of national unity.

Literacy and Reading Development

This great subject is important enough to justify a chapter by itself, or indeed a whole book. In fact many books have been written about it. But there are so many details that have to be worked out according to conditions in each country, and varying according to the system of classroom education and the campaigns for adult literacy, that we shall try to make only the one point that is more important than all the others.

That central fact is that literacy campaigns are wastefully expensive, and in fact morally unjustified, *unless* there is reading material for the new literate after learning to read. That is needed in order to keep the art of reading alive; and if books of the right sort are available it is possible to proceed steadily to higher levels. If there is no suitable material to read, the new ability will be quickly lost. Millions and millions of people are taught to read each year in a variety of literacy or mass education or public enlightenment campaigns in different countries, but the overwhelming majority of them have become illiterate again by the end of the following year. The follow-up of a literacy campaign is absolutely essential.

Literacy campaigns are usually thought of in connection with adults, but in all developing countries the high rate of school dropouts makes the problem of the juvenile new literate even more important. The cost of maintaining schools and teachers is so high that the teaching of reading to people who will shortly drop out of school cannot be economically justified unless there is some chance those people can retain that talent that was so expensively given to them.

New Literates' Magazines

As an interim step, before there are village libraries, or before the new literates are quite ready to use regular books, new literates' magazines have been attempted in a number of countries under sponsorship of the ministry of education or ministry of information and national guidance.

The general idea behind such publications is sound, but too often the people in charge have lacked an understanding of either the reading level or the natural interests of the new literates. As a result the publication has been too difficult for the new reader, and the subject matter has frequently been chosen entirely with child readers in mind.

There have also been cases in which the central idea has seemed to be not reading development but propaganda for the particular group in charge of the government at the time. Encouragement of national unity and explanation of the government's policies are entirely proper elements to include in a new literates' magazine, but even the government's propaganda purpose will be defeated if the publication comes to be regarded merely as a propaganda sheet rather than something the new literate will want to read for its own sake because it is interesting and perhaps also practically useful in personal day-to-day life.

Publishers' Cooperation with Libraries

For the obvious reasons of good citizenship mentioned at the beginning of this chapter, plus the special argument of the publishers' long-term business interest in having libraries produce more future customers, publishers should give high priority to a regular policy of cooperation with libraries.

Such cooperation can take many forms, some of the most important of which are referred to in the next chapter in the listing of things that publishers can do jointly. But perhaps the most important is development of a feeling of partnership with library people, and a recognition that neither library development nor book publishing development can proceed very far without full cooperation from the other.

Incidentally, wise publishers who succeed in building up this spirit of common interest are able to benefit in a special way through the feedback of information from libraries as to readers' interests. Alert librarians are in better position than anyone else, even including booksellers, to let publishers know the kinds of books that readers want to read.

Reference must also be made, once more, to the relationship of the mass distribution plans discussed in Chapter 13 to the spreading of universal education and an effective library system throughout a country. They are mutually self-supporting.

One of the most pleasing paradoxes in the whole book world is that free circulation of books through libraries automatically increases book sales, because of the numbers of new readers that libraries develop. And, as noted before, a mass distribution plan of offering good books for sale at low prices throughout a country is in itself an important educational institution and a powerful influence for more and better schools, libraries, and literacy campaigns.

Whether through joint efforts along lines suggested in the next chapter or through the individual action of the publishers acting separately, the wise publisher will do everything possible to help establish and strengthen institutions that produce more readers and lead more people to discover the personal rewards of reading.

17

Cooperation among Publishers

AN INDIVIDUAL PUBLISHER has sometimes been able to use imagination, courage, and capital to revolutionize publishing in a whole country. But it is much more usual to see a *cooperative* advance by a group of publishers. Even though they compete with each other in commercial terms, they nevertheless come together for joint efforts in the interest of all of them.

This chapter gives a checklist of the kinds of cooperation among publishers that have been practiced in various countries. We divide the list into six parts, though it will be seen that they are closely interrelated: (1) government relations, (2) book trade relations, (3) joint promotion, (4) facilities for the future book industry, (5) reading development and long-term promotion, and (6) book publishing associations.

Government Relations

The book industry is a small element in the total economy of a country. Educators and librarians, as well as book publishers, know how important the welfare of the book industry is to the nation, but finance ministers and economic planners tend to think of the small amount of money, the small number of people employed, and so forth, rather than the key function of books in national development. Individual publishers appealing to government or to the public to assist book publishing in some way seem just like other businesses seeking favors. If, however, the publishers can present a united front, and especially if they can mobilize the support of educators and intellectual leaders, they have a chance of making their points effectively.

But, as we said in the economic discussion in Chapter 3, the publisher has no right to claim public support unless truly serving the public interest, not merely from day to day but also in building for the future.

Discussed below are some of the areas in which government decisions *may* make or break a publishing industry, and about which the publishers may make joint representations to government, and try to enlist public opinion to support their position.

Import rules. Rules about foreign exchange, import licenses, and governmental red tape will always have a strong effect on publishers' welfare. Paper is the most important item because of the value and size of the import needed (unless the country happens to produce all the paper it needs). But other supplies and equipment are equally important, even though it may be the printer rather than the publisher who does the importing: printing presses, spare parts, ink, glue, films, chemicals, staple wire, and so forth.

The publisher's payment for translation rights is in a similar category even though the "import" in that case is not a physical object.

The booksellers' imports of books are also part of the total book industry picture which the publishers wish to improve. As so frequently noted, the book industry's interests are *common* interests, and publishers should be deeply concerned with the welfare of booksellers and printers. If the help of educators and librarians and intellectual leaders is to be enlisted in solving the publishers' problems, it is of special importance that publishers show *their* interest in helping booksellers, printers, schools, universities, and libraries, not merely the publishing industry.

Postal service. Publishers are interested not only in postage rates on book shipments but in the efficiency of the postal service in general. As we saw in earlier chapters, there are kinds of publishing that are virtually impossible unless there is an effective postal system.

Censorship. Each country has to decide for itself whether it will have censorship, and of what kind. But even if strict censorship exists, book publishers can, with patience and diplomacy, sometimes persuade governments to apply the rules in ways that will give as little obstruction as possible to the normal book trade, aside from the particular books that are forbidden. And in many countries the publishers have joined with other groups in seeking to modify or prevent censorship.

Copyright. Governments will not usually consider copyright laws, or the joining of international copyright organizations, unless there is pressure for this forward move from publishers as well as from authors and printers. And because of industrial interest in international piracy in the audio and video cassette fields, the music and film industries are among the book publishers' strongest allies on copyright issues.

Government competition. Especially in the textbook field, government-sponsored publishing enterprises can ruin private publishing. That may be a deliberate intention, in keeping with national policy. But if, as has happened in many countries, the country does not *intend* wiping out private publishing but merely undertakes state publishing as a way of meeting an immediate practical problem, there is much that the book publishers can do as a group.

Three things are of the highest importance: (1) a soul-searching examination of the ways in which the book industry had been failing to serve the public interest, thus giving the state the excuse and incentive for becoming a publisher itself, (2) a continuing study—with the help of disinterested experts in education—of the quality and educational effectiveness of the state-published books in comparison with books produced in a competitive system, and (3) economic studies showing the true cost, in national terms, of books produced under the two methods.

Book Trade Relations

After the first experience in cooperation of some kind, often in some joint representation to the government, publishers think of forming an association (see section on Book Publishers' Associations below).

If that step is taken, the continuing practical service in book trade relations attracts new members and helps make them willing to pay dues. Among the ways in which this practical service seems, all by itself, to justify association membership, the following ones are the most likely.

Booksellers' credit standing. One of the publisher's biggest problems is collecting the money the booksellers owe. Even aside from the occasional dishonest booksellers, all of them, even the most honorable, have trouble meeting their bills. Therefore every publisher wants to learn everything possible about the standing of a bookseller asking for credit the first time. Also, it is most useful to keep track of changes in that standing. If a bookseller is slow in paying, the publisher wishes to know whether this is merely a temporary difficulty or a sign of real trouble. If it is the former, the publisher may decide to send the bookseller a courteous warning but continue to ship books on credit; but if the bookshop is in real difficulty, the publisher will probably decide to impose a "cash with order" rule for that account.

To decide which policy to follow, the publisher may check with one or two other publishers, but cannot afford the time for inquiring further. The obvious solution for this problem is a cooperative credit bureau, and publisher's associations in a number of countries have established organizations of that sort. They work in different ways, but in general give information (confidentially and only to publisher members) on the credit standing of booksellers. This is done by putting together monthly reports from members (in ways so that the business of particular publishers cannot be identified) showing which booksellers are delinquent by how much, how long they have been in trouble, and so forth.

Although the main purpose of all credit bureaus is to warn publishers about booksellers who are falling behind in their payments, some of them recognize that it is against the publishers' interest to force booksellers out of business if they can be saved. When the credit bureau thinks booksellers are fundamentally sound, it may send a representative to talk with them and with banks in their community. Sometimes the publishers—in the light of the credit bureau's report—may agree to "freeze" the amount already owed, allow limited very short credit on new orders, and make arrangements for installment payments of past-due amounts over a period of time, possibly with the help of a bank loan to the bookseller.

Warehousing. Joint warehousing, which has been used for many years in developed countries, and has become more prevalent recently, will in some circumstances be useful in developing countries also.

Exchange of information. Among the kinds of information that can be usefully exchanged, besides the facts about booksellers' credit mentioned above, are rates paid to printers for book manufacture, salaries paid to staff, sales volume, and so forth. Many of these items of information may be regarded as trade secrets which publishers do not wish to share with their competitors. Usually, therefore, the questionaires through which the publishers supply information are sent to a chartered accountant, trusted by all and pledged to preserve secrecy. The accountant puts together the facts from the separate reports and sends the members only the consolidated summary.

Joint Promotion

Included in this category of cooperative efforts would be sponsorship of exhibits, prize awards, joint catalogues, reading lists, bibliographies of special kinds of books, book trade magazines, and so forth—as well as the long-term projects mentioned below (section on Reading Development and Long-Term Promotion).

Facilities for the Future Book Industry

Competitive though publishers are with their business rivals, they share a common interest in the future of their industry, and they can often act together along such lines as the following:

Capital. The problem of capital is one of the most difficult facing the publisher, as we saw in Chapter 3. It is therefore in the interest of all publishers to help persuade banks and "development corporations" of the need to provide business loans for book industry development. The publishers may also be useful to the printers who serve them and whose capital—or lack of it—may have an influence on the publishers' own capital problem.

Wholesalers and jobbers. As we saw in Chapter 8, there may be situations in which the lack of a good wholesaling organization prevents books from reaching remote areas. In such cases, publishers may decide through at least informal joint effort to encourage establishment of such a distribution system.

"Service industries" for the book industry. In industrially developed countries there are many specialized businesses providing services to the book manufacturers so that each printer does not have to maintain the expensive equipment and specially trained staff.

Among these service industries are gluemakers, ink grinders, "sorts" casters, engravers, roller casters, color separators, cover laminators, and bindery suppliers. Publishers can help encourage establishment of such industries—where they are justified—by letting printers know of their coming needs and assisting the printers in their own studies. The industry statistics gathered through exchange of information as suggested in the section above on booksellers' credit standing will of course be useful in such planning.

Book industry training. Cooperation among publishers (and sometimes also including printers and booksellers as well) can give a fine basis for book industry training. Some aspects of training programs are considered in Chapter 21.

Graphic art. Cooperative efforts at improving graphic art standards and the design of books have had notable success in many countries. Exhibits, prize competitions, and assistance to schools of fine and applied arts are among the methods used.

Reading Development and Long-term Promotion

Enlightened publishers can do some things individually in working for long-term reading development to "manufacture customers" for the future, but most of the important things require cooperative effort not only by publishers but also by librarians, educators, and public-spirited citizens interested in national welfare.

Improvement in schools, literacy campaigns, and everything relating to the teaching of reading comes to mind first. But it is in the library field that publishers have been most effective in helping to organize opinion to strengthen the institutions and provide them with additional funds for their work. Book purchases by libraries increase as a result of this, of course, but it is the long-run influence on book reading in general that has the most lasting effect.

Publishers have taken a lead, in various countries, in organizing and carrying out a national Library Week during which ceremonies, speeches, radio programs, and other public events focus public interest on the part the library plays in national life.

Book Publishers' Associations

Informal cooperation among small voluntary groups of publishers makes it possible to carry out some of the joint projects mentioned above. But an association open to all qualified publishers in the country gains wider participation and a wider sharing of the cost of these activities for the good of all.

Among specialized associations, one of exceptional interest in the International Association of Scholarly Publishers, founded in 1972. It publishes a newsletter packed with information about developments worldwide and holds periodic international meetings where publishers present formal papers and exchange experiences. The officers, of course, change from time to time, but the true internationality of the organization is demonstrated by the fact that at the present writing the president is at a Norwegian university press, the vice-president at one in the Philippines, and the secretary-general in the United States. An exceptional regional group is the African

Books Collective, formed under the leadership of the *African Publishing Record* in England, but now under full African control.

A few countries have founded their own associations of scholarly publishers, which hold meetings and, in some cases, develop training programs. They also provide an opportunity for the publishers to speak as one to governments and to international or national funding agencies. Too often, however, such organizations depend on the volunteer efforts of one person and as a result go up and down in vitality.

An association may start with no full-time staff but merely volunteer officers who carry out the work of the organization. Sooner or later, however, at least some full-time staff becomes necessary, and that is when the association really begins to be useful to the publishers and to society.

The cost of running the association is borne by its members in some way, sometimes according to a sliding scale of dues based on the members' total annual book sales in the previous year. As in the case of the exchange of information mentioned earlier, the facts about sales are given confidentially to a chartered accountant, so that no individual publisher's sales need be known to the fellow members who, in commercial terms, are rivals.

V

Special Subjects

18

Publishing Rights and Contracts

PUBLISHING METHODS and customs are so different from country to country, and there is such variation in the laws about property rights in general (whether or not there are specific laws about literary property rights), that it would be pointless to try to write down here the wording of a "model contract." Also, there are natural differences of opinion between authors and publishers about what a contract should say, even within one country.

We can start by remembering, from Chapter 2, that the author of a book can be thought of as something like an inventor. The author is the owner of the publishing rights to the book that has been "invented," unless the author has been hired by someone to produce the book, in which case that person or organization may be the owner, depending on the terms of the writer's agreement with the sponsor. Under the custom of most countries, and according to the laws of countries having laws on the subject, the author is recognized as the only person who can authorize publication of the book.

An author-publisher contract is an agreement under which the author permits the publisher to use those publishing rights under specific conditions. The payment of royalty or some other fee is usually one of the chief conditions, but there are other important conditions also.

Exclusivity is the most basic point in publishing contracts. When the author grants certain rights to a publisher, those rights are given *exclusively* to that publisher alone, unless there is a specific exception mentioned in the contract; and unless there is such exception, the author cannot grant the same rights to anyone else. That protection is absolutely essential for the publisher who risks money in issuing

217

the book and whose investment could be ruined by a rival edition brought out by someone else.

As is explained more fully in the section on Other Rights below, the author does not have to grant *all* kinds of publishing rights at one time. The author may, for instance, hold back the translation rights in order to make a separate agreement with a foreign publisher sometime later. But the particular rights that *are* granted under any contract are normally given exclusively to one publisher.

We shall devote the rest of the chapter to the listing of the chief provisions often included in contracts to handle the details of agreement.

Author's Warranty

A major point in most contracts is the *warranty* in which the author guarantees that he/she is the sole author and owner of the book, is legally entitled to grant or assign the publishing rights, and has not previously given them to anyone else.

The author is usually required to guarantee not only that he/she has not stolen anything from another author but also that nothing libels another person or is obscene or improperly invades privacy or any other right. It is implicit in the author's warranty that the author will secure all needed permissions for quotation from other sources, for reproduction of maps or illustrations, or for any other use of previously copyrighted materials.

These additional warranties are of course subject to wide interpretation and their value may be finally determined only in a court of law—if, indeed, the author has the financial resources for paying a judgment against the book.

In actual practice, under the laws of some countries, the publisher may be held equally responsible with the author, for instance for treason, no matter what the contract says. As to money damages, however, the author is usually required to agree that he/she will "hold the publisher harmless" (that is, that he/she will bear the cost of any damages) if the author's warranties prove to have been untrue and someone wins a legal case against the book.

Grant of Rights

Having declared, in the above warranties, that he/she is the owner of the rights, the author then says that he/she grants the publishing rights to the publisher "under the conditions stated in this contract." The grant tells what rights are given, and in what geographical area they are valid. (Restrictions may be in general terms here, and then may be stated in more detail under "other rights" as described below.) A Buenos Aires author, for example, may give the publisher "the right to publish, or cause others to publish, in all forms in the Spanish language throughout the world." Or instead of "in all forms" (which would include magazine series, for instance) the grant may say only "in book form." Or instead of saying "throughout the world" the grant may say "in the countries of Latin America" (which would exclude publication in Spain, for which the author would be free to make a separate agreement).

Usually it is agreed whether copyright is to be taken out in the name of the author or the publisher. (For discussion of some of the problems of international copyright, see Paul Gleason's article, "Copyright, Licensing, and Piracy" in the Appendix.)

Option on Future Books

Because a publisher, in bringing out a book, is in effect making an investment in the author as well as in the particular book—and may be launching the author on a profitable career—the author is often asked to promise to give the publisher an *option* on his or her next book. That is, the author agrees to let the publisher have the first chance to sign a contract on a new book, before offering it to anyone else.

The option clause does not usually give the details of a contract on a new book, nor does the publisher guarantee to publish it. There is usually wide possibility for either party to escape from legal (though not moral) obligations under the option clause, and its value may therefore be chiefly as a statement of mutual good will and good intentions at the time of signing the contract.

The author is often asked to agree not to write a directly competing book. This is of special importance in the textbook field, and
publishers are likely to bring legal action to prevent the author from
giving a competing book to another firm.

Agreement to Publish

In accepting the grant from the author, the publisher usually
agrees—if the manuscript is satisfactory in form and content—to
publish the book in a specified period of time or "within a reasonable time after receiving the manuscript." The time when the manuscript is to be delivered is stated specifically in the contract. The
publisher cannot be forced to bring out the book if there is a later
change of mind; but if the book is not published, the publisher can
be forced to give up the contract under the termination clause (see
the section on Termination below) and, under some conditions, may
have to pay damages to the author.

The publisher normally promises to issue the book "in suitable
form." Sometimes, if the author has enough standing for a good
bargaining position, other requirements may be imposed, such as a
promise by the publisher to consult the author about the design, the
selling price, the advertising budget, or other details that are normally regarded as being the sole business of the publisher.

Payment to the Author

The most normal kind of payment is a fixed percentage (for instance, 10 percent) of the retail selling price of the book for all copies
sold. The percentage may increase as the number of copies sold goes
up (for instance, if 10 percent is fixed for the first sales, the contract
may provide 12.5 percent after 5,000 copies and 15 percent after
10,000 copies). There is a growing tendency among publishers in
developed countries to base royalty not on the list price of the book
but on the net income the publisher receives from its sale.

Less than the full percentage may be provided for certain kinds of
sales or certain special editions of the book, for instance foreign

sales, sales in very cheap editions, and sales at very high discounts. A special category of the last is a sale at or below the manufacturing cost of the book—a point to which the publisher may finally be driven with a very unsuccessful book. For such *remainder* sales the contract may say no royalty will be paid at all.

The time of payment of royalty is fixed in the contract. The frequency of payment is sometimes greater in the first couple of years after publication than later on. In order to give the publisher time for making up accounts, actual payment is usually several months after the period covered. For instance, royalty earned by a book during the year ending December 31 may not be paid until March 31.

Other payments to the author, aside from the basic royalty, are usually described in the sections of the contract dealing with "other rights."

Advance Payment of Royalty

As proof of good will, and in order to persuade the author to sign a contract, the publisher may offer a lump sum payment to the author at the time of signing the contract (and sometimes an additional advance at the time the finished manuscript is delivered).

This is an *advance against royalty*, and is charged against the author's royalty account. No further payment is made until the royalty the book earns has repaid the publisher for that advance. Theoretically, this amount can be recovered by the publisher if the author does not deliver the manuscript, but usually not if the book is published but simply fails to earn that much in royalty. The cost of such unearned advances to authors can be a major factor of cost for firms that are careless in the making of advances.

Other Rights

The work an author did in producing a book can be presented to the public in many different forms besides the first publication in book form. The clauses of a contract dealing with *other rights*, or *subsidiary rights* as they are sometimes called, make clearer than the general grant (section on Grant of Rights above) just which of these additional rights the publisher is authorized to use or to handle on the author's behalf; and how any income deriving from those "other rights" is to be divided between author and publisher.

It is fairly well established in the publishing practice of many countries that the original publisher is justified in having a good share of the income from rights to use the work *in printed form* (books, magazines, newspapers, etc.), because publication in those forms relates so closely to the publisher's own business in handling the original book. But "publication" in *non*printed form (theater, film, radio, tape, videotape, and television) is much less closely related to the book business, and in those cases the publisher may not have any participation in the rights at all, or only a minor share of the income. For example, many contracts provide that any income from translation rights will be divided fifty-fifty between author and publisher; but if the publisher has any part in the handling of dramatic rights, the publisher may receive only 5, 10, or 15 percent of the income from that source.

The most important categories of the rights for use in printed form are: reprintings in book form (including licensing to book clubs), translations, serialization in newspapers or magazines, and use of excerpts in anthologies.

In recent years the value of the rights for reprinting in book form have become, in some countries, more important than all the other rights put together, including the basic royalties on the original book. This is because of the development of book clubs and paperback reprint publishing in which the quantity of books published may be some hundreds of thousands as compared with just a few thousand in the original edition. In early stages of publishing development in any country the clause related to reprints can be negotiated fairly easily between an author and a publisher because no great amount of money is at stake. But the more active the mass distribution book industry becomes, the harder the bargaining will be on this point.

Free Copies and Purchase of Books

The contract says how many free copies (perhaps ten) of the book will be given to the author, and the special discount allowed for buying additional copies. On this latter point, the contract sometimes refers to "purchase of copies *not for resale*," in order to prevent the author from using the favorable discount for competing with booksellers. Sometimes the author is allowed a special discount on *any* of the publisher's books.

Manuscript and Proof

The contract usually requires the author to present the manuscript "complete and ready for the printer," but as we have noted in Chapter 5, only an inexperienced publisher will believe that literally! The provision is useful, however, for protecting the publisher against an author who is entirely irresponsible about the condition in which the manuscript is turned in.

The contract also obliges the author to read galley proofs "promptly" (sometimes within a specified amount of time) and to pay for the excess cost of "author's alterations" beyond the free allowance, as explained in Chapter 5.

It is usual, likewise, to state in a contract whether the author or the publisher is to be responsible for preparing the index, or any other material not of the author's creation to be added to the book.

Arbitration

In order to save the cost of lawsuits, and to get a prompt decision, in the event of disagreement about interpretation of a contract, or about compliance with it by either party, provision is sometimes made for arbitration. If so, it is usually stated that, if such disagreement occurs, each party will choose one arbitrator and those two will select a third; and the majority decision of those three arbitrators will be accepted by both the author and the publisher. (In some countries publishers sometimes try to avoid arbitration clauses, which they think may be disadvantageous to them because lay arbitrators may be more likely than law courts to award speculative damages.)

Termination

A publishing contract in most countries lasts until the expiration of the copyright (and renewal) on the given book. It is usually provided, however, that the author can recover all the rights granted and cancel the contract if the publisher fails to publish the book or lets it go out of print and fails to reprint it within a reasonable time after the author has sent written notice.

Publisher's Obligation

The publisher's obligation to publish, to pay royalty, and so forth is usually stated to depend upon receipt of manuscript, illustrations, and other items at a certain date, in a certain size, in a specified physical condition (usually typewritten), and "in form and content satisfactory to the publisher." The last, of course, can lead to endless argument. In most court cases in Western countries it has been established that a publisher cannot be legally forced to publish a book it does not want. But to avoid disgrace in the eyes of a country's authors, the publisher choosing not to publish must be able to show that the manuscript was not "in form and content" what was expected when the contract was signed.

19

Some Notes on Accountancy in Book Publishing

BOOK PUBLISHING IS in many ways just like any other business. The system of accounting that is followed in any country (whether that system was locally developed or based on British or French or other foreign methods) will in general be the right one to use in book publishing houses just as in other firms; and in fact the systems do not differ in general principles very widely anyway.

But book publishing has a few characteristics making it different from other businesses. This brief chapter will describe some of those peculiarities and say a few words about certain accounting methods that have been used for dealing with them.

We do not mean to suggest that the peculiarities are found only in book publishing. In some degree they appear in other businesses also. But the particular combination may be new to people whose previous experience has been in more familiar forms of business activity.

This is *not* a technical guide to accountancy but merely a comment—for the book publisher who is not an accountant—on some of the distinctive aspects of the publishing business. The publisher's own bookkeepers and the chartered accountants who advise them will know better than a foreigner how the accounts should be set up in detail in accordance with local accounting practice.

Many of the special accounting problems of book publishing result from three things: (1) the large number of separate "products" (books) that are dealt with and the small size of the units of sale (perhaps single copies), (2) the relatively high cost and long period needed for the preparatory phase of producing each product, and

(3) the great variation in the length or shortness of commercial life of each product, and the variation in value during its life.

We shall look at the effect of those conditions on book publishing accountancy under these three heads: (1) the need for book-by-book accounting, sometimes called *title accounting*, (2) the value of the *inventory method*, and (3), as a result of those two considerations, the advantages of using an *accrual* rather than a *cash* method of accounting in book publishing.

The Need for Book-by-Book Accounting (Title Accounting)

A producer of rice or wheat deals with just one product, whether the amount is one ton or a million tons. An automobile manufacturer may deal with a single product (one model of one kind of car) or, more usually, with several, each of which has its own production cost, sales appeal, and special market. A large manufacturer of hardware has a much more complex business and may handle a fairly large number of separate items. But there are not many producers in the world who are concerned with as many different items as the book publisher. The book publisher who has been in business any length of time will have hundreds, or even thousands, of separate "products."

Every new book is a new product, with its own economic problems which are different from those of all the other products with which the publisher deals.

Many of the publisher's expenses (such as administration, rent, electricity, telephone, and shipping service) are incurred on behalf of all products; and the accounting system should include some method of dividing up those general costs and assigning them in proper shares to the particular books.

But each product also has its own specific costs which must be identified and charged to the individual book. These specific costs include royalty payments to the author, payments to the paper merchant and printer for materials and physical manufacture, and direct expenses for advertising.

Merely to lump together those costs for all the books would give the publisher no information about the profit and loss on the individual books. Therefore, an accounting system for a book publishing house normally has not only the general accounts for the business as a whole but also *title accounts* for keeping track of income and expense, book by book. The value of this information to the sales department—and even to the editorial department—is obvious.

For this title accounting there is usually a separate card or ledger sheet on which bookkeepers can record every item of income and expense for the given book. But a simplified method can be considered, at least for the beginning. That is to record on the title account the actual expense for the three specific items (author's royalty, manufacturing cost, and advertising), and to keep careful record of the number of copies of the book that are sold.

The publisher's studies of the general accounts will show what average discount has been allowed to purchasers of different kinds of books, and a fairly close approximation of the sales income for each book can be made if the number of copies that have been sold and the retail price of each are known. And to find out what general overhead costs should be added to the specific costs for each book, the method described in Chapter 3, basing it on the previous year's experience, can be used.

For policy guidance it is thus possible to make a rough estimate of profit and loss on any particular book at any time by combining the *actual specific costs* with the *estimated overhead costs*, and then comparing that total expense with the *estimated sales income*. For instance, if 4,900 copies had been sold of the hypothetical book studied in Chapter 3 (see Tables 1 to 4), the *estimated profit* would be §329 (see next page). It must be emphasized that this method of calculating profit and loss on particular books is only an approximation. Eventually the publisher will probably want to have a system under which the actual income for each book will be credited to its title account. In any event, the suggestion of estimating applies only to this special question of title accounting. For the accounts of the publishing house as a whole, full accuracy according to normal accounting principles is, of course, required.

Income

Sales income from 4,900 copies of a book with a retail selling price of §0.80, after deducting the estimated average discount of 30%	§2,744

Expense		§2,415
Royalty to author (10% of §0.80 × 4,900)	§392*	
Manufacturing cost	1,137*	
Advertising	200*	
Overhead cost estimated at 25% of sales income	686†	
Estimated profit		§329

The Value of the Inventory Method

Because the preparation cost of a book is high, and the time required may be long, and because the books produced in any one year may be sold over a considerable number of future years, an inventory method has great advantages in book publishing accounting.

If 10,000 copies of a book have been produced at a total cost of §1,983, the cost per copy is §0.1983. If a copy is taken from inventory to sell or to give away, that amount of §0.1983 is credited to the inventory account that "owned" it, and the same amount is charged to an expense account called something like "cost of books sold." Meanwhile the inventory account continues to "own" all the unsold

---

*These three items would be actual figures from the *title account*; the two others would be estimates for income and overhead.

†The overhead estimate of 25% is just an example. In many developed book industries a 40% overhead allowance is more usual.

copies of the book, and the value of the books in inventory is an asset for the publisher to show on the balance sheet along with the bank account and other assets.

If, after a period of time, the publisher sees that there are more copies of the book than can ever be sold, it may be decided to reduce the value of the inventory for that book, or perhaps to *write it off* entirely. If that is done, the inventory for that book in the future will be shown at no value. And the *write-off* is of course charged as an item of publishing expense for the year in which the adjustment is made. Publishers who use the inventory method review the status and prospects (that is, they re-estimate the probable value of the inventory) for each book once a year, deciding what new write-offs may be advisable.

The publisher has the unsold books in mind when looking at the profit-and-loss picture for each book. For instance, a calculation at a given time may show that the firm has about broken even in income and expense after selling 7,000 copies of a 10,000-copy edition; and if the book is still selling well to the public and it looks as if the whole edition will be sold eventually, the publisher can make a rough estimate of the additional income for the remaining 3,000 copies, and see that there will be good profit on the book as a whole.

The Advantages of Accrual Accounting

Accountants will see at once the direction in which the above discussion of inventories is taking us. The method described requires an accrual rather than a cash method of accounting. The accrual method takes account of assets and liabilities, whereas the cash method merely looks at how much money was paid out and how much taken in.

Under cash methods, the publisher's accounts might show, in a given year, payments of §50,000 and receipts of only §20,000. That would make it look as if there had been a loss of §30,000 in the year! But much of the money spent might have been for production of new books that had barely started to sell, or perhaps had not even been published.

The accrual method corrects this kind of inaccurate picture. Under accrual accounting, the publisher does not treat as current cost the full amount paid the printer but only that part included in the "cost of books sold"—that is, just the printing cost of those copies that were actually taken from inventory and sold. The value of the unsold books remaining in the inventory is an asset.

The example just mentioned shows how the accrual method lets the publisher see the true facts of what, under cash methods, would look like a business disaster. But accrual methods are just as useful in correcting misleading impressions of the opposite sort.

The overall cash statement might show that the publisher had paid out only §20,000 while, in the same year, the firm had cash income of §50,000. That would sound wonderful! But accrual accounting might show that the publisher had not yet paid the printer for a number of the books, and that royalties in large amounts were owing to authors for books already sold, and that much of the income came from books produced in previous years for which a large item of "cost of books sold" should be charged in the current year, even though there was no actual payment for manufacture of those books during the year.

Under accrual accounting, the major inventory assets are likely to be: *work in process*, the asset representing costs already incurred for books not yet completed (included here are advance royalty payments to authors, fees to illustrators, translators, etc., and installment payments to printers before the books are published); *paper inventory*, the value of paper purchased in advance but not yet used in producing books; and *book inventory*, the manufacturing cost of the books that have been produced but not yet sold.

Accrual accounting may seem at first to require more work than the cash method, but experienced publishers' accountants say it is actually easier in the long run. And it is the only way for a book publisher to have a realistic view of actual profit and loss and the value of assets.

These notes will seem most inadequate from the point of view of professional accountancy. But we have included them in the hope that they may suggest to a publisher the general *kind* of system that might be considered with the advice of chartered accountants or other qualified experts.

20

The Retail Bookshop

RETAIL BOOKSELLING is the source of lifeblood for the book industry. This is the point at which the public pays the money that
supports the book business. As we have seen in earlier chapters,
there are special ways of selling books to individuals—mass distribution, subscription sales, book clubs, and so forth. but the most
familiar method, and in most countries still the most important one,
is through the retail bookshop.

Even aside from publishers' possible direct part in retail bookselling through having their own bookshops, the bookshop is a subject
of major interest to all publishers. This chapter, therefore, deals
with retail bookshops in a general way rather than as if providing an
actual handbook for the bookshop proprietor.

The retail bookshop, anywhere, has a position something like that
of a school or library. This is even more clearly the case in developing countries than in societies in which the large number of school
and public libraries, and the policy of supplying free textbooks, give
young people less reason for looking to the bookshop as the natural
or perhaps only source of reading matter. Westerners have enjoyed
citing—as a rebuke to their own countries—the case of Barisol in
Bangladesh, a city of about 50,000, which some years ago had
twelve bookshops at a time when there were only three passenger
automobiles in the community.

Book publishers establish chains of bookshops in an attempt to
get good distribution, even though it would be better—and prefer-
able from their point of view— to leave the retail business in the
hands of professional specialists.

Retail bookselling is an art in which the right book must fit the
right customer. There are, consequently, almost as many ways of

selling books as there are books to sell. The bookshop proprietor must consider the location and appearance of the shop, the assortment of books in stock, the kind of clerks and the service they give the customers. The principles are the same whether the shop is a few shelves of books in the heart of an Eastern bazaar or a separate building on the main street of a great city such as Rio de Janeiro.

The purpose of retail shops is to make books of all publishers available to all customers. That purpose is defeated—and in the long run the business itself will suffer—if publishers who own bookshops try to give their own shops a monopoly of the retail trade in the books they issue. An independent bookseller should be in a position to secure copies of the books at a proper discount and be in a fair competitive position with the publisher's own retail shop. For that matter, rival publishers who own bookshops should likewise stock each other's books. The joint efforts of all of them will multiply, many times over, the total of all books that will be sold. In the United States some of the most famous publisher-owned bookshops, such as Doubleday, and Harper and Row, and McGraw-Hill, not only stock and actively 'promote other publishers' books but constantly give major window displays to books brought out by other houses. This is not only the basic reason for the large volume of sales those bookshops have but an important contribution to the multiplication of book-buying customers.

In some Asian countries, publisher-owned bookshops get their stock from other publishers not through purchase but through barter—each publisher receiving without payment a certain number of copies of each new book as it comes out. That method would be all right in itself, but one of the dangers is the tendency for the bookshop manager to think the stock was "free" and that selling prices can therefore be cut. This prevents the bookshop from profiting as it might from the operation. More serious, it gives unfair competition to the independent bookseller, discourages the opening of new bookshops, and thus holds back the multiplication of book customers that a proper retailing system could achieve.

The most basic need for a successful bookshop, of course, is an alert and intelligent manager, with an understanding of books and competence in business. But, after that, the first requirement is capital to provide the physical facilities and the stock of books to be sold, and to meet the operating costs. The capital requirements will depend, naturally, on the size and location of the place selected for the shop, the number and kind of books stocked, and the method of operation, including the extent to which the bookseller is able to receive credit from the publishers for purchases of books.

Capital

No general rule can be drawn for the amount of capital required for a bookshop, because conditions vary so greatly from country to country. It may be suggestive, however, to know that a study by the American Booksellers Association indicates that the amount of capital needed at the start is about one-third the amount of business in an average year. If a gross annual sales volume of §30,000 were expected, capital of §10,000 should be available at the start. Of course any new business has a hard time in its first year, so the new bookseller should have a good balance in the bank for working capital even after meeting the cost of establishing, furnishing, and stocking the shop. Furthermore, the proprietor should be able to draw on personal funds for living expenses in the first year while waiting for the business to develop.

One of the most useful ways for the bookshop to stretch its capital is to gain the confidence of publishers and get the privilege of ordering books on credit of 30 days, 60 days, or even longer. Another way of stretching capital is through use of the privilege publishers extend in some countries (but not in many others) of returning unsold books, as mentioned in Chapter 8.

Publishers are always looking for new outlets and will welcome a new bookseller, especially one who can provide financing during the period when the shop is in the process of building. It may even be possible to get some of the initial stock on consignment (that is, with the privilege of not paying except as the books are sold). However, it must be understood that liberal credit terms are given only to the bookseller who meets obligations promptly. The relations between bookseller and publisher should be most cordial, as they are working for the same objective—to sell more books to as large a public as possible.

An opposite consideration is the extra capital cost for the book-seller who allows credit to retail customers. Some capital will be tied up in unpaid bills for at least 30 days, quite aside from possible loss through bad debts and the extra administrative cost of maintaining accounts for the retail customers. Many bookshops, for that reason, have a policy of selling for cash except for sales to institutions such as schools, universities, and libraries.

The Bookshop

The physical location of the shop is of course one of the most important questions. It is always good to be in a well-frequented area, whether that means on a main street in the business or shopping district, near a university, or (in some countries) in a good location in the principal bazaar. Nearness to cinemas, buslines, and other natural gathering places can often be useful. Mere crowds are not necessarily an indication of a good place, for if they have limited buying power or are not the sort of people who would be interested in books, the numbers by themselves will not be useful.

Rent. A rule about the amount of rent to pay that has been used in some countries may be worth bearing in mind, though it is certainly not applicable everywhere. It has been suggested by some students of bookselling that yearly rent should not be more than 6 percent of the yearly volume of sales. In the example above, with an expected annual sale of §30,000, the rent under this rule should therefore be not more than §1,800 per year or §150 per month.

Size, shape, and layout. It would be unrealistic to specify the size, shape, and layout for bookshops in general, not only because of some difference of opinion among booksellers but also because the ideal space would not be available everywhere. (Various booksellers' associations have prepared sample layouts, which can also be found in booksellers' handbooks. These are especially useful when a new building is to be constructed so the size and shape can be suited exactly to the plans.)

Although general rules cannot be stated, there are certain important considerations to have in mind, whatever the size and shape of the space available.

One is that a stockroom absolutely *must* be available, and preferably as close as possible to the washroom, if there is one, so that frequent washing of hands will prevent the soiling of book stock.

If the ceiling is high enough for a balcony or mezzanine, that can increase the usable space, but special thought should be given to the location of the stairway leading to it. Stairs in the center take up valuable selling space on the main floor and prevent customers from having a full view of the shop.

Windows. The number and kind of windows depend on the space of the shop facing the street. Too many windows may become a problem both in the number of books needed to make a display and the amount of time the busy bookseller will need to give to them. Too many windows will also rob the shop of precious wall space needed for shelves and other fixtures.

Since the windows are the permanent advertisement of the shop, they must be made as attractive and eye-catching as possible. The window fixtures should be simple and functional. Too much decoration will distract from the books on display. The window fixtures should be designed so that it is easy to get to the window display space from inside the shop. It should also be easy to reach the windows for cleaning. The windows should be cleaned both inside and outside at least once a week.

Fixtures. The shop should be made as attractive as possible with functional fixtures, bright lights, simple decorations, and, if it can be afforded, air conditioning.

The bookseller may want all these nice things, but with only limited capital it would be hazardous to spend all the money they would cost. It is better to have a well-assorted and properly arranged stock than to use up capital for expensive fixtures.

The shelves and racks may be made of wood or metal, whichever is cheaper in the given area. Shelves along the walls must be low enough to enable a person of average height to reach the top shelf without use of a ladder. When there is space between the top shelf and the ceiling it can be used for display of posters, reproductions of paintings and drawings, colorful jackets, and other objects suitable for a bookshop. It should not be used for surplus stock, which belongs in the stockroom.

Adjustable shelves are adaptable to the many sizes of books, especially dictionaries, encyclopedias, atlases, picture books, and other outsize books. They are not a problem when adjustable metal shelving is used. Wooden shelves, however, must be planned in advance for metal strips and brackets on which the shelves will rest.

Because of the great output of mass market books and the increasing revenue from their sale, generous space should be planned to accommodate them. Wire racks are less expensive than wood. Racks that are too wide will take up too much aisle space, and if the racks are too high they will obstruct the full view of the shop and create "blind spots"—to the great satisfaction of book thieves. All fixtures should be designed and planned carefully to avoid alterations after they are built. Alterations are very costly.

Ideally, the shop should have, besides racks, some flat tables to display current publications. They should be small enough to be moved easily into the most convenient places where they can be seen by the casual browser. A shelf under the table is an advantage both for firmness and as a place for surplus stock.

The aisles between fixtures, tables, and racks should be wide enough for easy access to all parts of the shop for customers and clerks. Aisle space is not waste space.

A table for wrapping should be placed close to the entrance with plenty of space for a cash register, if one is to be used. Also one or two of the very latest and best-selling books can be on the table to entice the customer who is waiting for a purchase to be wrapped.

Bright lights are most necessary, from the show window to the remotest part of the shop where customers may wish to browse. It is false economy to save on lights.

Stocking the Shop

The physical facilities just described are important, but the only *really* essential thing in a bookshop is the stock of books. Buying the initial stock of books is only the beginning of what will become the most demanding part of the bookseller's job. One cannot let up for a minute.

Before any money is spent, the bookseller must have a good idea of the kinds of books that are right for the market. And in ordering stock the bookseller must learn how to use the basic tools of the trade—publishers' announcements and catalogues, bibliographies of books in print (when they exist for the languages in which the bookseller is dealing), and other bibliographical aids. If the shop deals in imported books in foreign languages, as well as locally published books in the national language, the bookseller has a large additional job—to learn how to order books from abroad, how to secure foreign exchange for the purchases, how to clear shipments through customs, and so on.

Buying can be direct from the publisher or through a jobber or wholesaler. For the small shop it may be best to do most of the buying from the wholesaler even though the discount may be smaller than the publisher will allow. The difference in discount, however, will be made up by the saving of time and money in ordering from one supplier. The advantage of writing only one order, receiving one shipment, checking one invoice, and paying with one check is self-evident.

All buying should be on the low side. A good rule is: Buy slowly, reorder fast. There is nothing a publisher likes better than a reorder, and the bookseller will have a much fresher stock and a smaller inventory. A particular book may be out of stock for a day or two, but it is better to miss a sale on one copy than to have a quantity left after the interest in the book is gone.

Display of Stock

All stock should be displayed on open shelves, open racks, and on tables. Except for rare books, nothing should be hidden from the customer. The customer should be allowed to handle any book. Avoid long counters or tables close to the entrance which may act as a barricade. People do not like barriers. The entrance should be as wide as the space will allow. A wide entrace is like a "Welcome" sign.

Stock Control

Stock control is an important subject for the bookseller's attention, not merely for the sake of good administration but because it can make so much difference in the amount of business the shop does. If, through bad control of stock, the shop runs out of its supply of a best-selling book, business will be lost. On the other hand, if the bookseller reorders too many copies because of not knowing how many have been sold thus far and how well the book has been moving recently, that will at least tie up an unnecessary amount of capital, and perhaps cause a permanent loss.

There are many different kinds of stock control. The method must be simple and easy to operate, because the number of different book titles is so great and the value of each relatively small. Booksellers' handbooks show some of the methods frequently used. The purpose is to keep a record (usually with one card for each book, with the cards filed by author's name) showing the price, the dates of orders, and the number of copies ordered each time. Then, depending on the system used, the manager checks the sales, perhaps at the end of each day, consults the cards to see the past history for the given book, and mails reorders to the publisher.

A useful but quite informal method used in many shops is to have a pad at the cashier's desk on which the clerk writes the titles of the books sold. The manager can use that list for checking the shelves and deciding which books to reorder, consulting the stock-control cards to see how well the book has been selling recently.

In the developed countries, many bookstores are now using computers to manage stock. One of the most widely used systems incorporates the International Standard Book Number (ISBN), since these numbers provide a unique code for each title.

Annual Physical Inventory

A physical inventory (stocktaking) is made at the end of each fiscal year. Usually the time for the inventory is set for the evening of the last day of the fiscal year when the shop is closed to customers and the work will not be interrupted. All members of the staff—sales, office, receiving, and shipping—are pressed into service. The staff is divided into teams of two; one reads quantities and prices while the other marks the figures on the inventory sheets prepared in advance.

Each section, table, and rack is numbered and an inventory sheet with the same number is placed on each fixture. Entries are made on these inventory sheets only by the number of copies and the retail price of each book, *not* by title. The title method of stocktaking was abandoned in the United States nearly fifty years ago when it was found that the quantity and price method is simple and efficient and gives a complete picture of the actual value of the stock after an average discount is taken off the total retail price.

When the inventory is recorded, the marked sheets are tabulated to arrive at the total retail value; an average discount is established for the complete stock, which is deducted from the total. What is left is the money value of the stock in the shop at the end of the fiscal year.

This method is of course only for accounting purposes. But the bookseller will also want to look at the facts in terms of particular titles—which are overstocked, which good sellers are getting low in number and should be reordered, and so forth.

About once a year it is advisable to have a clearance sale, at substantially reduced prices, of slow-selling stock. This will work to the benefit of the bookshop in several ways: it will clear the shelves of dead stock to make room for new books and fresher copies of backlist titles of what are called "bread and butter" books; it will turn dead stock into money with which to operate; it will bring in new customers who buy books only when they are offered at bargain prices. The best time for a clearance sale is before the physical inventory of the stock is taken at the end of the fiscal year.

Promotion

The successful bookseller does not just sit in the shop waiting for customers to come in, but does everything possible to bring them in. In countries in which direct-mail advertising is feasible, the bookseller's mailing list is one of the most valuable assets. Circulars prepared by the publishers may be used, as described in Chapter 9, or special mimeographed or printed announcements may be prepared by the bookseller. Also a certain amount of advertising may be placed in newspapers or magazines, especially if there is a cooperative arrangement, as mentioned earlier, in which publishers bear part of the cost.

Also, the alert bookshop manager and the best clerks will know the special interests of good customers and let them know when new books arrive that are in their field. This "personal bookshop" approach can take up a lot of time, but it is one of the best ways of creating loyalty in good customers.

In the final analysis, however, the most important promotion is the display of books—in the windows to attract the customers and draw them in, and then in the racks inside the shop to hold their interest when they get there.

The Ingredients of a Good Bookshop

The characteristics making a good bookshop might be listed in this way: good and accessible location; clean and attractive windows with good light (when there are windows), or at least attractive street displays; functional yet attractive fixtures; sensible arrangement of stock, so staff and customers can find books easily; a well-trained staff, paid enough so that turnover of personnel is infrequent; courtesy to customers; warm welcome to people who "just want to look," and a sign in the window, "Come in and Browse"; definite hours when the shop is open for business, with a sign at the entrace giving opening and closing times; ability to use standard bookseller's tools—catalogues, bibliographies, and so forth; familiarity with the special interests of good customers; and membership in a bookseller's association—or initiative in helping to organize one if none exists.

21

Book Industry Training

THE WORD "training" is normally used to mean the teaching of skills necessary to perform certain limited activities such as lathe operation, welding, cooking, or typewriting. But here we use the word in a much broader sense to mean equipping an individual with the professional knowledge, the specific skills, and, equally important, the confidence required to carry out certain activities. By this definition, training includes: (1) basic training for the beginner, either before employment or as an apprentice; (2) formal academic or vocational training (printing and printing-plant management are particularly dependent on such programs); (3) nonacademic seminars, workshops, and conferences, usually for individuals who have been in book publishing or printing for some time; and (4) a number of informal activities, usually initiated by the individual. A long list could be given, but a few examples will suffice: reading of books and professional journals; joining or helping to start informal clubs or associations of individuals with common professional interests for the exchange of ideas and discussion of common problems; observing and becoming familiar with the workings of all branches of the book industry. As an example of the latter, an editor, through frequent visits to local bookstores, can observe many things that will be indirectly useful; observation in local printing plants will likewise enrich one's background.

Training of all those kinds plays a part in the book industries of the developed countries, and we shall have more to say about this below. The point, however, is that for all parts of the book industry training must not be thought of in terms of a training program culminating in a license to practice editing, book design, or bookselling. Taking the industry broadly, it is unquestionably the informal activities indicated in item 4 above, coupled with experience, which have educated the successful European or American publisher, designer, or bookseller.

Main Objective

We mentioned above the three objectives of book industry training: professional knowledge, skills, and confidence. Of these, confidence may be the most important. A gambler would not necessarily make a successful publisher, but a publisher, to be successful, must be just a bit of a gambler. Without the professional knowledge and skills, confidence would be reckless; but unless one gains confidence along with professional knowledge and skills, the training must be considered a failure.

This matter of confidence has particular relevance for book industry personnel in developing countries. The publisher, editor, or bookseller in American or Europe works within a more or less firmly established tradition. In a developing country the new publisher, editor, or bookstore proprietor is often in "uncharted territory." Almost every aspect of the work may be pace-setting or even counter to such tradition as may exist.

Consider, for example, the author who has completed a manuscript. If European or American, that author may well have been in touch from an early stage with the editor of a publishing house, under whose encouragement the manuscript was written. There may even already be a contract. In some of the developing countries, on the other hand, an author's natural inclination, in the absence of a publishing industry with an established tradition, would be to take the manuscript to a printer and "publish" without a publisher. Even if going to a publisher, this author would probably question the right of the publisher to "interfere" with the manuscript through copyediting. Lack of confidence in the publisher's ability to secure the broadest possible market for the book, and to give an honest accounting of the number of copies sold, might lead to preference for a lump-sum advance payment (thereby imposing a strain on the publisher's limited capital) rather than take the chance of getting a larger revenue over a period of several years through royalty payments.

To break from the old tradition into a new one requires confidence—a great deal of it. Hence the emphasis on confidence as the primary objective of training.

Training in the Developed Countries

In a general way it might be said that in countries with long-established book industries training takes care of itself. Except for the special field of printing, in which carefully organized vocational training is usually required prior to employment, and printing plant management, for which an extensive post-secondary-school training program is required, there are no formally required or recognized comprehensive academic programs equipping an individual to go into book publishing in the way a school of journalism equips an individual to enter the newspaper world.

There are, to be sure, courses in editing and other aspects of publishing offered in academic institutions, and many art schools include courses in book design and illustration among their offerings. In the United States, there are short-term programs offered by certain colleges, particularly in New York, Denver, and the Boston and San Francisco areas, dealing with publishing procedures.

Training in book publishing has traditionally been a matter of learning by doing. One gets a job in publishing—perhaps as an editorial assistant, sales representative, or designer—or in a bookstore as a beginning clerk, and by working with the more experienced members of the staff passes through an apprenticeship, which might be very formally organized or very informal. Since advancement depends on experience and "learning the business," the beginner usually wants to learn not only about the specific job but about the book business broadly. In recent years, at least in the United States, these "apprenticeship programs" have become more formally organized in a number of the publishing houses.

Training in the Developing Countries

Now let us consider the problem of book industry training in the developing countries, where the situation may be quite different.

In many developing countries there are individuals with capital and a desire to go into publishing who must make a sudden leap into book publishing. There may be no existing publishing firms or bookstores in which to gain experience. There are no university courses. There is probably no trade association able to provide information or assistance of any kind, and book industry periodicals are either unavailable or deal with publishing and printing in developed countries.

We stated above that in the developed countries training more or less takes care of itself. It has never been a problem big enough to require the attention of the industry or of government. This is not the case in most developing countries, however. If these countries are to develop vigorous book industries without treading the long historical path of the West, training at all levels—but particularly the managerial level—becomes crucial.

To a certain extent training may be arranged in a country with a more developed book industry. But such training cannot begin to meet the total needs. *Local* training opportunities must be created to build the corps of people with the required professional knowledge, skills, and confidence to move forward.

How can this be done? In many ways, of course. The following list suggests some of the ways used in a few countries:

1. Schools of journalism should be persuaded to include courses in book publishing. The connection between books and newspapers is even closer in the developing countries than in the developed countries. Many newspapers in the developing countries, realizing that their presses are busy only a few hours a day, are using the *downtime* of these presses to produce books, and quite a few newspaper publishers have become book publishers as well. The future may see this repeated in many countries. It could be speeded up with the help of schools of journalism.

2. National and regional seminars and workshops should be organized and carried out on a recurring basis. Ideally the organizers would be the local publishers' association if one exists. But rarely

is there a publishers' association with the capability of taking this on without help, both financial and organizational. Governmental assistance (through the ministry of education or ministry of culture) seems logical but is seldom forthcoming. Such projects are not easily carried out. A considerable amount of organizational activity must be behind them if they are to be successful. Hence, they have usually been carried out with foreign technical assistance. The sooner such projects can come under local sponsorship, however, rather than through foreign technical assistance, the better.

An outstanding editing and publishing program in the developing world was inaugurated at the International Rice Research Institute in the Philippines by Ian Montagnes (to whom the present edition of this book is dedicated), on leave from the University of Toronto Press.

3. There is a need to increase and upgrade graphic arts training institutions and vocational training schools in printing. A number of developing countries today have graphic arts training centers. Book design and production should be included in the curriculum of these centers.

It must be frankly stated, however, that these developments are unlikely to come about through government initiative, though government support may be needed for them. The initiative must come from the local publishers, printers, and booksellers acting in cooperation.

Training Abroad

A system found practical in one country will not necessarily work in another. At the same time, however, there are certain common elements on which a successful book industry is based: (1) efficient management based on sound accounting for publishing houses, bookstores, and printing plants; (2) procedures that may vary somewhat from firm to firm but are more or less standard and get books produced rapidly and efficiently; (3) imagination and aggressiveness in developing manuscripts, getting books to the readers, and searching for ways of expanding the book market; (4) trade associations that carry out functions, studies, and projects that a single publisher or printer could not undertake alone; and (5) an "industry image" that commands respect and attracts talented young people.

It is these principles and attitudes of a developed book industry that can perhaps be exported. They do not depend on "hardware" or extensive capital.

And these principles and attitudes *are* being exported as publishers, printers, and booksellers from the developing countries visit the developed countries and get exposure to their book industries. For economic or other reasons, however, the number of individuals who can do this is small. Moreover, the number who can usefully profit from such an experience is perhaps even smaller. The ability to adopt, or adapt, ideas is not universal. The visitor from a developing country whose reaction is "But we can't do that in my country" has quite missed the point. Obviously the individuals best qualified to benefit from an exposure to book publishing or printing in the developed countries must be those with (1) more than average sophistication and judgment, (2) experience in the book industry of their countries, and (3) sufficient responsibility and scope to bring about change, if change is indicated, when they return home.

Perhaps the one area where the strongest case can be made for foreign training is printing plant management. The need for sound printing management, particularly in the public sector, is great in many countries. Governments have invested—and continue to invest—precious foreign exchange in printing equipment, and a strong moral obligation rests upon them to see that the equipment is properly selected and operated at the maximum possible efficiency. Printing management is a highly sophisticated business. An individual, no matter how well qualified as an administrator, needs skill far beyond administrative ability to manage a printing plant effectively.

To conclude this chapter, we might summarize the main points: (1) Training for most jobs in a book industry is a continuing process and much broader than the teaching of certain skills or procedures. (2) While this training more or less takes care of itself in the developed countries, it must receive top priority in developing areas. (3) Foreign assistance can play only a minor role in book industry training in the developing countries. The impetus must come basically from the local publishers, printers, and booksellers.

Appendix

Suggestions for Further Reading

Index

Appendix

Copyright, Licensing, and Piracy

By PAUL GLEASON*
Assistant Editor, International Monetary Fund

[By the kind permission of the author and publisher this article (somewhat abbreviated) is reproduced from the *Letter*, volume 9, issue 2, published by the Society for Scholarly Publishing (SSP). Copyright © 1987 by SSP.]

THE TERM "international copyright" is used to describe the collection of bilateral and multilateral agreements among nations to protect literary and artistic works—such as books, films, musical compositions, videotapes, computer software, audio tapes, television programs, and compact (audio) disks—through copyright. (Literary and artistic works are a subdivision of intellectual property—basically, works that require intellectual effort to create—which also includes industrial property: inventions, trademarks, and industrial designs.) At the center of this collection are two multilateral agreements: the Berne Convention, which had 76 member nations as of January 1, 1987, and the Universal Copyright Convention, which currently has about 80 member nations. Members of the two principal copyright conventions and those nations participating in bilateral agreements each have their own copyright laws governing treatment of works created, published, or otherwise produced within their boundaries.

The key principle under which both conventions operate is that of national treatment, which means in the case of books, on which this article will focus, that each nation adhering to the convention will afford copyrighted works of authors from *any other* member nation the *same* protection, under its domestic copyright law, that copyrighted works of its own citizens

---

*This article reflects the personal views of its author and should not be interpreted as reflecting the views of the International Monetary Fund.

receive. National treatment is essential to the orderly operation of the international book trade.

The History

National copyright laws began with England's Statute of Anne (1709) and spread to other nations of Europe. From their inception, copyright laws have served several purposes: (1) to guarantee an author a monopoly right to control, for a specified period, the uses made of his or her own work, including its sale to a publisher; (2) to guarantee a publisher a monopoly right to print (or arrange to print) and sell a work within national boundaries for a specified period; (3) to provide financial compensation to authors (royalties) to reward their creative work; and (4) to foster development of the country's arts and sciences and, indirectly, its economy. . . .

Copyright laws have often created considerable controversy. In particular the granting of a legal monopoly to publishers—which clearly has helped to provide them with sufficient confidence in their chances of recovering, through sales, their investment in editing, publishing, and distributing a work to justify their taking the risks involved in a publishing venture—has conflicted with the reading public's "need to know" and its desire for the freest possible flow of information, with publishers' prices for books the main bone of contention. (Although books are physical commodities sold at a particular price, the information they contain is a resource whose value to society is not diminished by the widest possible dissemination.) More generally, tensions among publishers, authors, government, and the larger society have caused the pot of copyright discussions to boil over from time to time.

Until the middle to late 19th century, copyright was largely a domestic concern. As the export of books from Europe expanded, and new communications technologies strongly affected nations, however, their perspectives on copyright began to shift. There was increased concern about book piracy—that is, the printing of counterfeit editions by individuals (pirates) who sell them (often at lower prices) in competition with books produced by the publisher holding the copyright. Publishers' revenues and authors' royalties were frequently reduced considerably by piracy.

Piracy had, of course, already existed for centuries. When the pirates operated from the publisher's own country, the latter could use the copyright law to shut down the pirates' plants and subject them to penalties; but when the pirates operated from another country, a publisher had no recourse, unless the two countries happened to have bilateral copyright agreement. In order to safeguard themselves against piracy and to otherwise protect their export markets, the nations of Europe made increasing efforts to reach a multilateral copyright agreement. Efforts to harmonize national copyright laws bore fruit when the Berne Convention was ratified in 1886.

European nations helped to guarantee themselves export markets by drawing their zones of copyright protection to include their colonies. As the international book trade grew in the 19th century and the first half of the 20th, the pattern of the book exports from mother countries to colonies became firmly established. During much of this period, Europe dominated both the production of scientific information, by being the locus of most serious research, and the distribution of the information, through its large, export-oriented publishing industry.

U.S. Copyright Policy

In the 19th century, the United States—then a fledgling nation—was the biggest book pirate in the world, freely reprinting European (primarily English) works without either requesting permission or making payment. This activity was clearly piracy in the eyes of Europeans, but it was completely legal under the U.S. copyright laws of that time. The U.S. government chose to enable its citizens to obtain copyrighted works (and the information they contained) at low cost and to encourage the growth of domestic printing and publishing industries by enabling them to produce books that were proven sellers in England, or elsewhere in Europe, without payment to copyright holders, thus greatly enhancing their chances of making a profit on their output. The downside of this policy was that it discouraged the publication of works by U.S. authors, since domestic publishers found the choice between best-selling books by European authors that were available at no cost and books by lesser-known U.S. authors that would have required payment of royalties an easy one to make.

After the formation of the Berne Convention in 1886, the United States remained aloof from it, primarily to avoid the suppression of domestic interests that would have been involved in adhering to Berne. (Actually, through a loophole in Berne, the United States was able, from 1928 onward, to obtain protection of its authors' works under the convention without adhering to it, by publishing editions simultaneously in the United States and Canada, a Berne member.) Nonetheless, the continuing growth of the U.S. publishing industry and European criticism of continuing U.S. piracy gave its government incentives to enter into copyright agreements with other nations. From the late 19th century, limited use was made of (U.S.) presidential proclamations and treaties to establish bilateral copyright relations with other nations. Since U.S. publishers' exports were very limited at this time, they had little interest in multilateral agreements that could have helped protect sales of their works in foreign markets.

World War II, which brought about many changes in the world publishing scene, marked the beginning of a new era in international copyright relations. The United States emerged as a major publishing power and began to take a greater interest in exporting books. Its reservations about joining the Berne Convention were still serious, however, so it chose to join the Universal Copyright Convention (UCC), which was established in 1952 largely to bring both the United States and the nations of Latin America into the international copyright system.

Copyright and Developing Nations

As the colonial empires of Europe broke up with the granting of independence to former colonies in the 1940s, 50s and 60s, large numbers of new, often weak nations appeared and set about the business of fostering their own economic development. Although these nations' resource endowments, climates, infrastructures, education levels, and political philosophies varied widely, they generally agreed that they would need to obtain scientific and technical information from the industrial nations, much of which was in the form of copyrighted works, if they were to realize their hopes for economic progess. More generally, these Third World nations sought to decrease their dependence on the information production and distribution system largely controlled by the industrial powers, since this offered hope of removing the fundamental inequalities between the two groups of nations.

As developing nations attempted to acquire more information from the West, the former's very limited means posed a major obstacle. Prices of books produced in industrial countries naturally reflected their own costs—wage levels, materials costs, etc.—and the ability to pay of consumers in their own domestic markets and primary export markets. Because copyrighted books published in industrial countries were very expensive in the context of developing countries, book pirates found ready markets for their unauthorized editions of, for example, best-selling U.S. or European textbooks. Copyright laws in developing countries were sometimes nonexistent, more often loosely drawn when it came to protection of foreign works, and tended to be loosely enforced.

Industrial countries, the United States the most prominent among them, attempted to meet the needs of Third World countries through a variety of foreign aid programs that subsidized the production of reprints or translations abroad. These programs reached their peak in the 1960s and received mixed reviews: they certainly helped them meet developing countries' growing needs for information, but they were also criticized for inhibiting the growth of indigenous publishing in the recipient countries—another means by which these countries hoped to reduce their dependence to meet developing countries' book needs by selling "international student editions" or "Asian editions" at prices well below those charged for the same books in their home markets.

Meanwhile, in various international forums—including the United Nations Educational, Scientific, and Cultural Organization (Unesco), administrator of the University Copyright Convention; the World Intellectual Property Organization (WIPO), administrator of the Berne Convention; and the United Nations Conference on Trade and Development (UNCTAD)—developing countries used their combined voting strength to press for a lessening of their economic inequality with industrial countries (the New International Economic Order) and, more particularly, a reduction in industrial countries' control of information production and distribution (the New World Information Order).

At two joint conferences of WIPO and Unesco, held in Stockholm (1967) and Paris (1971), the developing country members of those organizations pushed for concessions in the specifications of the two international copyright conventions from the industrial country members. After long and acrimonious debate, the Paris conference produced revisions of Berne and the UCC (often called the Paris Acts or Paris revisions) that allowed for compulsory licensing of copyrighted works—that is, for a publisher in a developing country to obtain from his national government, with the consent of the copyright holder, a license to reprint or publish translations of educational books for sale within his own country, in return for limited royalty payments.

Developing countries thus obtained a significant, though limited, concession from industrial countries, which agreed to compulsory licensing partly out of fear that developing countries might opt out of the international book trade, if some of their stated needs were not met. They could now obtain rights to publish reprints or translations of educational books copyrighted by industrial country publishers provided (1) the originating publisher had been allowed a period (generally 1-3 years) of exclusive publication rights; (2) the originating publisher had not made an edition of the book available in the developing country at a cost considered "reasonable" in that market;

and (3) the originating publisher had been contacted about the issuing of a compulsory license and consulted about arrangements for the payment of royalties according to the law of the applicant's country.

In order to issue compulsory licenses, with the agreement of the originating publisher, the government of a developing country must have first passed legislation implementing the compulsory licensing provisions of either Berne, the UCC, or both (depending on its membership). Despite the big head of steam behind compulsory licensing at the Stockholm and Paris conferences, only a few countries—for example, the Philippines and India—have actually enacted compulsory licensing laws. Nonetheless, the ability of *any* developing country belonging to Berne or the UCC to enact such legislation increases the leverage of *all* developing country publishers in negotiating normal (voluntary) licenses with publishers from industrial countries.

Although industrial country publishers have come to accept compulsory licensing as a fact of life in the international book trade, they generally have sought to head off the issuance of a compulsory license in a country by either issuing a low-cost edition for their own in that market or by negotiating a voluntary licensing agreement with a local publisher. There are several reasons for this. First, despite their countries' adherence to Berne or the UCC, some publishers object to compulsory licensing on the grounds that it interferes with the operation of markets. Alexander J. Burke, Jr., senior vice president of McGraw-Hill, says that "compulsory licensing is a form of legitimated piracy—legitimated in the eyes of the local government, not in the eyes of the world intellectual community."

Second, publishers have had a number of problems with developing countries' implementation of compulsory licensing as well. Countries' relevant legislation may not conform with the requirements of Berne or the UCC or, if it does, may not be adequately enforced by government authorities. Publishers have no satisfactory recourse under these circumstances, and the two conventions are not enforced by the administering organizations or any other authority.

Third, publishers have had a number of technical problems with compulsory licenses including delayed payment of royalties, taxation of royalties, and illegal exportation of books produced under compulsory licenses. . . .

Piracy in the Technological Age

Book piracy continued to expand during the 1960s, 70s, and early 80s. Technological improvements in offset printing and binding equipment have been put to use by pirates (to reduce their production costs), as have improved air and surface transport services. Obtaining data on the extent of piracy—an underground activity—is quite difficult. Estimates released in August 1985 by the International Intellectual Property Alliance (IIPA), a group made up of U.S. professional associations whose member firms produce copyrighted works, indicated annual losses to U.S. producers from piracy in ten developing countries (including most of the biggest pirate bases) at $1.33 billion annually, $427 million of which was losses from book piracy.

Industrial country publishers, which had long been concerned about piracy and its effects on their balance sheets, became sufficiently alarmed during the early 1980s to push for, and obtain, strong action by their governments to combat piracy. The United Kingdom negotiated with several Asian nations known to harbor major producers of pirated books, videotapes, films, computer software, etc., in order to win amendments and improved enforcement of their copyright laws. At the urging of the IIPA (which includes the Association of American Publishers among its members), the U.S. government has used the leverage created by trade preferences and aid it grants to convince such major pirate bases on Taiwan, Korea, Singapore, and the Dominican Republic to bring their copyright laws into conformity with the two major conventions and to beef up enforcement of these laws. Malaysia and Indonesia are expected to follow suit shortly.

Such government efforts have borne fruit, and piracy is now generally seen as declining, though far from eradicated. Industrial country publishers recognize, however, that piracy can only be minimized or eliminated over the long haul by reducing or eliminating the economic incentives that brought the pirates into publishing in the first place. . . . In recent years, publishers in the industrial world have responded to piracy, compulsory licensing, and the photocopying problem by making greater efforts to sell their own books in developing countries at afffordable prices and to sell reprint and translation rights more reasonably than they had previously.

As book piracy eases, the problem of unauthorized photocopying of copyrighted books in developing countries is receiving greater attention. There, as in the industrial countries, the reproduction of copyrighted material without permission or payment is commonplace. Indeed, after years of having the freedom to make copies for personal use, many people have come to consider such copying their personal right. There are also, however, copy shops that reproduce numerous copies of whole books, or chapters, for resale. Some of these operate around the clock and rival printing-press pirates in the quantity of the output. . . . Publishers have thus far taken little action against photocopying mills in developing countries, but may do so at a later date.

Meanwhile, the influence of the Third World on the international system of information production and distribution continues to increase, leading publishers from industrial countries to make greater efforts to meet the needs of these nations. Nonetheless, developing countries have muted, at least temporarily, their calls for such comprehensive reforms as the creation of a New International Economic Order, in the face of economic austerity and a hardening of attitudes toward such reforms on the part of some industrial country governments. As Philip Altbach has recently written, "For the present, most agree that the international copyright system, despite its inequalities, provides the best means of controlling the situation, especially in the light of massive technological change . . . . Despite the stresses, some piracy and the lukewarm adherence of some Third World nations, the international copyright system appears to be accepted as the basic structure to regulate the international flow of knowledge."[1]

---

1. Philip C. Altbach, "Knowledge Enigma: Copyright in the Third World," *Economic and Political Weekly* (Bombay), 21 (13 September 1986): 1649.

Suggestions for Further Reading

THE BOOKS LISTED here are in print at the time this *Guide* goes to press. There are of course many other books of high value though not now in print and to be found only in libraries.

These few books are not necessarily "the best" but seem likely to have broad usefulness for the different kinds of readers of this book.

Full addresses are given only for publishers not listed in *Literary Market Place* or *International Literary Market Place*. Because of constant changes and varying exchange rates it did not seem useful to attempt inclusion of prices.

Publishing in General

Altbach, Philip G., Amadio Arboleda, and S. Gopinathan. *Publishing in the Third World: Knowledge and Development*. 1985. Portsmouth, N.H.: Heinemann Educational Books; London: Mansell.

> One of the best overall summaries though strongest in the treatment of Asia.

Barker, Ronald, and Robert Escarpit, eds. *Book Hunger*. Paperback. 1974. London: Harrap; Lanham, Md.: Unipub.

> A classic, originally published by Unesco, by a British publishing specialist and a French professor of literature.

Collins, J. *Mail Marketing for Scholarly Publishers, a Beginner's Guide*. Order from Taylor Graham, 500 Chesham House, 150 Regent St., London W1R SFA.

> One of the several fine introductory books developed at the Primary Communications Centre, in Leicester, U.K.

Congrat-Butlar, Stefan. *Translations and Translators*. 1979. New York: Bowker.

> A compilation of facts rather than a discussion of problems and opportunities. Includes listings of centers, awards, and fellowships, and information about copyright and contracts.

Davis, Kenneth. *Two-Bit Culture: The Paperbacking of America*. Paperback. 1984. Boston: Houghton Mifflin.

Although dealing only with the United States, this telling of the story of the paperback revolution contains useful lessons for publishing in any country.

Follett, Robert J.R. *The Financial Side of Book Publishing*. Rev. ed., 1987. Alpine Guild, P.O. Box 83, Oak Park, Ill. 60303.

Self-study lessons in accounting for book publishers. Loose-leaf. Purchase includes the hardbound textbook *How to Keep Score in Business: Accounting and Financial Analysis for the Non-Accountant*.

Geiser, Elizabeth, ed. *The Business of Book Publishing*. 1985. Boulder, Colo.: Westview Press.

The best general work on book publishing now available. A symposium by specialists, in some ways replacing Chandler Grannis's *What Happens in Book Publishing*. And the Geiser book includes an updated bibliography by Grannis that is the best general list in print.

Gopinathan, S., ed. *Academic Publishing in ASEAN*. 1986. Singapore: Festival of Books, 865 Mountbatten Rd., Katong Shopping Centre; distributed by Advent Books, 141 E. 44th St., New York, N.Y. 10017.

Papers from a 1985 seminar about publishing problems and opportunities in five countries of Southeast Asia: Indonesia, Philippines, Thailand, Malaysia, and Singapore. The keynote address by Dean Edwin Thumboo of the National University of Singapore is a memorable statement about developing-world publishing under domination of the institutions and publishing agencies of the developed world.

Montagnes, Ian. *Editing and Publication: A Training Manual*.

Not yet published when this bibliography was compiled but surveyed in preliminary form. It provides a basic curriculum and related materials for training editors—specifically those concerned with disseminating research in the Third World—but its down-to-earth advice and approach can be useful to anyone in publishing. Nothing like it is available elsewhere. For further details write either International Rice Research Institute, P.O. Box 933, Manila, Philippines; or International Development Research Center, P.O. Box 8500, Ottawa K1G 3H9, Canada.

Pacheco, Esther M., ed. *Disseminating Asia's Scholarly Books*. 1987. International Association of Scholarly Publishers.

Proceedings of the IASP 1986 Asia-Pacific Seminar-Workshop in New Delhi. Order from IASP c/o Dorothy Anthony, University of Washington Press, P.O. Box 50096, Seattle, WA 98145-5096, USA.

PEN American Center. *The World of Translation 1971/1987*. PEN American Center, 568 Broadway, New York, N.Y. 10012.

Papers on problems of translation and on relations among authors, publishers, and translators.

Smith, Datus C., Jr. *The Economics of Book Publishing in Developing Countries*. 1977. Paris: Unesco; Lanham, Md.: Unipub. Editions in English, French, Spanish.

The specific figures used are of course far out of date and no longer valid, but the statement of general principles is perhaps still useful.

Unwin, Stanley. *The Truth about Publishing*. 8th ed., 1976. London: Allen & Unwin.

A famous book, a hard-hitting, straight-talking commentary on the publishing institution by a great British publisher.

Zell, Hans. *Publishing and Book Development in Africa*. Bilingual French/ English. Paris: Unesco.

This is a good place to note that Hans Zell is one of the most thoroughgoing and useful students of regional publishing anywhere in the world. The books and journals about African publishing that he has written and published are models that we wish might be found in other world areas as well. The Zell publications were formerly handled in association with Saur Verlag and their associated companies in various countries but now can be ordered direct from Zell, P.O. Box 56, Oxford OX1-3EL.

Editing, Design, and Production

Bly, Robert W., and Gary Blake. *Technical Writing: Structures, Standards and Style*. Paperback. 1982. New York: McGraw-Hill.

Not as "intellectual" as some more famous "style books" but perhaps of greater practical use to the working editor.

Butcher, Judith. *Copy-Editing: The Cambridge Handbook*. 2nd ed., 1983. Cambridge: Cambridge University Press.

Shorter and more descriptive than the *Chicago Manual* listed below.

Cambridge University Press. *Authors' and Publishers' Guides*.

A series of excellent very small books, including M. D. Anderson, "Book Indexing"; Judith Butcher, "Typescripts, Proofs, and Indexes"; John Trevitt, "Book Design"; Richard Hollick, "Book Manufacturing."

Chicago Guide to Preparing Electronic Manscripts, for Authors and Publishers.

Paperback. 1987. Chicago: University of Chicago Press.

A useful guide that publishers will wish to consult later on, even if they are not yet ready to think about typesetting from authors' tapes and disks.

The Chicago Manual of Style. 13th ed., 1982. Chicago: University of Chicago Press.

Probably the most widely admired and widely used of all style books, though it can be criticized for being *too* comprehensive for convenient use by inexperienced authors or editors.

Cogoli, John E. *Photo-Offset Fundamentals*. 4th ed., 1980. Bloomington, Ill.: McKnight Publishing Co.; distributed by Taplinger Publishing Co., 200 Park Ave. S., New York, N.Y. 10003.

A simple introduction that is quite popular in high school printing courses in the United States.

Craig, James. *Designing with Type*. Rev. ed., 1980. New York: Watson-Guptill.

A basic textbook, periodically updated and a fixture in many printing courses.

Feeney, M., ed. *New Methods and Techniques for Publishers and Learned Societies*. Order from Taylor Graham, 500 Chesham House, 150 Regent St., London W1R 5FA.

Another of the useful introductory books developed at the Primary Communication Centre, Leicester, U.K.

Gross, Gerald. *Editors in Editing*. Paperback. Rev. ed., 1985. New York: Harper & Row.

New edition of a famous collection of articles, letters, and other contributions showing editors in actual operation in different kinds of publishing.

Hill, Mary, and Wendell Cochran. *Into Print: A Practical Guide to Writing, Illustrating and Publishing*. Paperback. 1977. Los Altos, Calif.: Kaufmann.

Guidance on publisher-author-artist relations, with special attention to problems of illustrations, maps, and tables.

International Paper Co. *Pocket Pal: A Graphic Arts Production Handbook*. Paperback. 13th ed., 1983. Order from Pocket Pal Publishers, P.O. Box 100, Church Street Station, New York, N.Y. 10008.

A remarkable "vestpocket encyclopedia" of information on all aspects of printing.

Labuz, Ronald. *How to Typeset from a Word Processor*. Paperback. 1984. New York: Bowker.

A generally endorsed introduction and guide.

Lee, Marshall. *Bookmaking: The Illustrated Guide to Design/Production/Editing.* Rev. ed., 1980. New York: Bowker.

Expanded edition of a standard publishing/printing handbook.

MacGregor, A. J. *Graphics Simplified: How to Plan and Prepare Effective Charts, Graphs, Illustrations, and Other Visual Aids.* Paperback. 1979. Toronto: University of Toronto Press.

Terse, direct, descriptive commentary, republished from a series in *Scholarly Publishing.*

O'Connor, Maeve. *The Scientist as Editor: Guidelines for Editors of Books and Journals.* Paperback. 1979. London: Pitman; New York: Wiley.

Perhaps the single most valuable guide for science editors.

O'Connor, Maeve. *How to Copyedit Scientific Books.* Paperback. 1986. Philadelphia: ISI Press.

A companion to the above title, specifically for copyeditors.

Skillin, Marjorie, and Robert M. Gay. *Words into Type.* 3rd ed., 1974. New York: Prentice-Hall.

For a dozen years has seemed to lead the field among editorial reference books.

Smith, Peggy. *Mark My Words.* Editorial Experts, 85 South Bragg St., Alexandria, Va. 22312.

A practical guide to proofreading.

Stainton, Elsie Myers. *Author and Editor at Work: Making a Better Book.* Paperback. 1981. Toronto: University of Toronto Press.

A valuable guide for both authors and editors.

White, Jan V. *Editing by Design: A Guide to Effective Word and Picture Communication for Editors and Designers.* Paperback. 2nd ed., 1982. New York: Bowker.

Emphasizing the coordination of text and illustration for effective communication.

Williamson, Hugh. *Methods of Book Design.* Paperback. 3rd ed. London: Oxford University Press, 1983. New Haven: Yale University Press, 1984.

An updated version of an older work, still cited as an abiding classic.

Wilson, Adrian. *The Design of Books.* Paperback. 1974. Peregrine Smith Books, Box 667, Layton, Utah 84041.

An attractively written general work with special emphasis on the function of good design in giving "authority" to the author's message.

Periodicals

African Book Publishing Record. Hans Zell, P.O. Box 56, Oxford OX1 3EL.

Although basically a book-listing journal, this carries a great deal of other information about African publishing.

Asian Book Development. Asian Cultural Centre for Unesco, 6 Fukuromachi, Shinjuku-ku, Tokyo 162.

Although ostensibly dealing only with Asia this is the best journal in the entire world on the subject of developing-country book publishing.

The Bookseller. J. Whitaker & Sons, 12 Dyott St., London WCIA 1DF.

Along with *Publishers Weekly* (see below) the best source of continuing information on world publishing.

Horn Book Magazine. 31 James Ave., Boston, Mass. 02116.

One of the best ways of keeping up with developments in the children's book field.

Newsletter of the International Association of Scholarly Publishers. IASP c/o Edvard Aslaksen, Universitetsforlaget, P.O. Box 2959, Tøyen, 0608 Oslo 6, Norway.

Newsletter of the Society for Scholarly Publishing, 2000 Florida Ave. N.W., Washington, D.C., 20009.

By special arrangement, members of the society receive both this newsletter and *Scholarly Publishing* (see below).

Publishers Weekly, 205 E. 42nd St., New York, N.Y. 10016.

The most basic source of continuing information about North American publishing, and to some extent also following world trends.

Rights, a quarterly dealing with copyright and related subjects, jointly sponsored by International Publishers Association and International Group of Scientific, Technical, and Medical Publishers, 7 rue Gozlin, Paris 75006.

Scholarly Publishing, Toronto M5S 1A6.

Unique in the handling of its own subject and widely useful also to those concerned with other kinds of publishing.

Index